To Donna
with love
Carle

The Two Rosetos

THE
Two Rosetos

CARLA BIANCO

Indiana University Press
Bloomington and London

Published in Canada by Fitzhenry & Whiteside
Limited, Don Mills, Ontario

Manufactured in the United States of America .

Library of Congress Cataloging in Publication Data

Bianco, Carla.
    The two Rosetos.

    Bibliography: p. 222

    1. Italians in Roseto, Pa.   2. Roseto, Pa.—Social
life and customs.   3. Roseto Valfortore, Italy—Social
life and customs.   4. Folk-lore—Italy.   I. Title.
F159.R73B52   917.48'22   73-16523
ISBN 0-253-18992-6

To

Anthony Zilio' Falcone

and to all

Italian and American Rosetans,

with gratitude

Contents

PREFACE   ix

PART ONE
Roseto, Pennsylvania, and Roseto Valfortore

I	The Rosetan Emigration to America	3
II	The Two Rosetos: Two Related Communities	11
III	The Rosetan Migration and the Myth of America	34
IV	Traditional Life in Roseto, Pennsylvania	70
V	The Community and the World	122
	NOTES 143	
	WORKS CITED 155	

PART TWO
Rosetan Folklore

VI	Folktales	161
VII	Folksongs	200
VIII	Interviews in Roseto, Pennsylvania (excerpts)	207
	A NOTE ON THE METHODS	218
	SELECTED BIBLIOGRAPHY: THE ITALIAN IMMIGRATION TO AMERICA	222
	INDEX 230	

Preface

IN RECENT YEARS some fine studies and collections of immigrant folklore have appeared in the United States, and yet the folklore of the Italian immigrants has received very little attention. Phyllis Williams' *Southern Italian Folkways in Europe and America*, published in 1938, was designed as a guide for "social workers, visiting nurses, school teachers and physicians." It is a very interesting and useful book, although necessarily limited in its treatment of folklore material and not quite a folklore study. In addition, while the section devoted to Italian-Americans was up to date at the time of publication, the material dealing with the Italians in the Old Country was drawn from a much older source and did not refer to the same regional groups.[1]

Since then, aside from a few accounts of tales, songs or proverbs, no scholarly collection or study of Italian-American folklore has ever been published.[2] A great number of works on immigration have appeared, beginning at the turn of the century when the significant role of immigration in American life began to become apparent. There were books of all kinds: practical guides for the immigrants themselves, statistical monographs on the census and public welfare, semifictional accounts of the adventures of immigrant families, histories of American immigration, and sociological studies about such factors as crime, unemployment, and health conditions in Italian neighborhoods.

The following study attempts to examine the folklore of two related communities: one in the United States and the other in Italy. Owing to their common origin, both of these towns are named "Roseto," and both share common cultural and social traits. Over the past seventy years, however, they have gradually moved away from each other and an analysis of the field collections made in both communities indicates that two distinct, though related, cultural profiles exist beneath a superficial appearance of unity and repetition.

In the United States, where the adoption of mass-produced

models has earlier than elsewhere given a superficial pattern of uniformity to the culture, it is essential to be aware of the more hidden forces that have shaped and still influence life. Even where the most visible aspects of traditional life have disappeared, it is important to know what they were and how they have changed, for a better understanding of American history and society. My study of the two Rosetos attempts to show that, beneath the evident adjustment to certain aspects of American life, a whole world of traditional values, folk beliefs, and fantasies persists, in some ways as rich as that the immigrants left behind them in the Old Country. Deep changes have occurred and still occur daily in the life style of Rosetans and of most Italian-Americans. There are easily visible changes in the sphere of the social life, as well as in certain external habits acquired in the general use of the mass media. A deeper inquiry, however, reveals that both groups and individuals are—consciously and unconsciously—trying to preserve certain traditional values, once forming the core of their culture of origin. These values, combined with other variables, determine a well-defined set of behaviors among their bearers and favor the retention of the folklore.

My first experience in a transplanted culture was among the large group of Venetian farmers living in the countryside south of Rome, where Mussolini settled them more than seventy years ago.[3] At the same time, as a result of my field work in central and southern Italy, I became increasingly interested in the phenomenon of emigration, particularly to America, the evidence of which is ever present in Italian villages. I met a large number of returned migrants now living in their villages of origin, and I visited the relatives of old emigrants abroad, as well as those of present migrants to central Europe and northern Italy. In 1964, largely using personal connections and introductions obtained from the Italian relatives, I started my research of regional groups in the United States with a pilot investigation of eleven such groups in New York City, Chicago, and other places in Long Island and New Jersey.[4] What I learned about Italian-Americans in general and about their folklore at that initial stage proved very useful in the present book, for it provided me with a wider perspective and basis for comparison and testing with the Italian-American community at large.[5]

I chose Roseto from the many Italian settlements in America because it was both a homogeneous community closely related—thus comparable—to its sister village in Italy and a community that had not been isolated from the mainstream of American life. Roseto's very existence depended upon close contacts with other well-defined and long-established groups. This is certainly a significant factor in a study of culture contact and change: a purely rural or isolated community would not have been a good example of the Italian experience in America because the traumas of industrialization and inter-ethnic contacts are the primary characteristics of the immigrant's adjustment to American life.

I spent twelve months doing field work in the two communities and recorded nearly 150 hours of interviews containing hundreds of songs, tales, proverbs, habits, superstitions, beliefs, and life histories. The aim of the collection has been to record a fully representative sampling of the Rosetan tradition and to use this sampling as a basis for the study of the process of adaptation of this rural group to American conditions. In effect, the resulting study is a study of culture change based on folklore.[6]

The first Rosetans to come to America were farmers who were hired in New York City to work in the slate quarries in the "Slate Belt" of the Blue Mountain in Pennsylvania. Here they founded Roseto. Those who followed went immediately to Pennsylvania and settled there, making the drastic shift from an agricultural to an industrial way of life at the same time that they left their old home for a new one. In settling a new Roseto, the immigrants had to contend with hostility and distrust from the Welsh and the Germans who owned the slate quarries and who despised the new, unskilled laborers. Informants have told me that they were antagonized on the basis of both religious and ethnic differences, that most of them suffered poor living conditions long after they had arrived, and that social contact with the English, the Welsh, and the Germans was taboo. I recorded vivid descriptions of fights which took place on the hill where the Rosetans settled. It is only in recent times that a relative tolerance for one another and some intermarriage between the two groups has occurred.

The American Roseto was founded in 1882 by a group of eleven Rosetan immigrants and today ninety-five percent of its less than two thousand inhabitants are descendants of Roseto Valfortore, the namesake village of origin in southern Italy. The town suddenly came into international prominence in 1963, when an American cardiologist did a study of Roseto's eating habits and observed that the death rate from heart disease was unusually low—less than half that of the surrounding communities—despite heavy consumption of calories and widespread obesity.[7]

At first glance, the material collected in America may appear to duplicate the Italian collection, but its unique characteristics soon become evident. In many cases, songs, tales, or other folklore texts, which are only vaguely recalled in the parent community or are remembered only in a fragmentary form, have survived in the United States in older and completer versions. This is apparent both in the linguistic elements of the dialect and in the structure of the texts. The songs naturally undergo a slower process of transformation because of the close relationship between their metrical and musical structure. At the same time, reaction to the American experience has produced new songs and poems or the addition of new stanzas to the old ones. The most visible aspect of change in folklore texts occurs in the narrative, which because of its freer structure allows the narrator a wider range of personal interpretation and manipulation. Within the traditional forms we find here the addition of a large number of personal observations on crucial events and group experiences that often reflect the changes of the culture better than sophisticated sociological studies based on elaborate schedules, diagrams, and calculations.

Another aspect of change, perhaps more difficult to analyze but equally significant, is the investigation of the entire body of beliefs, attitudes, and habits held by the second-generation members of the community,[8] for their traditions lack the rationale and context which gave them meaning for the Italian-born immigrants. Part of the intricate totality of traditional norms, ranging from the simple act of crossing oneself at the sound of a death knell to the complex act of rejecting a transgressor of the traditional moral code, may be practiced by the second generation, but they are not necessarily still understood. A typical example concerns the imposition of norms on individuals by the group as a whole. Two godmothers will exchange a series of verbal formalities when they meet, and this may seem a senseless dialogue to the young Italian-American, who sees no reason for the women to give formal accounts of what the members of their respective families are doing. To the two godmothers the exchange is reasonable because they want it known that their daughters are at home carrying out their traditional domestic duties and are thus fulfilling the criteria expected from a girl. It seems important here to examine the factors that make the second and often the third generation follow these old patterns of behavior today, even when they no longer need to or understand why.

Italian immigrants, whether they came individually or in groups, often arrived with the idea of eventually returning to Italy. Their purpose at that time was to earn enough money to buy a small piece of land and a house in their native village and most of them shuttled back and forth across the Atlantic for several decades until the immigration laws of 1924 curtailed their freedom to come and go at will. The Rosetans were no exception. In Roseto Valfortore I met some aged informants who had retired there after twenty and even thirty years spent in the Pennsylvania quarries and factories.

One sector of immigrants, however, came with the clear intention of remaining in the United States and integrating into American society as quickly as possible. A whole body of jokes exists in the oral tradition emphasizing the comic side of the struggles of the immigrant who wishes to become an American, and there are songs expressing a clear determination to transplant to America, such as the one where the emigrant girl asks for her dowry before boarding the ship.

Disillusionment set in rapidly for many immigrants once in America. A great number of my informants spoke of how ugly America is, how the sky is never really blue, the fruit has no taste, the women are not loving, the flowers have no perfume, the sea is gray and not even salty enough, neighbors are not friendly and are secretive about their own lives and, finally, English is a crazy language because it is not pronounced the way it is written! Complaints of this sort, though most dramatically expressed by the immigrants living in urban centers, are often heard among Rosetans and even in Roseto Valfortore, where my informants used these arguments to explain their "choice" for staying in Italy. The same comments are very frequently made by recent immigrants, who are presently experiencing the difficulty of adjusting to their own fellow-*paesani* of the older immigration.

All immigrants came to America with an unrealistic view of what America was going to be like. This view changed as the immigrant faced the problems of adjustment, and the two sectors of the community—the immigrants wishing to integrate and those unwilling to do so—developed sharply different attitudes in regard to their new country and their homeland. They often transmitted these attitudes to their children and the differences remain perceivable today.

Many examples of Italian traits in the community could be mentioned, and this description might give the impression that Roseto is merely a duplication of Roseto Valfortore, an error perpetuated in all common references to Italian-American communities as "Little Italies." The Italian atmosphere of Roseto is undeniable: grapevines and fig trees in the gardens, the obvious physical traits of the people, the names on the shops and front doors, the foodstuffs for

sale, and many street names (Dante, Colombo, Garibaldi, Falcone).
However, striking differences are also easily perceivable. The questions here are what changed and how, what caused the retentions,
and what is now the result.

Let us consider the Italian-American group at large. If we are
aware of the situation of the peasantry in Italy and of Italian society
in general, we know that the cohesive factor which formed and
cemented for a while each of the innumerable Italian groups in
America has been the village spirit, the *campanilismo*, a term
coined from the Italian word for bell (*campana*) to indicate all
that is within the sound of the village bell. Metaphorically, it refers
to an intense regionalism existing in many southern European
peasantries but particularly in Italy. A tormented history of continuous invasions and foreign dominations, followed by a political
unity that came too late and has never been socially and economically effective, has made Italian society a cultural labyrinth without equal in Europe. The constant abandonment and exploitation in
which the subordinate and peasant classes have been left for immemorial times produced a permanent state of insecurity and diffidence in peasant society. The basic cultural unit for the Italian
peasant became his own family; beyond this, the small circle of his
immediate relatives and friends in the village is as far as his world
extends in terms of security, and the only place where his own
language is spoken in the fullest sense.

While the multiformity of cultural patterns derived from the
deep divisions in Italian society accounts for the rich variety of
Italian culture at large, it is also largely responsible for the contrasts dividing the various groups of Italians in America. Since the
village tradition constitutes the only cultural resource that the
emigrant brings with him to America, it is clear that it is the "little
tradition,"[9] using a term proposed by Robert Redfield, that kept
the Italian immigrants clustered in the so-called "Little Italies" and
not a sense of Italianism or patriotism, largely unknown or meaningless among Italian peasants. If a vague—sometimes fantastic—
notion of "Italianism" existed at one point among Italian immigrants in America, it was not a concept that came from the Old
Country. It was something that emerged later, as a consequence of
two main political and economic events developing in America and
in Italy: the Depression and the rise of Fascism. The Fascist-controlled Italian-American press, with papers such as *Il Progresso*,
contributed to the formation of spurious feelings which can still be
found among Rosetans and other Italian-Americans. The only common heritage that Italian emigrants did share at the time of depar-

ture was a distrust and fear of authorities, government, and all those outside one's own family or village group.

The theoretical framework of my research was inspired by works ranging from general surveys on immigrant folklore, such as those by Blegen, Christiansen, Dorson, Dégh, and Williams, to works on acculturation and peasant societies by Herskovits, Lewis, Redfield, and Gans and to historical and sociological studies on immigration by Handlin, Hansen, Jones, Glazer and Moynihan, and Eisenstadt. For research methods, I received suggestions and inspirations from such works as Toschi's handbook, Bronzini's questionnaires, Goldstein's guide, and Kluckhohn's studies on interviewing techniques. On the other hand, while a consideration of the above theoretical formulations underlies the whole research, this study tries, simply, to follow the process of change in its actual happening, without trying to make it fit into a pre-established scheme. It can be considered as both synchronic and diachronic as it studies the group as a whole but it gives the largest space to individual immigrants and their histories. In addition, I decided to avoid a complex terminology to define the various concepts involved in cultural change as I am not sure whether the terms—as well as the concepts—at our present disposal can really cover the process with any scientific completeness.

Both the content and the structure of Rosetan culture have been affected by deep changes and many new traits are easily identifiable as American or at least as non-Italian. Using folklore as the main field of investigation to study these changes, I hope to prove that the community's homogeneity and relative economic autonomy have helped a gradual process of change, avoiding most of the dramatic conflicts and pressure to conform that is often the lot of similar groups and individuals in urban areas. On the other hand, partly because the exposure to a contrasting culture took place at a slow, relaxed pace, Roseto maintained an interest in Italy, with Italian traditions reinforced by such contacts as the frequent exchange of visits and some new immigrants arriving from the "parent" village. I also hope to have ascertained, at least partially, to what extent the co-existing cultures are blending into a new whole with its own dynamic vitality, and to what extent they are merely an assortment of separate units and overlapping structures, with little chance of fecund development.

ACKNOWLEDGMENTS

THE PRESENT STUDY was made possible by the considerable help I received from several sources. First of all, I would like to mention the enthusiastic and generous contribution given by all my informants from both Rosetos, in particular, by Mr. Anthony Z. Falcone, whose intelligent assistance was most essential for me. The research grants and fellowships I received from the American Council of Learned Societies, the Wenner-Gren Anthropological Foundation, and Indiana University greatly contributed to the completion of this work. I am grateful to Professor Richard M. Dorson, Director of the Folklore Institute of Indiana University, for his encouragement and help in all phases of my work. I am also grateful to Professor Alberto M. Cirese of the University of Siena and to Dr. Linda Dégh of Indiana University for their valuable suggestions, and to my dear old mother, who took good care of the family during the long years of the research work.

The Two Rosetos

PART ONE

Roseto, Pennsylvania,
and
Roseto Valfortore

Garibaldi Avenue and Columbus Street in Roseto, Pennsylvania.

The "Street of the Americans" in Roseto Valfortore. Many houses in the village were left empty by the emigrants or the "Americans."

I

The Rosetan Emigration to America

The steamship is ready,
It is ready for the sea.
Mother, give me my dowry,
For to America I want to go.

THE tragic history of the Italian peasantry is the history of Italian agriculture and of the *contadini*,[1] the landless farmers or
small proprietors of the poor South. It is "the story of these hands
of mine," an informant in Roseto Valfortore said to me, "they
worked and worked as the Madonna wanted them to and yet the
balance never came even."[2]

Paradoxically, Italy was among the first of the European countries to develop sophisticated patterns of urban life, and city-states
and banking systems, and yet millions of country folk lived through
the ages in a totally static and slave-like condition. Life was spent on
the same plot of land with no change in view but the coming of
death. Nothing was ever done for the *contadino* and as late as the
beginning of the twentieth century a parliamentary investigation in
the South revealed that the peasants' wages had not changed since
1780. The poor farmer was abandoned to himself and to the land,
which he could only exploit over and over again, and the only assur-
ances in his life were his debts, poverty, disease, and the destruction
brought by wars.

Carlo Levi has eloquently described the conditions of peasant
life as he witnessed them during his political exile of 1936 in
Aliano, Lucania, a place near Eboli and similar, in terms of peasant

conditions, to Roseto Valfortore and to thousands of other southern villages (Levi 1947:3).

> Christ stopped short of here, at Eboli. We're not Christians, we're not human beings; we're not thought of as men, but simply as beasts, beasts of burden. Christ stopped at Eboli, where the road and the railway leaves the coast of Salerno and turns into the desolate reaches of Lucania. Christ never came this far, nor did time, nor the individual soul, nor hope, nor the relation of cause to effect, nor reason nor history. Christ never came, just as Romans never came. . . . No one has come to this land except as an enemy, a conqueror, or a visitor devoid of understanding . . . Christ did not come. Christ stopped at Eboli.

Many villages had—and still have—princes, dukes, barons, bishops, and cardinals. Names of the ancient aristocracy (e.g., Torlonia, Pignatelli, Borghese, Caetani, Corsini, Doria, Brancaccio) are still heard upon arriving in one of these villages today. The sumptuous palaces and life styles of the aristocrats were always arrogantly displayed under the eyes of the poor peasants, who thus witnessed living examples of the fantastic people of their own fairy tales. Even when a regular aristocracy was lacking, the village still had its Olympus of notables, in the priest, landowner, doctor, pharmacist, and other professionals whose self-image and behavior closely resembled those of the nobility. Class antagonisms were nurtured and institutionalized by the Bourbonic rulers, who used them as the foundations of their authority and strength. The peasant submitted wholly to the lord, believing that the proprietor was almighty, and that governments, tribunals, and police were one with him. Fearful of the *padrone* (boss), the peasant did nothing without consulting him. All Italian rulers cynically exploited the *contadino*'s miserable condition. Avenues of future glories and imperial destinies were promised as a return for present sufferings and renunciations. The large families of Lucania, for example, were praised for their fecundity by Mussolini, in a speech addressed to the Lucanian peasants soon after the 1936 proclamation of the Italian empire (Mussolini 1936:163).

> Lucania holds a primacy that makes her the queen of all other Italian regions: the primacy of fecundity! Peoples with empty cradles cannot conquer an empire and, if they have one, time will come when they no longer shall be able to keep it and defend it. The right to an empire is only for fecund peoples, that is those who have the pride and the will to spread their race over the face of this earth: the true virile peoples.

Ironically, Italian peasants did spread all over this earth, but certainly not as proud conquerors willing to expand their "virile race." The precariousness of the *contadino*'s life deeply affected his relationship with the land and with his own peers, as Lopreato writes correctly (1967:67), and my informants describe the land as "a Purgatory on Earth where Christians are condemned to eat each other." Regarding other peasants as potential rivals for the share of the limited resources, the peasant's confidence was restricted to his family and a narrow circle of relatives and friends. The picturesque term *"campanilismo,"* coined from the Italian word for bell (*campana*), expresses this restricted sense of community and the common feelings shared by all those who live within the sound of the village or parish bell.

Faced with these circumstances, the *contadino* sought escape in emigration, which runs like a red thread through the texture of modern Italian history, and which continues today in the form of an actual exodus. Emigration commenced in the northern part of the peninsula in the 1870's, and later, with the advent of industrialization and improvements in conditions in the North, shifted to the "boot" in the South, where it still continues owing to the persistent lack of a large-scale policy truly aiming at courageous social solutions. Speaking of the southern Italian peasants, Lopreato has written that they recognize emigration as the "most rational, perhaps the only feasible, way in which they can guide their destiny" (Lopreato 1967:257).

The 1861 Italian census provides the first data on Italian emigration and indicates that about 100,000 Italians were then living in America.[3] Since then, at least twenty-six million more Italians have left Italy for new homes. According to the Istituto Centrale di Statistica, more than ten million have emigrated since 1900. Considering their demographic increase, it is possible that about fifty million persons of Italian descent are permanently settled outside of Italy.[4] The first wave of Italian emigration came just before 1900, with a gross emigration of seven million persons. In this period migrations were chiefly on an individual basis, mostly from the northern regions, and were largely directed to European countries. In a second period, from 1900 to the outbreak of the first World War, about nine million people left Italy, and nearly one million in 1913 alone. Emigration was now regulated by the government, according to norms formulated in 1901,[5] and the emigrants came largely from the South and proceeded to America. World War I brought a shift back to European-bound migrants of northern origin up to a maximum of 100,000 a year. A fourth period, between 1919 and 1927, saw a new rise in southern emigration with the peasants dispersing about evenly for overseas and European destinations. Restrictive legislation of both the Fascist and the United States governments[6] forced emigration down to a total of 1,300,000 from 1928 to 1940. In this period, as during World War I, the majority of migrants left northern Italy for other European countries, but over seventy percent of these people eventually returned to Italy. After World War II, emigration revived once more, and in the past twenty years eight million emigrants departed from the central and southern regions, of whom sixty-six percent remained in European countries and the others returned. Evidently important changes are now occurring in the *contadino*'s life which give him different goals and new attitudes toward his adopted country, at the same time that they give modern Italian emigration new trends and characteristics.

The southern Italians, who began to emigrate in great numbers in the later 1880's, were following the northern migrants to Latin America when an epidemic of yellow fever broke out in Brazil claiming 9,000 Italian victims. The Italian government temporarily halted emigration to South America, and the *contadini* flocked to the United States from Sicily, Calabria, Apulia, Campania, Abruzzi, and from Latin America itself. Along with Russians, Austrians, Poles, Hungarians, and Greeks, they arrived at the turn of the century, a part of what American historians have termed the "New Immigration," in distinction to the earlier wave of English, Dutch, French, Scotch, Irish, and German migrants. Out of a total of 4,981,331 Italians immigrating between 1820 and 1961, the distribution by decades is thus represented, according to *Historical Statistics of the United States:*[7]

1821–1830	409
1831–1840	2,253
1841–1850	1,870
1851–1860	9,231
1861–1870	11,725
1871–1880	55,759
1881–1890	307,309
1891–1900	651,893
1901–1910	2,045,877
1911–1920	1,109,524
1921–1930	455,315
1931–1940	68,028

1941–1950	57,661
1951–1960	185,491
1961	18,956
Total	4,981,331

Before World War I, most Italian immigrants were single males who usually came for short periods, hoping to earn enough money to return and buy property in the Old Country. This temporary migrant was often called the "bird of passage" (C. F. Wittke 1939:436), and he could also be a married man who had left his family behind. After a few years had passed and they had made several trips to Italy, most immigrants discovered that they no longer wanted to return home, their jobs and their new homes no longer appeared unstable and strange, and their traditional pessimism and ancient fears had faded (M. Ascoli 1944:33). This gradual adjustment was also due to the fact that Italian women had begun to immigrate to America in large numbers, either to join their men or on their own. The interviews included in this book tell of the adventurous trips of Italian girls who came to America all by themselves. In addition, the immigrant's skills were becoming more diversified and he no longer needed to depend solely on brute strength for earning a living. Some had saved enough money to buy small businesses such as fruit stands, barbershops, and shoe repair shops, and thus had the independence and the confidence to settle permanently.

Statistics show that Italians, like the Hungarians and other immigrant groups, became almost totally urbanized after their arrival in the United States. According to the 1960 United States Census,[8] 91.7 percent of the Italian-born immigrants settled in those urban-ethnic neighborhoods usually called "Little Italies." These neighborhoods bloomed strictly following loyalties and kinship obligations of the respective native homes in Italy and rarely were (or only at a later stage) what their literal name means: a sampling from all of Italy. The variation, within any such group, was mostly limited to provincial or regional areas, with exceptions for culturally related groups. If the main nucleus was, for example, from Matera, Lucania, the rest of the community would have come from nearby villages and towns and some from all of Lucania or even from Apulia, but it would be difficult to find there any Venetians or Piedmontese. This pattern is fully confirmed by the Rosetans in Pennsylvania, where the few cases of non-Rosetans living in town and those of intermarriage with outsiders were largely within provincial or regional affinity. This pattern has not been so strictly followed by northern Italians, although the Tuscans from the tiny village of Colle di Compito still clustered off Western Avenue in Chicago seem to prove the opposite. Once formed, group settlements followed different developments according to a wide range of factors: from working reasons to a gradual autonomy from kinsmen and village. Often the immigrants realized how the function of the ethnic group was at once protective and helpful but also retarding in terms of occupational-social mobility and moved elsewhere to try at least an outward integration with the host society. At the beginning, however, the kinsmen and village-clusters were the rule and, in cities such as Boston, Cleveland, Philadelphia, and Buffalo, thousands of these groups still resist the overwhelming socioeconomic pressure toward dispersion.

When the emigrant was unable to pay for his sea passage, he would try to obtain a loan from a relative or a *compare* (godfather), or he would resort to a well-established emigrant, preferably from his own region. Most often, he was approached by emigration agents, who operated in his village or province in connection with shipping companies and, at times, even with racket groups abroad. Once in America, the chain continued, for he needed further assistance in finding jobs and accommodations, and again he was forced to turn to the influential individuals within his own group of origin. Most of the life histories narrated by my informants, both in Roseto, Pennsylvania, and in urban America, conform to this pattern. Here is an excerpt from Carmela Martellotti's life history:

C: His parents [her husband's] were already in Boston at that time. And I was there, too, but I didn't know them. He came after with his younger brothers and his uncle Louis, that is his mother's brother. His brother, his sisters, all, all his people came. Little by little, one after the other, see? We did, too. Like a string of sausages. Then, they got the best jobs in Boston, you know? They had *u cumbare* [godfather] from near Campobasso, he knew everybody! Oh, he helped everybody around there! I must say the truth now, no joke. The best jobs! Two of them worked in the cement mill, two brothers, and another one was with *u cumbare* in a business I forget now. Of course, they were grateful to him. I mean, one had to pay such and such amount for a few years. But it helped them a lot![9]

Family and village loyalties were also reflected in the early geographical distribution of Italians across the country and persist to this day. Joseph Velikonja (1967:26) found that Italian immigrants of the mid-sixties still preferred central urban districts and the Atlantic seaboard, while the rest of the population tended, more than the Italians, to abandon the central districts for the suburbs. He gives these data relative to a 1960–65 report:

DECLARED DESTINATION OF ITALIAN IMMIGRANTS, 1960–65

City	Total	Percent of total
New York City	30,952	28.9
Chicago	6,452	6.0
Newark–Patterson	3,699	3.4
Philadelphia	3,075	2.9
Rochester	2,053	1.9
Boston–Cambridge	1,896	1.8
Detroit	1,532	1.4
Cleveland	1,255	1.2
Pittsburgh	1,052	1.0
San Francisco–Oakland	986	0.9
Hartford	939	0.9
Los Angeles	939	0.9
Total for 12 cities	54,826	51.2
TOTAL FOR U. S.	107,184	100

The unending caravan of immigrants coming from southern Europe and passing freely through the American gates stirred a crescendo of fears and hatreds among those who were already there. A body of literature emerged enumerating the perils for the "purity" of the American "race" and elaborating the myth of the "Nordic" superman and the image of southern European "human flotsam." The liberal immigration policy was strongly attacked from every side, from motivations which ranged widely, according to the economic, political, and psychological interests and attitudes of the various sectors of American society. Historians and free-thinkers of Spencerian tradition (such as Fiske and Cabot Lodge) insisted on continuing the Teutonic and Anglo-Saxon origin of social and public life in America. Protestant churches were hostile to Catholic—as well as to Jewish and Orthodox—immigrants, and so was the puritan sector of society which renewed the anti-Catholic inspiration of the previous "Know Nothing" movement and fostered the formation of the "American Protective Association" (Livi-Bacci 1961:10 ff.). Even leaders of the newborn unions (like Samuel Gompers) were against the new immigrants, for fear of competition of cheap labor and, later, for the widespread identification of Italian workers with "red anarchists and rioters aiming at over-throwing the American democracy with violence and blood" (Dore

1964:331). Feelings of fanatic patriotism were expressed in such works as Madison Grant's *The Passing of the Great Race* (1928:v) :

> The conviction grows that the Republic will perish, from internal, not external, causes. The assault upon the Republic, upon its traditions and institutions, are from within and are constant and progressive. One major danger lies in the influx of alien races. . . . To call it merely a major danger is to minimize. . . . Our danger lies in our steady and increasing degeneration into a democracy—and, thereupon, will follow chaos. Were peoples from these other races—alien as they are in mind, in outlook, and in instinct—actually needed for any purpose?

A result of this supposed threat were the two quota laws of 1921 and 1924, which drastically reduced the number of immigrants permitted to enter the country from Italy and other southern European countries. As the fears faded somewhat with time, Congress amended the 1924 Act in 1940 and revised it in 1952,[10] while its final form in 1965 moved away from a quota system toward family and occupational considerations.[11]

Meanwhile, the community of Roseto, Pennsylvania, along with the other groups of the vast Italian influx, had sunk its roots into the American soil. The many decades separating the arrival of the first Rosetans in the slate quarries of the Blue Mountain to present-day Roseto are a part of American history known only to the men who lived through it. Their experience, however, has been a meaningful one, worthy of interest and memory.

II

The Two Rosetos:
Two Related Communities

Roseto Valfortore, Foggia, Italy

ROSETO Valfortore is on the border of the province of Foggia,
Apulia, on the western side of a branch of the Appennine
Range. It lies on a small plateau against Mt. Stillo in the upper
valley of the Fortore River, about 700 meters (around 2,400 feet)
above sea level. The town is 54 kilometers (30 miles) from Foggia
and is within two to six miles of the surrounding villages of Alberona, Biccari, San Bartolomeo in Galdo, Montefalcone, and
Castelfranco.[1] Typical of mountain villages, the climate is very cold
in winter, when Roseto can be isolated for several days or weeks
because of snow. Spring and autumn are mild but short, while
summer is usually very hot and dry with breezes both from the
mountains and from the Adriatic Sea.

The best way to get there is from Foggia, which is located on the
Rome–Bari railway route. A private bus, driven by a Rosetan, runs
between Foggia and Roseto twice a day, touching a few other villages along the way. A straight provincial road crosses part of the
Tavoliere di Puglia[2] before reaching the medieval city of Lucera. A
curving country road continues up the mountain from Lucera, leaving the Tavoliere visible for a long time, before passing to the other
side of the mountain, and disclosing a very beautiful panorama all
the way. Roseto appears suddenly, from above, resting in a niche
and facing the faraway highest Appenine peaks—Mt. Gran Sasso,
Mt. Majella—and the Matese Mountains. Just before entering the
village, there is a spot called *Piano dei Morti* (the place of the
dead) with an old watering trough for animals, where tradition

Italy

100 MILES
100 KILOMETERS

SWITZERLAND
AUSTRIA
FRANCE
Trento
VENETO
Turin
PIEDMONT
Milan
LOMBARDY
Venice
LIGURIA
EMILIA-ROMAGNA
Bologna
YUGOSLAVIA
Genoa
Ligurian Sea
Florence
MARCHE
Ancona
TUSCANY
Perugia
Adriatic Sea
UMBRIA
CORSICA
(FRANCE)
LAZIO
Aquila
ABRUZZI-
MOLISE
ROME
Rosero Valfortore
Lucera
San Bartolomeo
Foggia
Tyrrhenian Sea
Benevento
APULIA
Bari
CAMPANIA
Potenza
Naples
LUCANIA
SARDINIA
Salerno
Eboli
Gulf of
Taranto
Cagliari
CALABRIA
Messina
Palermo
Reggio Calabria
Ionian Sea
SICILY
TUNISIA
Mediterranean Sea

Ray

has placed a number of legends and beliefs. The *Via Nova* (new street, dialect name for via G. B. D'Abanzo) leads to *Piazza Castello*, or *Piazza Ranne* (town square) in front of the *Palazzo Marchesale* (the palace of the Saggese Marquis). Judicial cases were once administered in this open square and a legend says that the anonymous marble head overlooking the spot from the castle façade was the head of a local prince, maybe Bartolomeo di Capua, whose ever-present face was an assurance that the law would be maintained. Another legend I heard in Pennsylvania says that heads of executed brigands used to be placed there in the past and that the present one was once a real head. Today this square, as well as part of the main street, is used for celebrations, markets, and fairs and it is the center of public life and entertainment. The square and the main street have sidewalks, benches, trees, and some of the newer houses; they are situated in the central part of the whole village area, along the mountain ridge. *Piazza Vecchia* (old square or old main street) is the oldest section of the village, extending from behind the castle to *Porta Ranne* (main gate). A semicircular street terrace, overlooking the Fortore Valley and facing a beautiful landscape, encircles the section of *Sottasanta* (literally, under the saints), which is the oldest and the lowest cluster of houses and alleys. *Piazza Vecchia* crosses this whole section of successive rows of stair-like alleys and narrow archways. The *Arco della Terra* (an archway through the castle) leads from the town square to the *Madonna del Carmine* (Our Lady of Mt. Carmel), Roseto's main church, which is artistically ornamented with marble work and fine doors. Keeping orientation in the intricate net of alleys forming the picturesque section of *Sottasanta* may seem hard to the newcomer; before long, however, he will discover that nearly every street has short cuts leading to the city square, besides being itself ultimately connected with it. The houses are built so close to one another that an American-born informant, commenting on his recent trip to his parents' village, compared its structure to that of an artichoke, using a realistic and indeed responsive image. All old houses are two-storied, the ground floor being divided between the kitchen and the stable (which is often used as a storeroom or working place) and the upper floor for the bedroom. The stairway is mostly an external feature and the houses are made of stone and stucco.

The furniture and the other items inside the house are limited to essentials: straw chairs, iron beds with both wool and cornhusk mattresses, traditional wooden trunks for clothing, and simple cooking utensils made of wood, copper, or aluminum. Ornaments consist mainly of sacred images and family photographs displayed behind cupboard windows, while curtains and carpets are only to be found in the houses of the upper classes, away from *Piazza Vecchia*. Floors are usually made of red clay tiles while the stable has beaten dirt. A wood-burning stone fireplace with a chimney, which was used for both heating and cooking purposes, is being gradually replaced by bottled-gas ranges but most houses also keep a smaller brick fireplace for burning charcoal, a *furnacedda*, used for cooking special dishes. Many houses have been recently equipped with running water and a toilet; otherwise, water is fetched by women from the public fountains with a wooden barrel, *varrila*, or a copper or clay container.

The roofs are made of alternate rows of flat and round red tiles and have an approximate inclination of 25 degrees. Although small, windows are a very important element in the community's life. They are conceived of as an extension of the cramped interior and are a means of communication and social control, as well as a place to dry the laundry and even store food items for preservation (red peppers, tomatoes, figs, etc.). Always ornamented with flowers or spices (the ever-present basil plant is famous in the oral tradition), they often have an iron railing, which gives them the added function of serving as balconies, after the Spanish style common to all southern Italy.

Besides the *Palazzo* and the main church, the other buildings and places of public interest are the elementary and junior high school, the town hall—which since 1898 has occupied a house originally meant to be a sanitary center, eight other churches, and a "new" cemetery.[3]

Men and women meet at different gathering places. In good weather, men meet in the square or on the main street and remain there until late at night, sitting on benches or at café tables, but more often standing or just strolling up and down the main street. In winter, they spend two or three hours after dark inside the four bars, which are all located near the square and on the main street. Rosetan bars are a combination of taverns, coffee shops, pubs, and social clubs.

Women socialize on the curbs outside their doorways in small groups. There they accomplish much of their domestic work during the daytime, and there they rest and chat at night until their men come home and join them for another hour or two before going to bed. In wintertime, they remain by the kitchen fire, alternately grouping at a neighbor's house, to save fuel. The fountains, the public ovens, and washing places are the other meeting places for women, while children of all ages spend their time in the streets. On festival days, processions, fireworks, band music in the square, markets, and fairs are important social occasions for men and women of all age groups and economic conditions.

Agriculture, based on the cultivation of wheat and corn, is the primary means of subsistence of the whole village. Since the best arable land is far away from the village, peasants must travel three to ten miles a day on foot or by mule to reach their land. Until the redistribution of land (after Unity and again after World War II) all the land worked by the Rosetans belonged to a few landowners, while today most peasants can till their soil as owners, *mezzadri* (sharecroppers), renters, or hired hands. Of these, the first and the third are the most common forms, since the land reform resulted in the emergence of a number of very small landowners. As elsewhere in southern Italy, this "atomization" of the land did not bring unqualified success, for the poor income earned from a small piece of land did not permit the peasants to acquire modern techniques and tools. Many of the latter are still wooden and plowing is done by men or mules. In the past, before massive emigration to America, no rotation of crops was ever practiced and agriculture suffered greatly from poor management. Now, the endless exodus of working hands, together with the absence of a large-scale plan of radical solutions, makes southern agriculture sink more and more behind the rapid general advancement of the North.

There are no industries in Roseto, and trade is limited to a few shops and periodic open-air markets. Since pasture land is scarce, animal husbandry is limited to sheep, goats, pigs, and chickens, and it is now definitely designated to women or children. A local marble quarry supplied the raw material for stone carving, which flourished until the turn of the century and was a craft passed on traditionally from one generation to the next by two or three families in the village. In the past the Bozzelli family were Roseto's leading stone workers, widely known outside the village, but today members of this family have either turned to agriculture or have migrated to the United States. A few artisans are still active in Roseto such as shoemakers, tailors, carpenters, barbers, blacksmiths, and coppersmiths; but they are noticeably fewer in number and more impoverished than their counterparts of two or three decades ago, and their ancient pride and prestige are now totally gone.

There is no post office in town and the mailman, who is also a farmer, distributes the mail brought in by bus. A semiprivate telephone-telegraph office is run by an American-born Rosetan who returned to live here with his family before the Fascist regime came into power. Rosetans in need of medical checkups usually go to Lucera and Foggia, while for more serious cases Naples or even Rome may be chosen.

The ex-farmers who have not emigrated are now engaged as laborers in construction plants in Lucera, Foggia, and other vicinities, while most of the land near the village is cultivated on a reduced scale by women and old men.

The Saggese family (former aristocrats) have not resided in Roseto for centuries; its surviving members live in the big cities and only come to the village for the annual festival of the patron saint, the Madonna del Carmine. The Town Hall had to support a long and difficult series of judicial cases against the Saggese for the settlement of their former possessions (Facchiano 1971:269).

Social distinctions still follow the ancient hierarchical patterns and closely reflect the occupational and economic realities of life. The landless farmer has thus always been on the lowest rung of the social ladder, followed by those who own a little piece of land, a "handkerchief of land" as it is often called. Although the two groups are equal financially, the difference in their status is determined by the fact that one owns the land and the other does not. The little landowners constitute the largest group since the reorganization of land under the Land Reform Act. Above them is a small middle class of landowners with medium-sized holdings (*massari*), shopkeepers, and artisans. A little higher in status than the *massari* is a small group which has more education and includes the municipal clerks, the teachers, the mayor, and the pharmacist. The old nobility and the archpriest, who traditionally occupy the top level of the society, are the class of the so-called *Signori* (literally, the lords). Due to the absence of the Saggese family and to a certain upward mobility caused by such factors as emigration, mass media, education, and greater participation in national politics, this top level of the social structure has become merely a symbolic factor. The local clergy still enjoy their leading position, but while their actual power is still intact, they no longer seem to receive the ancient *rispetto* (reverential obedience) once shared with the nobility and now appear much more worldly in the eyes of the peasants.[4] Ever since 1946, Rosetans have voted for the Christian Democratic Party, with a few voting for the Socialist and Communist parties, and the other political groupings getting no votes at all.

Following the typical peasant diet in the South, Roseto's consumption of meat has always been very low. Recently, due to the

A shoemaker works outside his doorway in Roseto Valfortore.

A returned emigrant in Roseto Valfortore.

Old Mariuccia works outside her doorway in Roseto, Pennsylvania.

Traditional gardening in Roseto, Pennsylvania.

penetration of some city life style through the media and emigration, more people are eating meat than in the past. Individually produced goat- and sheep-cheese, chicken, rabbits, and pork constitute ten percent of the whole diet, which otherwise is based on starch and vegetables. Olive oil, mostly imported from the nearby village of Biccari, is the only kind of shortening used by Rosetans, while butter, milk, and sweets are practically a luxury reserved for festive days.

Illiteracy was extremely high at the turn of the century (De Mauro 1963:32–39), and despite the increased availability of elementary education, the continued exodus of the most gifted individuals in the population—men and young people especially—has kept illiteracy high in the village. The Education Act of 1962 extended compulsory education to the fourteenth year, and all children today attend both grade school and junior high school. However, most peasants in the age group between twenty and thirty-five have only completed the five years of elementary school. Earlier schooling was accomplished under very poor conditions and classes were often taught in dialect. Attendance was irregular because many poor children were also engaged in field and housework. The next age group of people, between thirty-five and fifty years old, includes a few illiterate and many semi-illiterate adults,[5] while illiteracy is common among the peasants over fifty years old.

Roseto's history is not available in any complete form but an outline is offered in a recent book by a Rosetan priest (Facchiano 1971). References begin with the year 1000. Norman chronicles indicate that Roseto belonged to William II from 1166 to 1189 and that there was at least one Rosetan soldier on the Crusade (Del Re 1845: passim). A good, though not official, source for Rosetan history is the *Liber Baptizatorum*, chronicles of a sort maintained by the local priests in different periods.[6] There we read that Prince Sanseverino di Salerno owned Roseto in the early Middle Ages and then lost it following a series of murders in the royal family. During the threat of a Turkish invasion from the Adriatic Sea, Roseto was taken over by another Salerno prince, Dottor Domenico Rinaldo. At this point, an undetermined disaster drove the inhabitants out of the town, and they resettled at nearby *La Rocchetta* (the little rock) on a lower hill close by. According to the *Liber Baptizatorum*, a later landslide forced the Rosetans back to their original location, where the village was reconstructed by Prince Bartolomeo di Capua in the late Middle Ages. The ruins of La Rocchetta are still clearly visible, and a folk legend maintains that a horde of gigantic ants destroyed that place, thus completely ignoring the slide factor which is one of the most serious problems still affecting a wide mountain area around Roseto. For centuries, Roseto shared the unstable history of all southern Italy, virtually passing from the hands of one feudal ruler into those of another, down to the last Marquis Filippo Saggese.[7] The 1948 census indicated a population of about 6,000 people in Roseto Valfortore, but by 1961 only 3,436 were still living there. The latest census, taken in 1968, shows that the number of permanent residents has shrunk to about 1,800, with present emigration continuing to drain off still more of the active and best part of the population.

One does not need to examine statistics to realize the extent of emigration from Roseto. A walk through its old alleys, away from the busy town square, reveals entire sections which have become deserted, and the only inhabitants visible on the streets are women, children, and old people. Economic deprivation and social injustice have perpetuated a stagnant society with no hope of improvement. A growing awareness of the existence of a better way of life else-where has stimulated Rosetans to seek new opportunities through emigration to northern Italy and such cities as Rome, Naples, Foggia, and Bari and to the United States, Canada, Australia, and central Europe. For over ninety years emigration has been the only alternative to misery and defeat for Rosetans, as it has been for the peasants of thousands of similar villages. Of those who emigrated to America, only a few have returned to live in the village, while some have permanently settled in Foggia or in other large cities. Contacts with the Rosetan communities in the United States and Canada are very frequent, and while hundreds of families emigrated to Toronto and Hamilton, Ontario, in the past ten to twenty years, several families have still succeeded in emigrating to the United States, particularly to Roseto, Easton, Bangor, Philadelphia, Boston, and Washington, D. C. The present migratory trend, however, is typically one of "birds of passage"; that is, single males or young couples seeking temporary residence in the "industrial triangle" of northern Italy—delimited by Torino, Genova, and Milano—or in northern and central Europe, with frequent visits home—where many leave their children—and a common intention to settle eventually in urban areas, such as Foggia, Bari or Rome.

Roseto, Pennsylvania

The Borough of Roseto is located in the northeastern corner of Northampton County, Pennsylvania, in the shadow of the Blue

Mountain, not far from the "Pennsylvania Dutch" settlements. The terrain is very steep as the land rises from Martin's Creek, a tributary of the Delaware River, to the hill of Roseto, against the Pocono Mountains. Roseto is in the so-called "slate belt" area, and is about fifteen miles from the county seat at Easton, eighty miles from Philadelphia, and ninety miles from New York City (Basso 1952:50). Thick green forests cover the local mountains and the area is scattered with the dark, rounded hills of refuse from the quarries.

Roseto is surrounded by the boroughs of Bangor, Pen Argyl, East Bangor, and Wind Gap and by the villages of West Bangor and Martin's Creek.[8] In the 1950 U. S. census, its population was 1,667 and the 1960 census indicated a slight decrease to 1,630. Roseto's municipal authorities anticipate that the population will increase as a result of an improved highway system serving the borough and the recent annexation of new land. The following data are taken from the Town Hall records:[9]

	1930	1940	1950	1960
Population	1,746	1,778	1,667	1,630

The ethnic composition of Northampton County is heavily Italian. Although the cities of Easton and Bethlehem contain the highest concentration of southern Italian residents in this area, they have no distinctively regional groups (Grifo 1960:10). Roseto's population, on the other hand, is probably the most homogeneous ethnic enclave in the nation. The entire community is Italian, with about ninety-five percent of the people originating from Roseto Valfortore. There are several families of "mixed" ethnic origin in the sense that some of their members married the descendants of immigrants from different villages or provinces in Italy. With very few exceptions, however, their original homes in Italy are not far from Roseto Valfortore or from Foggia, such as Biccari, and other villages near Campobasso, Salerno, Potenza, and Benevento in the bordering regions of Campania, Lucania, and Abruzzi-Molise. Of the neighboring communities, Pen Argyl, three miles from Roseto, is the only one containing a large group of northern Italians, and these inhabitants all came from the same Venetian town of Vittorio Veneto.

Roseto was initially built at a walking distance from Bangor, but the two boroughs have practically become a single, continuous town in the last thirty to forty years, with Division Street and Front Street as their approximate boundaries. The steep hillside connecting Roseto to Bangor is called Fourth Ward and most of the houses there belong to Rosetans who settled beyond their borough because of the convenience of living near the factories or the quarries where they worked.

As many as twenty-five percent of the 5,766 Bangor residents are Italian, with many Rosetans among them, although the predominant ethnic groups come from the mining city of Bangor, Wales, and from parts of England and Germany. The settlement has been in existence since 1863, mostly engaged in slate quarrying and commerce, and it is still an important shopping center for the neighboring boroughs and villages (Basso 1952: passim).

The railroad line between Bangor and Pen Argyl which crossed Roseto in the middle was discontinued about twelve years ago and no other public transportation system has taken its place. A local bus service between Easton and Bangor was also discontinued in 1966 so that most transportation in the area is private now. Roseto's main street, Garibaldi Avenue, is a long, quiet street crossing the center of the borough in a south-northeast direction starting at the Catholic Church, running through the oldest and most populous section of the town, crossing Columbus Avenue and then turning east, toward Pen Argyl and the Blue Mountain.

Many of the social and economic activities take place in this old part of the Garibaldi Avenue which is the heart of the settlement. Here are most of the public buildings, such as the Church of Our Lady of Mt. Carmel—called *la Chiesa del Carmine* by the older immigrants, the Catholic Cemetery, the Post Office, the Travel Agency, the Marconi Social Club, the Town Hall and the Columbia Fire Company, the Roseto Hotel, and the Presbyterian Church. Also on Garibaldi Avenue are some of the oldest shops and mills such as the Castellucci Shoe Store, Mary's Luncheonette, De Franco Meat Market—still called *la chianca* by many residents, Ronco Pharmacy, Le Donne's Bakery, Cacciagarro Groceries, the Roseto Paper Box Company, Mat's Barber Shop, and Casciano "Connie" Blouse Company. The houses on Garibaldi Avenue—which was originally a wagon road—are the oldest in town, built directly on the sidewalk, with no space for front lawns. While little or no room is left between one house and the next one, all of them have long, narrow back gardens intensely cultivated by the oldest members of the families and still very reminiscent of southern Italian gardening. Here grapevines, tomatoes, fig trees, zucchini, broccoli, garlic, and onions are the most recurrent items while all of the traditional Italian herbs and spices, such as *malva* (a plant of the mallow family), parsley, mint, *origano*, basil, and the "precious" camomile, are given the greatest care.

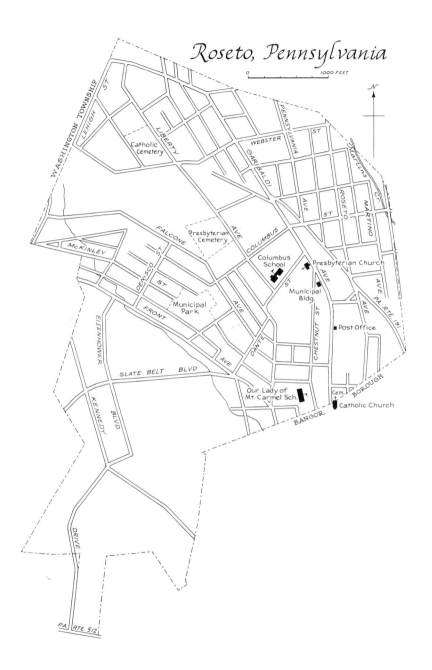

Roseto, Pennsylvania

0   1000 FEET

N

With the exception of the newest buildings, all of the houses here and elsewhere in town follow the two-story pattern, with the living room and the kitchen on the ground floor and two or three bedrooms and the bathroom on the upper floor. Most houses have a basement for food storage and wine-making facilities, where lined up on the shelves housewives keep hundreds of jars with home-canned vegetables and fruit. In their basic outline, most houses follow a general Pennsylvania style and what distinguishes them as Italian is more a matter of details and use than of architectural style. Kitchens are very large and are used as family rooms, while living rooms are reserved for guests and special occasions. Often the front porch was not an original feature of the house, but it was added later, reducing the space left for sidewalk use. Many buildings are painted white or dark red and white, regardless of whether they are built of wood or bricks, while the few stucco houses are usually beige.

A quick look at this old section of the borough around Garibaldi Avenue, Dante Street, and Columbus Avenue produces an image of a dignified but modest community: neat, compact, and well kept up. But the picture somehow changes if one goes beyond the central area to the outskirts, where young couples or wealthy families have recently moved. Here the houses tend to be surrounded by large green lawns with trees that shelter them from neighbors and there are no grapevines or vegetables in the gardens which are purely ornamental. These are invariably one-story houses, expensive suburban stone constructions, with an evident pretense of elegance and very similar, on the whole, to the patterns proposed by such popular magazines as *Better Homes and Gardens.* The interiors of these homes also reflect an effort to aspire to middle-class values. An enormous amount of space is devoted to the living rooms, while the kitchens are smaller than the traditional ones, and equipped with all sorts of automated facilities, wall-to-wall carpets, and decorations so that they resemble another living room rather than a place for cooking or eating. Curtains and carpets are particularly abundant as are vases, statuettes, and other kinds of knickknacks. Bathrooms are numerous: normally three, also lavished with colored carpets and ornaments as if to conceal their primary characteristics. Such homes are all centrally air-conditioned and often provided with two or three TV sets and fanciful telephones scattered about. The basement is also quite different from those found in the older houses Even its name has been changed—and it may be called a "bar" because it has a counter for serving liquor, complete with mirrors and bottles, as well as sofas, carpets, and expensive equipment for parties and receptions.

The most impressive public construction is surely the Catholic Church. The original wooden structure, built in 1893, was subsequently rebuilt in 1923 in native stone. The exterior is vaguely reminiscent of the Romanesque style, especially in the façade, with its colored rose window, while the interior is decidedly baroque, with arched windows and two rows of fake-marble columns supporting the indented walls of the central nave. The numerous sacred objects and ornaments on both the central altar and the side ones and the many statues of the Virgin and saints give it an unmistakable Italian character. In particular, the statues of the saints in the many niches along the side walls closely recall the naïve style of the artisan-made *santi* existing in the churches of Roseto Valfortore in Italy. The Presbyterian Church, also built on Garibaldi Avenue in 1893 and continuously served by Italian pastors until 1953, displays an architecture typical of most American Protestant churches, both inside and outside.

The municipal building and the Marconi Social Club, both on Garibaldi Avenue, are rather simple buildings, square in shape, entirely of brick. The former houses the Town Hall as well as the Columbia Fire Company, while the latter, enlarged and modernized several times, was designed for the entertainment of its members, with an auditorium, banquet rooms, and large kitchens. It is now used for the rehearsals of the Roseto Cornet Band and for parties and social dinners of the various sodalities, clubs, and political groups.

Besides the numerous boarding houses of the past, the borough until recently had a regular "Roseto Hotel," which was purchased by the local American Legion Post, and now there are no hotels in town. There are only parochial schools in Roseto: the Columbus School on Columbus Avenue, the Salesian Sisters Convent and Kindergarten, and the Pius X High School facing the Catholic Church.

In the past the great majority of men worked in the slate quarries, while several score worked as unskilled laborers in various plants in the Easton area or in Bangor and Bethlehem. The artisans were the only immigrants who retained their former occupation after the move to America, and there are still a few Rosetan shoemakers, barbers, and tailors living either in Roseto itself or in the immediate vicinity. Some individuals acquired new independent skills, usually through a previous period of apprenticeship in New

York City before settling in Roseto. Photography and flower shops, as well as plumbing establishments, are examples of these trades.

The blouse mills existing before World War II multiplied rapidly after the war, and Roseto has now seventeen such mills, all family businesses, with two or three brothers or cousins as joint owners and an average of ten to thirty-five employees. Men are usually employed here as pressers or cutters, while women operate the sewing or finishing machines. Husband and wife are often employed in the same mill as well as one or two of their children. As a rule, women did not go to work in the past, and besides housekeeping and sewing they only engaged in such activities as picking and selling berries and wood gathering in the nearby mountains. It is calculated that about seventy-five percent of Roseto's women are now employed in the shirt factories, while some of the younger ones are working as beauticians, clerks, or nurses outside the town.[10]

Two of the nearby slate quarries are owned or directed by Italians: the Capitol Slate Quarry, which is owned and directed by Joseph Capozzolo, and the Stoddard Slate Company, directed by Ferdinando Tedesco. Fourteen of the forty-five workers in the Capitol Quarry and eighteen of the fifty in the Stoddard Company are Italian, while the majority are Welsh and German. The Rosetans living in the Bangor area are rarely slate miners, most of them being artisans, shopkeepers, clerks, blouse mill workers, professionals, and contractors. Dr. Romano and Dr. Farace, Rosetan physicians, live and practice in Bangor, while Dr. Turtzo, who is also a Rosetan, practices in Pen Argyl. There are several Italian physicians in the Easton and Bethlehem areas and many Rosetan residents go that distance to be treated by them.

Aside from the slate and blouse industries Rosetan commerce is comprised of three beauty shops, two barbers, a bakery serving a wide area outside the town, two shoemakers, one pharmacy, two florists, one funeral home, two restaurants, one gas station, one part-time photographer, one butcher, and three groceries. Superficially, Rosetans give the impression of being a classless society, maybe because their behavior has retained much of their peasant Italian background. In the community's eighty years, however, clear differentiations have emerged, some of them reflecting the distinctions brought over from the Old Country. While none of the emigrants belonged to the upper classes at the time of their departure, smaller differences did exist among them. A few were highly regarded artisans, such as the Bozzelli family of marble carvers, and others were the poor relatives of Rosetans who had acquired some kind of social distinction in the past, such as the Capobianco and

Wine-making in Roseto, Pennsylvania.

A slate quarry in Roseto, Pennsylvania.

the D'Avanzo. These small differences were not forgotten in the new country, and in spite of the initial sense of unity and common poverty many of the Rosetans explicitly claim social superiority because of distinguished ancestry. Wealth had long been a powerful means of social distinction in the Italian past and, consequently, those families which became successful in their American business ventures soon formed a small elite group representing the new local power structure. This elite group enjoys recognized prestige in Roseto and often sponsors undertakings of public interest—like the elite groups in Italy who sponsor celebrations and other public events but do not participate in the local life—but it does not join in the real life of the community. Socially, this elite group cultivates relations outside Roseto and often outside the ethnic group.

Names such as Falcone, Rosato, and Policelli are regarded as highly distinctive as they correspond to the names of Roseto's founders: Nicola Rosato, Lorenzo Falcone, and Giovanni Policelli. Other names of old settlers such as Ronca, Tedesco, Ruggiero, Donatelli, Cacciagarro, Sabatino, and Cascioli are also regarded with esteem. Most members of these families still live in the old part of Roseto around Garibaldi Avenue. Children of these families have rarely married American Rosetans not originally from Roseto Valfortore or non-Italian Americans.

As it happens in Italy, nicknames denoting regional origin in Italy other than Rosetan, such as "Viccarese" (from Biccari), "Alberonese" (from Alberona), and "Marchesciana" (from Marche), can be transmitted from parents to children. These nicknames show that names of towns are only used when the place of origin is close to Roseto Valfortore, whereas those of provinces or regions refer to more distant, alien places. In addition to the place of origin in Italy, nicknames such as "Maria la Forestera" (Mary the foreigner) and "Carmela la Taliana" (Carmela the Italian) show that the time of immigration is an important factor of social distinction. I could easily notice—and I heard bitter complaints about it—that the new immigrants are kept at a certain social distance, are given nicknames reminiscent of their recent immigration (i.e., "Italian" in an all-Italian community), and are forced into a subordinate role similar to that suffered by the first Rosetans when they encountered the already established non-Italian settlers. The latest arrivals must go through a sort of apprenticeship before they are truly accepted into Rosetan society. Recent immigrants from Roseto Valfortore would not be allowed to communicate in the Rosetan dialect with the American Rosetans who would only speak English to them. It was only after the newcomers had shown some knowledge of English that they were allowed to communicate in the Rosetan dialect! The fact that several American-born Rosetans have married the children of other settlers, such as Sicilians, Campanians, Lucanians, Abruzzesi, and Marchigiani, was thus a matter of some social consequence in the community life.

The greatest public festival is the annual celebration of Our Lady of Mt. Carmel, on the last Sunday of July—as it is in Roseto Valfortore—which gathers Rosetans and non-Rosetans from all over Pennsylvania and from localities in Florida, California, and Canada, wherever relatives and friends live. Just as in Italy, it lasts three days and involves a procession and other kinds of communal recreation, both outdoors and indoors. Fireworks have been recently discontinued and many Rosetans complain that the festival has lost much of its ancient splendor and vitality.

Other occasions for public gatherings are the traditional "Spaghetti Dinners" at the Marconi and Columbus clubs, the Carnival dances and banquets, the various meetings of the sodalities and political parties, and the fund-raising dinners for Roseto Valfortore's Mt. Carmel celebration, or for public disasters such as the flood in Florence or the earthquake in Sicily. Family reunions, bringing together hundreds of blood relatives and in-laws from all over the nation, are held annually in Roseto's park.

Street socialization, so prevalent in the past, is becoming less and less relevant and the pedestrians in the streets today are rarely the young members of the community, who prefer to use cars. Families often sit on the porch or in the gardens, especially in the warm summer nights, women will chat in the doorway, and old men will occasionally sit on the bench outside of the butcher store or stand in front of the barbershop, but the outdoor life that once prevailed has definitely gone and a pattern of increasing privacy is becoming the present life style.

Nearly everyone devotes Sunday morning to church. Older people spend festive afternoons visiting while younger inhabitants mostly drive to nearby resorts or sporting events. Most adults speak and understand the Rosetan dialect while the younger children can often comprehend it but are unable to speak it. The Italian-born Rosetans rarely read or speak English fluently, while the oldest American-born usually know both languages and some of them even seem more at ease in the dialect. There was, for example, the sad case of an American-born lady who had forgotten her English in her old days and could not communicate with her nurses and doctors at a hospital far from Roseto where she had been taken. The lack of any real linguistic communication between grandmothers and grandchildren is an everyday matter.

Education is becoming a matter of great concern for the parents, who work hard in the mills in order to provide high school and possibly college education for their children. The superintendent of the Bangor High School told me that the students of Italian extraction had a marked desire to succeed, were more willing to submit to discipline, and tended to choose the fields of law and medicine when they went to college. The children of Protestant Rosetans attend the Bangor schools, while many Catholic children from Bangor attend the Catholic school in Roseto.

Catholic Rosetan residents are roughly 1,230, the Roseto Presbyterians number around 270, and the Jehovah's Witnesses count over fifty members, mostly among the various branches of the Tedesco and Finelli families.

Local channels of communication that permit a rapid spread of news in the community vary from accidental meeting to visiting and from daily contacts with relatives and neighbors to informal gatherings at the shops. De Franco Meat Market is a good meeting point for such an exchange. On the whole, in spite of the quiet and almost empty appearance of the streets, rumors seem to circulate quite rapidly and a visitor is hardly in town when most people will know it. *"Paese,"* the Italian word for town and village, is still widely used here to refer to both the place and the people in it, and expressions such as *"lo sa tutto il paese"* (the whole village knows it) and *"ma il paese non vuole"* (the village doesn't want it) clearly illustrate this identity of place and people.

Italian family solidarity, which has often served as a classical example in sociological literature, has been largely retained here and reciprocal support among relatives and godrelatives is one of the few pillars on which the community still rests. The structure of the family is still pyramidal—at least formally—with the father as its head, *capo di famiglia*, with complete authority over his wife. His authority over the children, on the other hand, is becoming less stable and clear, and his traditional leading–protective function over his unmarried sisters and younger brothers can only be observed in a few cases. At the same time, the children are taught, by word and deed, that membership in the family carries with it duties and obligations for the common benefit and many still give most of their wages to the parents, as is still done in Italy. The ambitions and the interests—both social and material—of the college students, on the other hand, are focused elsewhere, on undefined horizons of life and freedom. "This place is dead," "There's no freedom here," "I don't like the way people live here," are frequent remarks heard among the eighteen- or twenty-year old nonworking youths.

Like Roseto Valfortore, the American Roseto has had very active city bands. Members of both the first and the second generations agree that Roseto's famous cornet bands were often invited to such places as Boston, New York City, and Philadelphia, where they won numerous prizes. Nearly all of my male informants, in fact, have been or are now members of the Roseto Band, which is presently directed by Fred Vario, the chief of the fire company. Everyone in town is very proud of the past musical traditions and of the Rosetan musicians who have acquired nationwide reputations such as maestri Imgaro and Donatelli and Professor Leonardo Falcone, present director of the Michigan State University Band.[11]

After the first group of eleven Rosetans came to work in the Bangor quarries in 1882 (Basso 1952:7), increasingly large waves of immigrants came from Roseto Valfortore. They first lived in the poorest barns, the "shanties," scattered around the slate quarries, working for as little as forty cents a day and rejected on both social and religious grounds. In 1887 the first house was built on the hill near Bangor in the place that soon expanded into the group of houses called "New Italy" by Rosetans and "Italy Town" by non-Italians. There is much controversy among the Rosetans as to the man who built the first house and I have often listened to contrasting versions of the story. The county records, however, seem to indicate that Nicola Rosato was the first to acquire a piece of land there in 1887. In that same year, Lorenzo Falcone and Giovanni Policelli arrived, and these three men are regarded as co-founders of the settlement. Since then, all Rosetans arriving from Italy, South America, and other places in the United States settled "up hill" in "New Italy," which rapidly became a village of considerable size. There followed a long, tormented history of hard work and endurance, patient saving, and long and bitter feuds with the Welsh and English groups in the vicinity. As most immigrant peasants in America, the Rosetans had to be initiated into industrial life, and the problems stemming from their inexperience created frictions between them and other ethnic groups which often resulted in bloody battles along the hillside dividing "New Italy" from Bangor and the other communities. Today, with the third generation becoming adult, an attitude of tolerance has developed, while both the first and the second generations maintain quite evident traces of the old resentments.

The first twenty to thirty years of the community's life were marked by frequent trips back to Italy, either to find a bride or to fetch parents or younger sisters and brothers. A few returned to live permanently in Italy, while some came back to America before the restrictive laws on immigration were passed. Some went to serve in the Italian army up to World War I.

Since becoming a borough in 1912, all Roseto's mayors and councilmen have been of Rosetan extraction, except for Mayor George Giacquinto, whose ancestors came from near Naples. The 1912 incorporation of "New Italy" as Roseto Borough[12] and the World War I period were years of central importance for the transition of the community and for the uncertainty which many felt about whether their identity was Italian or American. During those years, many of the people realized for the first time that they were going to remain in Roseto and decided to acquire American citizenship or urged their children to do so.

Since then, the history of Roseto has been a slow and uneventful one for this ethnic group so contained in itself and yet so continuously engaged in vital contacts with different groups. Written records are very scanty and mostly deal with a few memorable dates such as those for the construction of the Knights of Columbus Hall, the Town Hall, the opening of the Martocci–Capobianco American Legion Post, or the colorful celebration of the Roseto Golden Jubilee in 1962.

The majority of old immigrant women did little or no traveling outside Roseto after their arrival from the Old Country, while many of the men made frequent trips between America and Italy at the turn of the century. Besides this special experience, totally confined to their youthful age, few immigrant men did any extensive traveling elsewhere until recently, when summer trips to Italy became common again. After World War II, the example of American life patterns, as well as increased financial affluence, have made traveling a more common feature in the life of all Rosetans. Usually, however, visiting with relatives or attending ceremonial occasions are still the primary motivations for traveling, at least for old and middle-aged persons. Besides mutual visiting with the Rosetan settlements in Toronto, Ontario, and the numerous other settlements all over the United States, more groups and individuals are traveling to Italy every spring and summer. The older tourists prefer to take guided tours to Florence, Rome, and Naples and then rent a private car for a trip to Roseto Valfortore, where some of them stay two or three months. Some even send their relatives passage money to come to America for a visit.

This continuous contact with Italy and with other Rosetans in Canada and elsewhere brings about a series of interesting phenomena and observations, from both the Italian and the American points of view, which will be analyzed in this book. Rather than from written records, the true history of Roseto emerges from the individual lives of Rosetans, from the accounts they give of their personal and communal experiences, and from the examination of their present culture, which bears both the vestiges of the old tradition and the fresh traces of their American life.

III

The Rosetan Migration
and the Myth of America

Yes, New York, rather than Rome or Naples, would be the real
capital of the peasants of Lucania, if these men without a
country could have a capital at all. And it *is* their capital,
in the only way it can be for them, that is, as a myth . . . as
an earthly paradise.

The peasants who emigrate to America remain just what
they always were, those who come back twenty years later are
just the same as when they went away, like stones, which a
rushing stream has long coursed over but which dry out
under the first warm rays of the sun. In America they live
apart, they live next door to the earthly paradise, but they
dare not enter (LEVI 1947:123-24).

STUDYING the effects of a recent historical phenomenon such as
the Italian immigration to the United States requires the use
of a variety of approaches and techniques. Written records rarely
deal with the individual culture of immigrant groups and the study
of oral traditions seems the primary means to discover the very core
of that culture. While Italian-American folklore does not include a
very large number of new texts resulting from the migratory experience, many important adaptations have occurred in the pre-
existing folklore traditions. These significant changes are clearly
perceivable both in Italy and in the transplanted groups abroad and
constitute a powerful illustration of the migratory phenomenon as
a whole.

I shall here examine all those forms of oral tradition which reflect the Italian migration: from emigration songs to adaptations

of older ballads and from personal historical accounts to proverbs, letters, messages, and folktales. As for the historical accounts resulting from the interviews, I regard this material as both richly informative and as a form of authentic traditional narrative. These accounts are eloquent evidence of the social and psychological implications of real events, but it is also evident that the presentation of those conflicts and tensions is largely based on traditional concepts and beliefs. In Roseto these narratives have been transmitted orally through generations and concern the critical points of the migratory process: emigration, arrival, search for work, primitive standards of living, the fight for survival against established settlers, and first accomplishments. These accounts are often expanded rationalizations of events and attitudes and they mostly refer to personal experiences, but they are largely applicable to the group as a whole. They are passionate, quick to magnify the courage and the virtues of Italians in confrontation with a hostile and insensitive society, and they are popular among the second and third generations whose only contact with the emigration experience is through these narratives. We can find in them the immediate expression of those intimate values which constitute the core of the culture and which rarely emerge from direct questioning, either from the difficulty of formulating objective judgments or from the fear of contradicting the official expectations of approved social behavior.

In the interviews and the traditional texts America often appears as a mythical land, immense and magnificent, opulent with food and flowers. This theme recurs in the proverbs, tales, and songs of Italy and of other countries which have experienced the large-scale emigration of their citizens to America. While some of these texts were created in the new settlements, others originated in Italy before and after emigration among both the emigrants and those who remained at home. It is irrelevant to try to establish whether a certain song originated in the new or in the old country, as the intense diffusion in both places indicates a continuous stream of reciprocal borrowing of themes and texts which actually followed the movement of the migrants to and from their native land.

The image of a marvelous land, a promising escape from age-old miseries, often recurs in folksongs. The following stanzas refer to the time of the first emigration to South America, with a powerful image of that immense and wondrous "third part of the world."

> I bless Christopher Columbus,
> Who discovered the third part of the world.

He discovered three parts of the world,
And we Italians are called to work there.

And coffee is all over the land,
Long live America and those who are there.

And America is long and wide and beautiful,
It is all made of roses and flowers,
It is all covered with roses and flowers,
Long live America and those who go there.

Refrain. . . .[1]

I recorded several versions of this song in Roseto Valfortore in 1965. All of the versions I collected in central and southern Italy are basically identical to this one although the tune may differ slightly. In spite of its being popular in Italy, in Canada, and in the United States, the song has not, to my knowledge, been included in any published collection. Several other songs were similarly inspired by a romantic view of America as a paradise:

What shall America be?
A little bunch of flowers.

I want to go there,
though it is a distant land.

I wonder what it is like,
I wonder what they do there.[2]

Proverbs, however, seem to reflect a more materialistic, though still admiring, view of the "promised land":

He who becomes American can eat and drink like
a Christian.[3]

He who can see America becomes as rich as
a king.[4]

Besides promising beauty and vastness, the opportunity of finally becoming human—becoming a Christian—is envisaged in the abundance of food and money. The conviction that economic and social fulfillment would never be allowed at home continues to motivate the major part of the peasant migration. The traditional lore teaches the peasant that no human dignity is possible in total poverty, no beauty for women, no peace, and thus centuries of ancient hopes and dreams crystallized in a modern dream: America. The following proverbs reflect the bitter realities of the peasant lot:

> A woman can't be beautiful if she has no
> flour in her house.

> If you lack a little bread, you'll be kicked
> like a dog.

> There is no hope for those who are in need.[5]

Once the idea of emigration penetrated the community, it created a tremendous turmoil of practical problems and decisions in what had always been the most static style of life. Writing letters became an everyday problem—and it would be more so after emigration—as did the collection of such items as documents, photographs, and luggage. None of those issues had been dealt with by the peasants, who were not even accustomed to traveling to the next village unless on foot or on a donkey. The objects and money needed for the trip and the problems connected with it are often mentioned in the songs about emigration. *Mother, Give me a Hundred Lire* is surely the most popular ballad on this subject. It can be found from one tip to the other of the peninsula as well as among Italian immigrants everywhere. I recorded it among all groups I visited in the United States and in Canada. The following was collected in Roseto, Pennsylvania:

> "Mother, mother, give me a hundred lire
> For to America I want to go."
> "I won't give you the hundred lire
> And to America no, no, no!"

> "If you don't let me go to America,
> Out of the window I shall jump."
> "I won't let you go to America,
> Better dead than dishonored."

> Her brother is at the window:
> "Mother, mother, let her go."
> "Mother, mother, give me a hundred lire
> For to America I want to go."

> "Go ahead, evil daughter,
> May you drop in the deep, deep sea!"
> When the ship sailed half the ocean,
> To the bottom she did sink.

> "Oh ship, you're sinking to the bottom,
> To the world you'll not come back!
> My good fisherman, as you're fishing,
> Fish out also my pretty Gina."

Now the pretty hair of pretty Gina
Feed the fishes of the sea.
The pretty eyes of pretty Gina
Feed the fishes of the sea.

The pretty hands of pretty Gina
Feed the fishes of the sea,
The pretty body of pretty Gina
Feeds the fishes of the sea.

"These for sure must be the curses
That my mother put on me!"[6]

My informants refer to *Mother, Give Me a Hundred Lire* as *the* emigration song. It tells of a girl who wants to go to America at all costs, even though her mother refuses to grant her permission to do so. She finally leaves, but her mother's curse follows her and the ship sinks in the middle of the ocean, taking the girl with it. However, this song was not originally inspired by the emigration movement but it is a later adaptation of the ballad *Mother's Curse.*[7] The old motifs of the eloping girl and her drowning under her mother's curse have been maintained, but love as the cause of the elopement and the horse as its physical means are here substituted by America and the ship, respectively. The 100 lire[8] request seemed too little to my informants in America, and thus some Pennsylvania versions speak of 500 lire or even of 1000 lire.[9] In general, I found the American texts longer than the Italian ones, with a marked stress on the girl's request, which is often repeated several times, following each of the mother's refusals.[10] In Italy, on the other hand, it is not infrequent to hear unfavorable comments on the stubborn girl.

The following songs were not adaptations of pre-existing texts, but they naturally make large use of traditional themes and concepts. They are very different in terms of musical and metrical pattern, diffusion, content, and emotional attitude. The first song belongs to the group called *partenze* (departures), popular in central and southern Italy, where the theme inspired wedding songs (the bride leaves the paternal home), shepherd and fishermen songs, as well as serenades. Its tone is very sentimental and only the Italian side of the migration is described. I found this text among the Tuscans living in Chicago in 1964 and slightly different versions in Newark, New Jersey, among a group of former shepherds from Abruzzi-Molise:

I am leaving for America,
On board the long steamship,
My heart is full of pain
For I'll see you no more.

> But before I leave,
> I shall go to the square,
> To see if there is a girl
> That I can take with me.
>
> In the square there are no girls,
> There is only my sister.
> Adieu, my beautiful land,
> I shall come back no more.[11]

I recorded the following song in Roseto Valfortore and the surrounding villages of Alberona, Biccari, and Castelfranco. The Rosetans abroad—United States and Canada—seem to remember more stanzas as they probably sang it more often. It is also possible that the song is of American origin, which would explain its abundance of details about American life and its greater popularity in the new country. While the tune is the same in all the forty-two texts I recorded, the variations are mostly a question of selection of motifs, with the request of the dowry being rare in America, where the song usually starts with the girl's departure. Quite logically, the Italian texts start with the girl's request for her dowry and insist on the motif of departure but most do not go beyond Gibraltar and details on the American experience are missing. The following text was recorded in Roseto, Pennsylvania, from a seventy-six-year-old lady who emigrated from Italy at the age of sixteen:

> What does America mean?
> A little bunch of flowers.
>
> The steamship is ready
> It's now ready to leave.
>
> When we arrived in Gibraltar,
> The land closed and the sun got dark.
>
> When we got to the Battery,
> All people spoke and I didn't understand.
>
> When we got to New York,
> The train went down and the water on top.
>
> When we got on the sidewalks,
> Just like soldiers all women look.
>
> Oh, America is a silly land,
> Even the peasants wear evening suits.
>
> Here the poor artisan has his art:
> A shovel in his hands, he plows the asphalt![12]

Here is a text of the versions commonly found in Roseto Valfortore and sung by an eighty-year-old informant, nicknamed "Garibaldi":

> Mother, mother, give me my dowry,
> For to America I want to go.
>
> Farewell, my dear sweetheart,
> We will not meet any more.
>
> I leave you with a "goodnight,"
> I shall see you no more.
>
> Tomorrow I shall leave
> To go to America and to New York.
>
> What does America mean?
> A little bunch of flowers.
>
> The steamship is ready
> It is now ready to leave.
>
> When we arrived at Gibraltar,
> The sun got dark and the earth closed.[13]

The motif of a temporary residence in America and an eventual return to the native village is often present in songs and tales as this was a common pattern in the real life of the emigrants. It is interesting to note the peasants' view of the various levels of success that are possible in America. In Italy, the people know that those who become really rich never return to their original village.

C: They go there, they make a ship of money, they write home less and less, they get married, they disappear. They forget about us here. They become like those kings there, we don't see them any more.[14]

Those rich people become fantastic characters lingering in the peasants' memory, filling their imaginations with dreams of wealth and magic and reinforcing their desires to emigrate.

Despite this fantastic view of America reflected in some folksongs, the characters impersonating the returning migrants in the folklore texts never seem to be the very rich kind. On the contrary, whenever the dramatic or comic adventures of returning fellow-villagers are described, they never acquire a distinguished stature and, as *Americani*, they are just ordinary peasants, returning with very modest savings. What happens to them is what usually happens to the characters in the traditional stock of jokes and anecdotes. They rarely appear as more skilled or clever than the local villagers as a result of their life in America. Common stories about the numb-skull man from a neighboring town or village are usually adapted to fit the situation of the departure and return of migrants, just by adding or substituting the American element to the local and pre-existing one. The story often involves a returned emigrant who loses his little American fortune because shrewd fellow-peasants are quick to capitalize on his slight disorientation caused by the long absence. *Campanilismo* is widely reflected in emigration stories involving those set in America and those with an Italian setting. In-appropriate behavior is thus rarely attributed to a Rosetan emi-grant and it usually involves someone from San Bartolomeo in Galdo—the rival nearby village—or from Alberona just two miles away from Roseto Valfortore. A typical example of this kind is the story of the farmer emigrating from San Bartolomeo who, upon seeing the calm and flat ocean for the first time, exclaims: "That's what I call plenty of land to plant my cauliflowers!"

Although the folktale type Th 939/A: *Killing the Returned Soldier* does not seem to exist in Italy in prose form, it is very popu-lar in a long ballad called *Bruno Comes Back from America*. The young man goes to America where he saves a good sum of money. When he comes back, he goes to eat at his parents' tavern and, characteristically, is not recognized by his old folks (America can change people), who plan to kill him for his money. In both Rosetos I recorded variants of this song in which Bruno is saved at the last minute by either the Madonna of Mt. Carmel or the Holy Trinity, who inform him of the tragic mistake. Interestingly, old informants in Roseto, Pennsylvania, did not seem to remember this song, while two middle-aged women who have made summer visits to Italy know it.[15] Here is the text I collected from a retired cart driver in Roseto Valfortore whose daughter emigrated to America:

> Gino made up his mind to go to America,
> To go and get himself a good position.
> He told his father what he had in mind,
> His mother was tormented with great agony.
> One day she told him, "Son, before you part,
> Let's go visit the shrine of the Holy Trinity."
>
> Gino went to America and from that land
> No letter to his father he ever sent.
> The money that he made there day by day
> During all that time of his long stay
> He put it in a bank for times to come,
> And on March twenty-three he got back to Rome.

When he got to the tavern it was by night,
He said to the host, "Please, bring me some wine,
I happen to pass by this place of yours
And you'll do me a favor if you'll put me up.
From traveling so far, I feel worn out,
I come from America and I'm heading for Rome."

[To me: Do you understand what this is, Carla? They're his mother and
father! They don't recognize him!]

They served this youth in all he wanted,
But as he was paying, he drew a nice purse:
Inside they could see there was a good bundle,
Two thousand good dollars, which was much gold.
His father who saw it went straight to his wife,
Their mind was to kill him and rob him all clean.

Gino went to his bed to take a good rest,
His mind was tomorrow to reveal himself.
The first dream he had as he went to sleep
He saw the Holy Trinity right there at his feet.
It said, "Dear Gino, try and save yourself,
For your savage father your life wants to take."

Gino got up and was all full of fear
As that apparition was still in his mind.
He knocked on the door and he called so loud,
"Your true son is here, won't you hug him again?"
When his father had seen that it was his true son,
All full of regret and sorrow he was.

His mother her dear son she held so tight,
With joyful tears her cheeks were all wet.
She said, "Oh, my son, how were you so wise
To guess all that was in our cruel minds?"
He said "Oh, dear mother, the Holy Trinity,
It saved my young life from your evil cruelty."

Reference to the scarcity of male population as a consequence
of emigration—another dominant feature in the real-life situation
—is also reflected in tales and songs, where the common hardships
accruing to the abandoned families are described. Many men leave,
send letters and money from America, but sometimes they gradually
stop writing and never show up any more. What happened?

My husband went to America and doesn't write
I wonder what offense have I done.

The deserted bride says that she finally turned to another man and now has more babies and problems than before. The song has a satirical opening, in which the woman describes the ridiculous efforts of hiding her irregular position from social sanctions, and it closes with the bitter realization of how the best young men are taken away by emigration.[16] Almost all the Italian-Americans I met know and like this song which is also very popular in Italy. The reason for such popularity is probably its realistic rendering of an important aspect of the whole emigration experience: the loneliness of the close relatives left behind.

The main characteristic of the peasant view of America is a mixture of realistic knowledge and folk attitudes and fantasies. A variety of impressions, dreams, and opinions, often inconsistent with one another, is to be found in many other songs, tales, and proverbs; and it is this contradictory body of beliefs that proves the existence of a myth of America in the peasant world: an America which is both earthly and heavenly, real and unreal; real, as a land for work, sweat, and sacrifice; unreal, as a magic universe with infinite possibilities for fabulous strokes of luck, a truly superhuman world, comparable to the peasant world of miraculous saints and madonnas. This is what Carlo Levi called the "dual nature of this myth" (1947:116–17) among the peasants of Lucania. This dual myth is both believed and not believed. The peasants are well aware of the hardships and failures existing in that world, and yet it can be magically wondrous for them. Just as is their Madonna, whom they worship and implore with absolute faith in her infinite and miraculous powers and who, at the same time, is viewed as a poor peasant woman, a suffering mother, totally impotent against the malignity of men and life.

Most families in Italy have a close or distant relative in America and tangible signs of these connections are visible in all rural houses. One can see calendars of American shipping or construction companies, framed dollar bills, photographs of religious celebrations in the United States, relatives photographed beside their luxurious cars or in front of their American cottages, and even posters advertising some Italian-American brands of food such as Del Monte, Delmonico, and Gallo. But the most striking thing I have seen, illustrating the dual nature of the peasant's view of America, is the combined portrait of President Kennedy and Pope John XXIII. These two genuine folk heroes are often pictured on the walls of Italian homes on both sides of the ocean, where their function is not different from the protective one secured by the images of St. Nicholas, St. Anthony, or the Madonna del Carmine. As Levi stated in his *Christ Stopped at Eboli* (1947:122) :

> ... the eyes of the two inseparable guardian angels that looked at me from the wall over the bed. On one side was the black, scowling face, with its large inhuman eyes, of the Madonna of Viggiano; on the other, a colored print of the sparkling eyes and the hearty grin of President Roosevelt.

Ambivalent feelings toward America are displayed by returned emigrants:

(B: Bianco;   A: Antonio)

B: So, how long were you there?

A: Twenty-seven years, yes. Oh, Madonna, oh!

B: But why did you come back?

A: It wasn't me, oh, no! The family. The family didn't want to stay, I mean my wife. The air wasn't good, you see? There is nothing like your native air, nothing!

B: Wasn't the air good there?

A: Oh, yes! It's beautiful over there! Lots of trees, green, huge plants—gigantic! Nice. The air, I suppose, was all right, but what can I say? Native air is native air, that's all. No comparison.

B: And, apart from the air, how was life there? Work? Where did you work?

A: In the cement mill, down in Easton. Outside Easton, a huge thing—great! They paid good money there. I made hundreds of dollars a week there. Oh, I tell you, thousands and thousands of dollars! A lot! [He has obviously forgotten how much he was earning.]

B: Really? That much?

A: Much more, much more! It's not like here, like this miserable place here! There is gold, there are jobs, plenty of jobs, I know it. I worked like a dog, with the furnace, and foreman was always mad at me. Oh, boy! He was a *Germanese*: No good! He wouldn't give me time for breathing. I had to hurry all the time, all day, "Yes, Sir. Yes, Sir." I had to say "Yes, Sir." Here it's different: You can sit here in the square, resting, chatting in the sun. It's peaceful here, it's restful, oh, yes, it is!

[Another man sitting on the bench with A. interrupts with a proverb.]

Man: Had the peasant known all this, he wouldn't have gone to America.[17]

[All men around us laugh at the rhymed proverb.]

A: Oh, you shut up! I am not speaking against America. It's a great country! What do you think? I love it. Those are civilized people—not like us here, not like you, scratching the soil with your fingernails! It was not a place for me, that's all!

B: No? But why?

A: You see? You can't meet your friends there. There is no love there, you cannot count on your own people, on your own wife and children there! They tell me I'm dumb. Oh, I don't know. Maybe.

Antonio's vacillation perfectly reflects the mixed feelings toward America typical of most returned emigrants, at least of those who returned to an agricultural life in the village, after the industrial interlude in America. Like most other peasants, Antonio has blind faith in the magic properties of "native" air (a belief which was often reinforced by all sorts of exploiting propaganda), and he also enjoyed returning to the restful peace of his village. On the other hand, he was obviously dissatisfied with the frugal life to which he has returned and America lingered in his memory as a challenging giant, both fair and unfair, ugly and beautiful: the myth of America. Most interviews with returned emigrants in the Italian villages contain similar attitudes.

The final stanza of the ballad of Christopher Columbus, in contrast to the opening lines describing a vast and magnificent land, contains sober and more realistic messages from the American experience: the reverse of the medal.

> We came here from our villages,
> We didn't find any straw or hay,
> We had to sleep on the hard ground,
> Just like animals. This was our rest.
>
> *And coffee is all over the land,*
> *Long live America and those who are*
> *there.*

Another song contains similar opposing themes:

> What can we find in America?
> Mountains of gold and mountains of work,
> A golden cross, but still a cross,
> A diamond cross is still a cross.[18]

Very successful emigrants usually lose contact with their village of origin and enter a fantastic paradise of semigods and fabulous heroes, the "American dream" that survives in the peasants' minds.

Unacceptable life conditions in Italy and the extraordinary success of some individuals sustain the need for continuing emigration and the belief in the "earthly paradise." Actual experience taught many emigrants, though in a confused way, that their basic condition was not changed. Even when hard work and endurance were able to afford some material improvement and thus some rise in human dignity, the immigrant could see that he still was a total alien in the society for which he worked, just as he had been in his native country outside his village society. He still was—and even his children might often be—a member of a totally subordinate social class, where he had no other function than fulfilling material needs. There was little chance of improving his condition of being an exploited, forgotten piece of a superior and unknown mechanism. He had more money—though not always—to secure physical survival, but he had lost the reassuring factor of living in the familiar world of his own village. In addition, his family was suffering from the disorganization and breakdown fatally associated with the urbanization process. His uneasiness was increased by slum-like housing settlements, which offered all the disadvantages of low-class urban dwellings and none of the few benefits typical of rural ones, while ironically he was often engaged in the construction of beautiful buildings and entire cities.

Consequently, the ambivalent dual attitude toward America held by the immigrant—and especially by the returned emigrant—may be explained as the result of two main factors: the undying hope for a dignified human condition, fulfilling the simple man's dreams of justice and equality, and the frustrating experience of the narrow chance for real change in the existence of the peasant, no matter where he goes to work. Hence, the contradictory view held by both the immigrants in the United States and the peasants in the Italian villages: America can make one happy with its gold, freedom, justice, vastness, beauty, mechanization, and abundance of work. And yet the same persons will define America as bitter, ridiculous, unjust, dangerous, unhealthy, crazy, incapable of love and friendship, and will even deny that American food can have a taste and flowers a perfume!

To conclude this brief review of the dual nature of the "American dream" I shall quote from a poem by Emanuel Carnevali (1925:161–62). Returning from America, where he had spent all his adult life, he wrote:

> I come from America, the land that gathers
> The rebels, the miserable, the very poor;

The land of puerile and magnificent deeds;
The naïve skyscrapers—votive candles
At the end of supine Manhattan.

I come from America where everything
Is bigger, but less majestic;
Where there is no wine.
I arrive in the land of wine—
Wine for the soul.
Italy is a little family,
America is an orphan,
Independent and arrogant,
Crazy and sublime,
Without traditions to guide her,
Rushing headlong in a mad run which she calls
        progress.
Tremendously laborious America,
Builder of the mechanical cities.
But in the hurry people forget to love,
But in the hurry one drops and loses kindness.
And hunger is the patrimony of the emigrant.

America, you gather the hungry people,
And give them new hungers for the old ones.

The Rosetans Tell Their Story

(M: Maria Antonia)

M: My father, my mother, my brothers, and my uncle—we all came together, see? In 1907. When we arrived here, it was the twentieth of October 1907. And when I left from my village in Italy—from Roseto Valfortore—I walked half the way holding onto the tail of our donkey, you know? I was walking after our mule, holding her tail, and my uncle was leading the mule. Do you know who is my uncle? He is my father's brother, Custanza Zito's father, so that she is a cousin to me. So I was crying and crying and my father repeated over and over: "Keep walking! We must get to Naples." And I said, "No, no, I don't want to come, I want to stay with Grandma!" And the man—you know what he did? He couldn't take it any more and—you know, like the Italians do—he took off his belt and gave me so many blows! And my uncle was afraid he'd kill me. But you see, he had to do it, because I was stubborn. We were going to Naples—to America, that is—and I was walking back to Roseto, see? He *had* to do it.

B: Was this the road down from Alberona?

M: No, the other way. To come to America, we had to go through Castelfranco, and all those other places, see? Then, to Naples, to take the boat.

B: And how was it on the boat?

M: Oh, it was so beautiful! My mother was always sick. Not my father, though, no. He had already done nine or ten trips back and forth. He came and went, he went and came, see? My mother didn't like to come to America because in her family she was an only girl, and five brothers to take care of, see? All farmers, and she was the girl and she didn't want to leave them. But she had to realize that my poor father was going and coming all the time! So he said to her, "If you don't come now, I take another woman. And then it's worse, see?" And you sure know the proverb!

B: Which proverb?

M: *Americane e soldate sonne mal'aspettate* [Soldiers and Americans are not worth waiting for].

B: That is to say?

M: That is to say that after a while, they don't come back any more! See why? I was about ten years old then.[19]

Maria Antonia, 68, later told me that after she came on the S/S *Spartan Prince*, she never went back to Italy or left Pennsylvania. She visited Philadelphia for some special occasions, but, otherwise, spent her whole life in Roseto, only going to the nearby settlements for errands and necessary purchases.

The previous account and the following ones are fairly representative of the two most common patterns of immigration. The first pattern is that the family group, in order to preserve its own unity, eventually leaves the village, after as many as ten or more round trips to America. The childhood memories of the crossing remain as a series of vivid fragments, each focused on a critical aspect: exhaustion from the journey to Naples, her mother's reluctance to leave her kin, the beauty of the ship, the long route to Naples through "all those places," the mule—or donkey—as means of transportation. Not all my informants went to Naples by mule and walking, some of them had the chance of going by horse cart to Foggia, where they could catch a train to Naples.

The second oft-repeated pattern was that of the trip to America of the young bride, whose wedding had been arranged through photographs and letters between her relatives and friends in the two Rosetos. This second pattern was common to all southern Italian groups in the United States. Luisa Strippone's mother was such a bride:

(L: Luisa)

B: What is your name?

L: Luisa Strippone. My grandfather was *scardalana*, that is, he made mattresses, in Roseto Valfortore. Then, Mamma came to America but Papa came first, see? But they didn't know each other, or maybe they did, but Papa used to live in one side of the village and Mamma in another. But Mamma came here because she was supposed to marry Pietro Cistone. Then, when she arrived at New York, Pietro Cistone didn't show up, see? Now, my mother had come on the boat with a man: They say he was godfather with my grandmother and his name was "*Cacamele*," that was his nickname, yeah! At that time, my Mamma was seventeen, so my grandmother had told him, "You watch my daughter!" See? And the godfather said, "Yes." Now when they arrived at New York, my mother was scared, 'cause she saw that Pietro Cistone wasn't there! But *Cacamele* said, "Don't worry," and he took her and he left her with Domenico Stefano. When they arrived in Roseto, she stood there and Papa was with Domenico Ronca, across the street. Within seventeen days they got married! They didn't marry for love, though. In those days they took each other, but not for love. She thought, "I came up here and who knows what's gonna happen to me! It's better I take him." See? They didn't marry for love, what love? Anyway, we were glad that Mamma took Papa. It's good she didn't take Pietro Cistone, *nu cazze de mbriagone*, a drunkard![20]

There is a similar story of an eighteen-year-old bride who had been entrusted by her parents to the Captain of the S/S *Madonna* in Naples. The girl sailed alone and was supposed to be met in New York but, once at the port, nobody called for her.

(G: Giovannina)

G: When I came from Italy, nobody showed up for me in New York, so I started crying and I said, "I wanna go back, I wanna go back! No one came to meet me!" But there had been a trick with my name, see? My people asked for Giovannina while my papers said "Maria Giovanna" and so it was a mess! They couldn't find me and went away. But I didn't know it, see? Everyone spoke different, I couldn't understand a thing and I was so scared! I had my suitcase and the money was on my breast and I held it all the time. I said, "Now they can rob me, they can do anything to me!" See? Everyone shouted English and I wanted to go back. I cried. But there was a fellow from Benevento on the ship, and he said to me, "You must go to Roseto? I know Roseto, they're all Italians over there. You must go, it's easy: You go to Bangor and all roads go to Roseto from there, see? Then, if Americans speak to you, you just say, 'I no stand,' and they understand that you don't understand, see? You say that word and show this note with the address. You just say, 'I no stand' and they won't touch you."

B: And then, what happened?

G: Then he took me to the train station and left me there. There were only men there, men reading newspapers. I said, "Oh, Madonna! Do I have to spend the night in here?" Because the train for Bangor was at 3:00 A.M. see? So, I put my bag on the seat, and I sat on the bag. I didn't want to go to sleep because I was afraid so I kept my hand on my breast where the money was and just sat there. But I did fall asleep for a while, and then somebody pulled my arm and I was awake. I saw a woman, tall, lean, huge. I said, "Oh, Madonna, she must be a witch! What does she want from me now?" She spoke to me and I said, "No stand! No stand!" But she went right on speaking and I said again, "No stand!". I was mad because I *had* said "No stand" and yet she continued. Then she even pushed me and took my bag from under me to the other end of the room! Oh, boy![21]

It then turned out that the witch was the station clerk who was kindly trying to tell the girl to lie down on a couch and rest until three o'clock and that she would check the luggage. But how could Giovannina imagine all this? It wasn't just a linguistic problem. It is true that she did not "stand," but even if she had known English, she surely would not have believed the woman's innocent intentions. By night, a station full of men: what was that woman doing there? She finally saw the couch and agreed to lie down but insisted on keeping the suitcase as a pillow and did not go to sleep until the train came.

The psychological and practical situation of the arriving immigrant is revealed in these accounts through abundant details, comments, and descriptions which also indicate the adherence to the traditional values and beliefs embedded in their culture of origin.

The letters the immigrants sent home from America are another valuable and often exciting source of information about the migratory experience. Theodore Blegen (1931) has brilliantly used these letters to illustrate his work on the Norwegian immigration to America. Maybe because of the high degree of illiteracy common among southern Italian immigrants in those days, I could find only a few such old letters in all my contacts with Italian-Americans and their relatives in Italy. As can be seen from the following letter, many immigrants had to use another person to write home, and the people in the village were then confronted with the problem of reading it.

Dear Mamma:

I hope the *Madonna del Carmine* and all the angels protect you and my sisters and my brothers. This *paesano* is writing this letter because he is lucky and can write better and I hope the Madonna will protect him. We work all day and night, too, and I eat at cumpare Francisco's boarding house but we never sleep and I want to tell you that the foreman promised me more money after February and I hope it's true because the expenses are high and if all goes well we can buy the land with that fountain, mamma, and I do what you told me to do and I never forget to do that way. Our room where we sleep is warm because the stove is in the corridor and we are not cold and yesterday cumpare Filippo brought me the camomile for my stomach and the *malva* and I gave him fifty cents. Now I finish this letter and send you a hundred kisses and be in good health and kiss Carmelina and aunt Cristina and the relatives at home and that you write soon and I send my blessing from the United States of America.

Your affectionate son Bonanno Giuseppe.

While doing field work in the Italian villages before going to America, I often recorded messages to take to the American relatives. Very significant human material poured into my tape recorder through this particular form of correspondence and the important aspect of contact between relatives divided by time and space is here illustrated with great immediacy and ethnographic realism.

(M: Menica)

M: When you go to Roseto, Pennsylvania, you find a niece of mine there.

B: Yes, and did you say you wanted to send her a message?

M: Here? Ah, well, you'll say, "Your aunt wants to know how you are—your aunt Menica from Roseto Valfortore—"

B: But you can speak directly to her, if you want.

M: Here? With this? Well. But it must be precise—clean—the address, no?

B: No, you'll give me the address later.

M: All right then—I forgot your name——

B: Carla.

M: Ah, Carla, well! "Dear niece, dear niece Carmela: Your father wrote me and he sent me the money for *Sant'Antonio*, for the *festa* of *Sant'Antonio*. I told him that he's got to come to Roseto, that he must take a trip to here! But he doesn't want to come, see? Encourage him to come, to come and see me here. Tell him—all of you tell him to come here: You and his brother Filippo and his sister Rosina and you, too, come on! Hurry up here, you and this *cazze* [obscene] of Ferdinando you married there! *Addio*, Carmela! I kiss you." Is it all written up there now?

B: Oh, sure!

M: Oh, no kiddin'?[22]

The following message was delivered with great excitement in the presence of a large number of relatives, all of whom were very touched at the idea that their names, now being mentioned one by one on the tape, were going to be heard in America.

(G: Giovanni)

G: "Dear cousin Giovanni: I am your brother-cousin Giovanni. I am in the *paese*, here in Calabria. My sisters Filomena and Nunziata are here near the table and they are your cousins, too. Giovanni, we are lucky that this lady came here today because she will come to you in America where you are. We gave her your address in Brooklyn and let's hope that all the brothers and sisters with the children will be there when she comes there with this instrument. Giovanni, do you hear me? I am old and ugly now, see? But you live in America and with the help of la *Madonna di Pettoruto*, who knows? Maybe we shall meet again! My sister wants me to inform you that we sold our mule last Saturday and we also sold grandma's vineyard this year—the land near the road, remember? The weather was bad this year and we couldn't manage, with the boys in Germany and everything, see? Giovanni, my brother-in-law Rocco wants to thank you for the money you sent for his daughter and, Giovanni, we are the same blood and you know my affection for you. Aunt Michelina is here and sends you her blessing and also your old *cumare* Domenica blesses you and her son Antonio. And now we must tell you that tomorrow there will be the funeral for *mastre* Donato, the shoemaker near us, remember? Well, now kiss your daughters, Carmela and Nunziata, and be well. Goodbye, up with America![23]

Most interviews reflect the conflicts resulting from interethnic contacts once the immigrants settled in their new homes. The informants in the following excerpts are drawn from the second and third generation and a variety of age and social groups, and all related the difficult relationship between Roseto and Bangor, that is, between the Rosetans and the Welsh, Germans, Irish, and Venetians. In these relationships, I found no significant differences among the various age and social groups, but it appears that the initial struggle for survival has by now stabilized itself in the usual patterns of *campanilismo*—Roseto in opposition to Bangor or Pen Argyl—just as in the old country it had been Roseto Valfortore in opposition to San Bartolomeo, Alberona, or Biccari. They believe that the Rosetans alone of the many groups in the area were capable of distinguishing achievement and this in spite of the hard situation created for them. Goals were achieved thanks to the extraordinary characteristics of their own group, because of physical qualities ("we are strong") and thanks to their cultural heritage ("we are southern Italians"). Consequently, the group is eager to defend and preserve those characteristics which they think proved rewarding in the struggle, and to reinforce the in-group tendency even more. Much of the present attachment to traditional values and even contact with the Italian village may be due to the reinforcing effect played by Roseto's success as a group against a hostile environment. A. Z. Falcone is regarded as the most prominent and respected figure in Roseto, Pennsylvania. Aside from his personal qualities of generosity and active participation in the improvement of the town, he has the additional distinction of being the first male born in the new Roseto.[24] This explains his nickname, *"Americanedde"* (Little American), by which Rosetans still identify him and even occasionally his relatives. The appellation belies his ethnic affiliation, which is with the Italian rather than with the American portion of the society, while his in-group reaction characteristically leads him to identify Germans, Irish, and Welsh as "Americans," but never the Italian-Americans.

(A. Z.: Anthony Zilio')

B: Is there much contact with the other Americans around here?

A. Z.: Well, you know what I mean. Especially the Americans: They are under us here and yet they call us "Shoemaker, shoemaker!" Yeah, they call us "Wap" and "Dago," sure! Now, of course, they don't do it as they used to. Well, first of all, we served

them right, you know? A lot of sound blows, yes, a lot! We killed
them, we ran after them all the way down the hill inside Bangor!
That's true! But we *had* to do it, because, you see, they gave us hell,
see? It exists now, still now! I don't care, but it does exist now, yes,
sir. My daughter, A., she married one of these Americans, yeah!

B: Is he from Bangor?

A. Z.: Irish! Yes, from Bangor, of course. That one! He eats
like an animal and drinks like a wolf. Well, I don't know—in their
minds, these other races here—they think they are one point ahead
of us all the time! You don't know, but we Italians are too humili-
ated—you know what I mean? They say things to us, they call us
names, and then they come up to Roseto to fill up their stomachs.
We have too much of a good heart! Those were pretty bad times
for the United States: Depression—have you heard of the Depression?

B: Yes, I think I have.

A. Z.: Exactly. But up here in Roseto we had everything! We
worked in our gardens, we cultivated every inch of land. We gath-
ered wood and berries up in the mountains, we grew chickens, goats,
pigs, yes! Yes, sir, we had all we needed and I tell you why: because
we like to work! And then, in the quarries, they would—well, like
myself or a fellow like Luigi, you know, Filomena's poor husband?

B: Yes.

A. Z.: Well, all of us. The Americans managed to give us the
hardest jobs—jobs for animals, yes! And little pay because they
wanted us to leave, see? And God forbid you made a mistake and
picked up their hammer or their chisel? Damn! It was real hell.
I used to say, "All right, God, you made these damn fellows. But
why did you have to put them in front of my eyes?" Oh, Carla, I
often wanted to throw them into the quarry, right into the water!
It happened to a fellow, he could not resist it. Because they are
jealous of us, do you know what I mean?

B: But I suppose time has changed things, no?

A. Z.: Well, in a way, but then, of course, our younger people
nowadays are just as dumb as those foreigners, see? Now it's the
Americans who come up here for work. Yes, in our mills, because
they were good for nothing, all that drinking, no saving—well, now
they have to watch, and yet, they think they are better! *La Ma-*
donna! [He curses.] Like yesterday, remember? Well, those are all
Italians: Sicilians, Rosetans, Abruzzesi, Neapolitans. They had
named their place *Pompeo*, I mean, *Pompei* in the first place, you
know? Out of respect, see? But what respect! These Americans
know no respect and they renamed it West Bangor. West Bangor!

Carmine Malpiedo and his grandson during a storytelling session.

Anthony Zilio' Falcone. As the first boy born in Roseto, Pennsylvania, he is called *Americaneddu,* the little American.

La Madonna! Oh, it was no joke, let me tell you! Those streets there, see? I made them all. I was with the highway company then.

B: But how was this place at the beginning, do you remember? You were a little boy then.

A. Z.: Oh, I remember—I remember everything. My parents had just a one-room shanty, right on the slate, near the bushes. Yet, they made a second room against it and took in boarders, they made *la borda* [the boarding house] and we slept four, five, six together. I remember the mattresses: we used to go to the Dutch down here— they had the corn. We would fill the sacks with corn leaves and Mamma made the mattresses for *la borda* because she was *la bossa,* see? Our people came from their home up in Italy and they were hungry, no joke! The English here, we call them *Johnnybull,* they are like bulldogs, see? But they like the Venetians all right. Did you see Pen Argyl? A long line of houses, that's Pen Argyl—no shape or anything, just a line. Well, one side of the street is all Johnnybull and the other is all Venetian, true! Do you know that proverb?

B: Which one?

A. Z.: *Die li fa, poi l'accocchie* [God makes them and then puts them in pair]! [He laughs.] Now, Pen Argyl is Johnnybull, Bangor is Welsh. Roseto is Rosetan. Carla, our fathers—they were hungry for money! Just this morning I was telling Peter, the postmaster— Pietro Rinaldi, you know him. I said, "Pietro, do you remember when we used to go pick *roccabalà* [Italianized corruption for huckleberries]?" Forty, fifty baskets up in the mountains, then we used to sell them in Bangor, see? Oh, but the Welsh didn't like that, no sir!

B: But how was it for the Italians who settled down in New York City, do you know?

A. Z.: They were worse off! I know that! I got people in the Bronx and I used to visit them. Here we got our town and we always got it since the beginning. They gave us hell all right on the job, but home was home! You know what I mean? Up here we are like kings. They used to attack us down there, they would throw stones and tomatoes, they said we smelled, we were Dago, Guinea. But not up here in Roseto! No! No! I told Dr. Wolf, I said, "Doctor, this is why we have no heart attacks: We are happy." Yes, I told him all right, oh, I did![25]

Another informant of the second generation called those first decades "our fathers' frontier days." Although twenty years younger than A. Z., Carmine was just as emotional and in-group oriented as

A. Z. His speech is very excited and his highly patterned gestures add a great deal of meaning to what he says.

(C: Carmine)

C: Well, the fights we used to have—we were kids. We used to go down there to the brickyard, to swim. The Welsh boys of our age would get our clothes and they would put knots in it, you know?

B: Knots?

C: Sure. They tied our sleeves, our pants badly and then they chased us. Well, we couldn't dress up that way 'cause there were knots in our pants, see? So, we'd run up the hill naked, and by the time we'd get home, we'd get hit by our fathers, see? First thing, my father didn't want me to go and swim at all. Every time I'd go there I'd always go for a beating. We used to go to the moving picture house there in Bangor, we didn't have any up here, see? Well, some of the Welsh guys would start a fight. They'd hit us in the movie, or they'd wait for us outside and they'd beat us badly if we were few. Those times in Roseto we didn't have no sidewalks, see? and we'd make a little wagon with wheels and we'd go down to Bangor on the side of the road. So those Welsh boys they'd jump on us and they'd break the wagon! The dirty bastards! We had to run. But sometimes we beat them bad, too. So, one Sunday, I was comin' out of the movin' picture and one fellow hit me on the head. He had a stone—he broke my head for no reason! I was Italian: that's the reason! Because we was Italian, that's all. They used to call us Guineas, they called us wop. But I recognized that boy. I recognized this boy and on the Big Time, when we have the Mt. Carmel feast, you know, on the last Sunday of July—well they had the nerve to come up here, the pigs! To eat our good food! To provoke us! Well, I saw this boy and he saw that I spotted him. So he started walking with a man: He thought that I figured that was his father, see? But it happened to be that I know his father! So that I took a stone and followed him. Boy, I got him, boy! He said, "Don't hit me, don't hit me!" Oh, but I hit him. His name was Warren and I was nine or ten. Yes, I started to work at nine, so I was ten. We once decided to burn down Bangor!

B: Burn it?

C: Sure! We tried. We put their club on fire—they had a club there. But they put it off soon. Damn!

B: How about the adults? Your father, for example?

C: The big ones? The big ones, too. Their big people would pick on our big people, see? We used to fight hard. They used to holler at our daddies, "Guinea! Wop!"

B: Why did they say that?

C: Oh, I don't know. That I don't know. They would holler at them, "Go back to Italy, Wops!" They didn't want us here. But when we'd catch them up here—wow! [he whistles], we'd give them a lesson!

B: Any reason why this happened?

C: Well, jealousy, I guess. Because they saw we were better. This town was starting to build and they could see that everything was booming down with them, they was gettin' less money. In other words, the Italian people was slave, they was always labor, until someone started making blocks and things, and they got wise, see? Then, we had good music! The musicians of different nationalities didn't have the air, the power, the blow, the notes—they was flat. Just like you take a good professor, you know, when he makes a preach?

B: Yes.

C: At certain times, he raises his voice, when he's supposed to, and then he calms down. Now, you take another professor that is not an Italian—he talks just like if he reads. Our children, our grandchildren here, they know this well. He doesn't give you the expression of the story—that's what counts! Once our band won against Bethlehem and Easton and they threw eggs, stones, everything, and the band had a big fight, with mandolins and violins: they had to hit, yes! They was just jealous! But all the Italians, they are all strong, they eat well! When an Italian hits one of these Welsh people here, or a Johnnybull, they'll all remember! Then, if they gang up—like three or four—and get an Italian, naturally, then he uses a knife! Of course, to defend himself.[26]

A third-generation Rosetan, who is a painter and elementary school teacher, represents the younger, college-educated generation; and yet, despite her remoteness from the experience of the settlers, the stereotyped concept of the first integrating years persists very clearly. Although she lacks the aggressiveness and hostility of the older informants, she maintains their traditional attitudes and beliefs.

(A: Anne)

A: It's still a problem, though not as much. Until lately, even to go around with a boy that wasn't Catholic, or that wasn't Italian, was a big problem up here. Especially a non-Italian, yes. Because we were antagonized, always.

B: I see; but which group was most antagonizing?

A: The English! The English! We found that the Polish and the East Europeans were easier to get along with. But the Northern people—like the English, the Germans, the Welsh—they used to be badly against us, because they thought to be better than we were, do you know? I think they treated us like the colored people are being treated today. Do you understand?

B: Yes. And what about the other Italians? Those from different villages, like Biccari or the Sicilians? Did they get along well with the Rosetans here?

A: Oh, there were lots of arguments. There still are! Every group thinks to be better than the other one. Like my father: he would pick on my mother because her parents were from Biccari and his from Roseto Valfortore. I mean, they were both born here, but their folks came from different villages. They would call each other names—they would even fight for this. And their dialects differ.

B: But you couldn't tell the difference!

A: Oh, I can tell right away! I can tell if one speaks *Biccarese!* There is a different accent!

B: I see; and how about the Venetians?

A: Oh, those are so different!

B: Yes? How?

A: Look, we have those up here in Pen Argyl. Well, they don't have the initiative that we have here in Roseto. They're—they're nice-looking people: tall, blond, blue eyes. They're quiet people, too. But they're not as easygoing as we are, and not so smart either. We are friendly, we love each other—they don't. The Venetians— oh, I think they—they have an idea of superiority, anyhow! They are more like—like the English—that's it. Cold.[27]

The social and psychological need for the Italian-American to be considered as valuable as other groups makes them boast of some impossible roles in the progress of the nation. There are a few legends among them which reflect this need to raise the group's prestige and the desire to be looked upon as socially and culturally influential in the society. Legends about Garibaldi, Colombo, and the "invention of music," do not circulate in any significant measure in Italian villages, yet I found them quite popular in America, especially among southern Italians. One reaction to a reputation of being low-class late-arrivals and ignorant and dirty people took the form of a sort of folklorization of such historical themes as Garibaldi fighting oppressors among different peoples. With the exception of the Poles and the Black Americans, the Italians appeared to have the lowest status of any of the other groups, far below the status enjoyed by the British, Scandinavians, and Irish. The Blacks, therefore, where often rejected as inferior by the Italians, who were eager to designate an ethnic group with a lower social status than their own, to be despised or pitied. The Sicilians, for example, who are the most discriminated against of all Italians, have nicknamed the Black Americans *mulagnane* (Sicilian for eggplants), and the Tuscans in Chicago call them *Mori* (Moors). Racial discrimination, however, rarely erupted into violent hostility, and during my field work in different parts of the United States and Canada I never observed hysterical and violent rejection of the Black people, taboo against socializing with them, or hatred for them. Actually, in the southern United States, southern Italians were often reported "too close" to Black Americans and thus were viewed as a possible menace to the white "American race." An historian of immigration has written:

> The arrival in the South of increasing numbers of dark-skinned immigrants seemed likely, moreover, to raise new racial problems for a section which already believed it had its quota of them. In particular, the tendency of the newcomers, especially the Italians, to associate freely with Negroes, threatened to blur the color line (Jones 1960:266).

Because of a reputation as criminals and murderers, as strikebreakers, and as members of the Mafia, the southern Italians incurred various levels of discrimination:

> The strength of the K.K.K. in the South was aimed at three groups: the Negro and his associates, the immigrant, and the non-Protestant. The Italian was threatened by all three biases. Mob violence against Italians took place in Louisiana on several occasions, the most prominent being the lynchings in New Orleans in 1891 (Cunningham 1965:25).

Italians were even alleged not to be white, as Förster (1919: 408n) in his important book on Italian immigration to America reported in these significant statements collected from southern American employers: "One white man is as good as three Italians" and "It makes no difference whom I employ: Negro, Italian, or white." Rosetans are not in close contact with Black Americans because none lives in the town itself. The following legend of Garibaldi as a "liberator of slaves" touches upon the problem of racial issues.

(P: Piscianzinu)

B: What about the others? English? Welsh?

P: Oh, no. They're American! They are not like the Dutch.

B: I see. And the Negroes?

P: Oh, that's a long story! I can tell you that.

B: Tell me the whole thing.

P: All right. When Garibaldi went to the United States, he went to the South, because the Negroes were ill treated in the South, see? They were treated like the animals—worse than that. They still rebel now because they don't want them in the schools with the white people! A shame! You can see that on TV. So, when Garibaldi came here, he went to the South and he said, "No, this is bad. This cannot continue like this. No!" Because, you know, Garibaldi came here and when he came he had the power of an officer. He was a superior officer: he was Officer of Science! Do you understand?

B: Yes.

P: Well. He is also the one who made the Italian unity. However, when he came to this country, he saw that the Blacks were slaves and he said, "Why should human blood be treated so badly? This is human blood!" And he called all the doctors he could and made them visit the Negroes. And the doctors found that Negro blood was purer than our blood, better than ours! Therefore, their brain is better than our brain—they are more intelligent than we are. So, Garibaldi ordered everybody here in this country to let the slaves free because, you know, Garibaldi knew the Negroes well, he had Negro soldiers in Italy, too. So, Garibaldi freed the Negroes from slavery, you see? That's the story.

B: I see.

P: Now, these new generations don't want their children to go to school with Negro children! They want to cancel what Garibaldi did! Well, some of them are different, they are malicious. But the others—they are bright, they are good. You should see some of them on TV: You would go out of your clothes! [He means from laughing.] There is even a Negro singer at the Metropolitan Theatre in New York singing Italian Opera! They don't want them. It's an infection of jealousy, the same they have against us Italians here![28]

The negative judgments that Italian-Americans often give of Black Americans are exactly the same as those usually given by other Americans of southern Italians:

G: They are all right, they all belong to America, they are all Christian, they are not animals. They have brain, good brain. I know it because there is a family next door, so I know that. But they are not very clean, they are lazy boys, that's all. They riot, they don't keep quiet and nice, they're noisy, too. They have all those children, you know? But they are lazy boys, that I know, and they don't clean their back yards and all that, you know?[29]

It seems that while the first conflicts were of a more violent nature, involving a crude struggle for survival on occupational and territorial grounds, now the antagonism with other ethnic groups has shifted to a smoother, quieter level. In Roseto, the Italian-born immigrants have played a passive role in later interactions, as they no longer have personal contact with the outsiders. They only narrate repeatedly to their children and grandchildren what the situation was in the past. The second generation is still very resentful. Despite their bitter feelings and the narrations of the "frontier days," however, they are beginning to give more attention and thought to their children's attitudes. Their children are now receiving high school education, which means new contact with non-Rosetans and non-Italians, both in their own town—where the Bangor Catholics come—and in Bangor—where the Protestant Rosetans go to school. Some of the third generation are attending college, and with them the very nature of the interaction is beginning to change. It is no longer a question of the whole community standing as a bloc against outsiders in violent but clear terms; the Rosetan children now face different, more subtle problems of ethnic and social differences. They must interact on different terms with the children from the other groups—the same groups which are so bitterly disliked by their elders. Many of them are thus expected by their parents to retain their group identity in a school which is totally American and, at the same time, to become successful American citizens.

Among the few letters I was able to collect, the following one, addressed to Mrs. Sabatino Cirino in Roseto, Pennsylvania, by her son Onorio Cirino during the war in southern Italy, is certainly the most touching. It describes the enthusiastic welcome given by Roseto Valfortore to this young American soldier when he went there to see his old grandmother for the first time in his life. The long-interrupted contacts between the two Rosetos were re-established by this visit, which is still a memorable event for both communities. I shall quote the entire letter which is an invaluable picture of the wartime difficulties suffered by close relatives on both sides of the ocean.

Dear Mamma:

I left here from [somewhere in Sicily] Dec. 1, got the 10 p.m. plane out of here and reached Naples where I had a delay before leaving for Foggia and I traveled the rest of the way to Roseto Valfortore partly by jeep where I arrived about 5:00 in the evening.

I stopped at the first house I saw and a man by the name of Luigi Di Franco came up to me. "I am a *Rosetani* from Roseto, Pa.," I told him, "I have a grandmother here by the name of Rosa Santucci Sabatino." Well, to cut this letter short, he brought me to grandma's.

It was dark and I awoke grandma, who was in bed, and called, "It's your grandson Onorio, son of your daughter Giuditta!" "Tomorrow is another day!" grandma said and she just wouldn't believe it. But finally she did and I can't express the joy there was. We hugged each other so tight! I kissed her for you, Mom, and she said I looked just like you. She said God has answered her prayers that she would see me and she said she would die of happiness. Grandma looks so pretty at her age which is 89! She has all white hair.

Gee, Mom, how we both cried when we met! I'm crying again as I'm writing this letter. I was scared to ask for grandma because I thought she might be dead since we haven't heard anything from her for five years. But she is in good health and she's so pretty!

The village of Roseto wasn't touched at all by the Germans and I was so happy to see that when I got there. Of all the ruined places I've seen in Italy, it was in the best shape and untouched, don't worry about anything like that and there is food to eat.

I stayed over at Uncle Nicola Romano's daughter's place. Her name is Giuditta like you and she has a son 4 years old who has never seen his father. He is a prisoner somewhere in Africa.

Tell Uncle Tony that his sister's son Tony [Antonio] is somewhere in Greece. They haven't heard from him for a long time.

I had so much fun with all my cousins there. They were afraid I couldn't speak Italian and were amazed to find out that I talked just like they did, just like that.

My cousin Giuditta, Uncle Tony's niece cooked hand made *macaroni, cicateddi* and *prechlatella* for me. Gee, I really ate there; I bet I gained ten pounds. I had a time sleeping, though, because the mother church of Roseto is there and the church bell rings every hour and more and that's the way people tell the time here. In the morning early they'd have mass and the bells rang every half hour then.

It's plenty cold there and you have to stay near the fire to keep warm. They burn wood and boy! does the house get full of smoke! All the people work hard there: you see them carrying wood on their back and they go to the fountain for water.

All the girls there asked me if American girls wear woolen stockings and I said they didn't, they wear only silk stockings so you can see their nice legs. As soon as I'd tell them I had a wife, they'd grin and walk away!

When I was in the house lots of people came to see me, one after the other, and when I'd try to take a walk everyone would stop me to ask about their relatives in Roseto. You should see, Mom, all the names and addresses they gave me and told me to write for them. Honest, it'd take a year to write all those letters! I'll do my best for them, though.

The *Rosetani* said I was the first American soldier to stop there. I sure felt like a big shot there. They would say, "There goes *le rosa da Onorio.*"

Grandma gave me the gold ring that grandpa gave her when they were married, and she asked me to think of her when I wore it.

Mom, tell all the people there in Roseto that in Roseto all their relatives and friends are fine. Everybody is fine.

When this letter was published by the *Bangor Daily News,* it stirred deep emotions in the whole community and among Rosetans living in the nearby settlements of Bangor, West Bangor, Wind Gap, and Martin's Creek. I found that several families even kept the newspaper clipping carefully framed in their scrapbooks. Another Rosetan soldier went to Roseto Valfortore in that period, Fred Vario, who also had very close relatives there. The triumphant welcome given to these boys by their parents' village had a symbolic value besides its realistic one of family reunion. They arrived as part of the "Liberation Army" and to the villagers it seemed as if liberation from the German oppression actually came from their own people abroad. The atrocious period in which America—which included their own fathers, children, and brothers—had been Italy's enemy had come to an end, and the American planes crossing their sky were no longer feared as death messengers which could even be piloted by one of their own relatives. This event, which was soon followed by a resumption of correspondence and shipments of packages from America, helped to revitalize the myth of America as a "land of salvation" after the long interlude of Fascism and war.

The nightmare of war had been equally hard in Roseto, Pennsylvania, for all those who feared for their relatives, and the issue became a particularly tragic one whenever a Rosetan soldier was sent to Europe or, worse, to Italy. After the war, a renewal of interest in the village of origin arose again among Rosetans and, in time, physical contacts followed that first connection re-established by Onorio in the winter of 1943. Many members of the second generation developed a deep attachment to Roseto Valfortore as is still proved by the extensive visiting, writing, and exchange of gifts.

Since the end of the war public initiatives—such as collecting funds for Roseto Valfortore and inviting the mayor Giuseppe Falcone and the archpriest Luigi De Cesari to visit, with gala receptions, parades, and municipal band music—have helped to polarize the attention of the community on its namesake town. The community as a whole looks at Roseto Valfortore as at the humble but wholesome origin of their successful American town, and this attitude reveals the group's need of finding a gratifying comparison, a reassuring basis for its own prestige and identity in America.

Some American-born Rosetans hold a particular view of Roseto Valfortore and the life there. They are so fond of Italian village life in general that they have almost mythicized the peasants, their generosity and friendliness. They travel to Italy often but usually avoid the big urban centers or just go through them in a hurried tour. Although they often brag about the beauty of famous Italian cities—especially when speaking to non-Italians—they are alien to the sophisticated but stressful life of Rome and Florence as well as to their art and history. Many such Rosetans came to see me in Rome during the past three or four years and I could see how they were truly alien here, except for their names, their somatic traits, and the dialect they spoke. They generally avoid the North or pass rapidly through it, because they grew up in a southern Italian environment and thus feel removed from the Northerners, and because it is rumored among them that Northerners ridicule their heavily southern and archaic dialects and openly treat them as inferiors. In addition, none of the northern cities matches the idyllic image that this group has of Italian village life. This image was transmitted to them by their elders, who used to tell them about the poverty in the Old Country, but recalled it as healthier and happier than American life. The second generation grew up under the influence of these narrations, and Rosetans who had never crossed the ocean knew by heart the names of streets, piazzas, and fountains of Roseto Valfortore, as well as all the names of relatives, of haunted places, and of surrounding villages and towns.

Roseto Valfortore and trips to Italy are thus a favorite topic of conversation and entertainment. Returning Italian-American tourists give parties and show films and slides; they discuss these souvenirs, making comparisons and rationalizations of situations and values:

(L: Luisa)

L: Like the proverb says: *Le mondagne non s'affrondano, li cristiane sembre si confrondano* [Mountains never meet, but people always do]. It means that only the mountains don't move, while people can travel and always get to meet again, see? Like me.

B: You went to Italy. Tell me about it.

L: Oh, yes. I love it! No matter whether we suffered a lot for the toilets and all that, but people loved us too much! Too much! And I would go there all the time, any time, honestly. I wouldn't go to Rome and all that: I was in Rome enough. I would go to those little places, for the sake of those people there. They were too nice, those people with us. Oh, they're very nice! Just for that alone, I'd go now. I write to all of them!

B: Oh, yes? In Italian?

L: Well, I was born here, you know? I didn't study written, high Italian. But I write—half Italian, half Rosetan—what I know, that's it. Yeah! I write to them. The affection I have for them people, oh, I can never forget them! Biccari, Castelluccio Franco, Roseto Valfortore, oh! And they like me and my husband, you know why?

B: Why?

L: 'Cause I was no show up! The way you see me now here, this way I went over there, see? I was just like anybody there. Somebody here—they go there with lots of gold, dresses, and this and that—not me! No. You see, no? They'd resent it. As a matter of fact, they told me, they said, "How come you don't do like these other Americans? They come here, they put on all those things—gold and silver?" All those scenes there, see? Those scenes are bad! I was natural, that's what I was, natural.

B: I see. Where did you stay in Roseto?

L: At the tavern, you know, the Goduto's?

B: Oh, yes, I was there, too.

L: Poor place, not too clean either. But they're poor, but they're nice and happy, too. And then, in the morning, I could see Maria Pasquala [her cousin] and Francesca, sitting on the steps in front of the tavern—I could see them from my window when I got up. They were waiting for us to get up, see? They'd bring us an *espresso* coffeepot—sweet people, sweet. When we got up, at nine o'clock, they had already spent three—four hours out in the fields already, plowing, or something, see? And then they'd come to town, they'd sit there and they'd bring us coffee. Oh, I'll never forget that.[30]

Both the previous and the following informants were born in America and visited Italy on a guided tour, which they soon left to go to Roseto Valfortore. Family connections as a sort of identity card to present oneself in the village emerge from Bozzelli's interview:

(Bz: Bozzeli)

B: So, you left your tour in Naples, right?

Bz: Yes, we took a car and we drove to Roseto, see? I found it easily: Lucera, Biccari, Alberona, and Roseto! That's the way my mother used to tell me. She told us what the conditions were, what it looked like—the people, the *piazza*, and everything. And I found no difference; with very few exceptions, no difference. They now have the electric light and they didn't before, right. But the rest looks as I was told it was. The people are wonderful, just wonderful—the same people as here, see? The same names, the same faces, the same words—unbelievable! The thing that impressed me the most was that I remember we had the same habits here, years ago, as they have there now. People here used to gather in the *piazza*, too, in front of the church, you know? They'd stay there and sit and talk. Over there—in Roseto there, they still do this in the *piazza*. People come there, they gather and they talk of their problems—what happened and this and that. That I thought was very, very nice. And you should see when I got there! I stopped in the square and in a few minutes the whole village was there: "The Americans! The Americans! They are here!" They'd shout like that. Then, they asked which families did we belong to, who was our father and all that. They knew we were Rosetans from the way we talked, see? We said we were Bozzelli and Finelli, see? Finelli is my wife. Then, all the Bozzelli and the Finelli started coming to us: to see if we belonged to them, see? Madonna! What a crowd! They spoke just like us, just like Mamma and Papa—same. Of course, we are the same people, that's why!

B: And did you find any of your relatives?

Bz: Did we find any? Lots! Lots! A woman came to us, she said, "They told me my sister-cousin is here, I want to meet her." So, my wife asked her what her name was. "Maria Giuseppa," she said, and then my wife said, "Like my sister! And is your brother's name Donato?" She said, "Yes!" and my wife then said, "My

brother is Donato, too, and then your father must be uncle Giovanni, right?" That woman said, "Yes!" and my wife said that they
were sister and cousin then, she said, "Then we are sister-cousins!"
And they hugged and kissed and they wept! Oh, boy, what a scene!
What a scene! The people there were crying, too. See why? Because
my wife's uncle, Giovanni, was here but he didn't like this American
air and he went back there and this is why Maria Giuseppa was
born there, see? That's why.

B: What about Naples, Rome, Florence?

Bz: Oh, it was rough, rough! Expensive, noisy! In Paris they
nearly robbed us! No, that I don't go for, no.

B: Were you in northern Italy, too?

Bz: Only Milan. And then I took a plane back. I didn't like that,
you see? It's an American city, you don't notice you're in Europe
there, no sir! Everything is like New York: Westinghouse electric
razors—everything the very same! And the people they aren't nice,
they have airs, they—who knows what they have in mind? They
knew we were from Foggia right away.[31]

The satisfaction at finding everything familiar, "the same
names, the same faces, the same words" is the main theme of the
interviews relating trips to Italy. They add value to the hypothesis
that at least some Rosetans try to solve their problems of ethnic
identity in America by strengthening their affective links with
peasant Italy. They fail to relate to American society at large and
thus find gratification in comparing themselves to their ancestors.
In many ways, their cultural isolation in the United States is similar
to their parents' previous isolation from the dominant society in
Italy and the old pattern has repeated itself. Like their parents,
they have not quite entered what they call the world of the "northern people." They share America's material culture in all its
evident and external aspects, and therefore their non-American
culture traits are less perceivable than with their Italian-born parents, who still manage to retain some of their old way of dressing
even when using mass-produced new clothes. Their intimate culture,
however, is deeply divorced from American culture at large and
this is clearly reflected in the patterns examined in the next two
chapters.

An American Rosetan and her Italian cousin during the patron saint celebration in Roseto Valfortore.

Ex-votos—U.S. and Canadian dollars—are sent by emigrants, framed with roses, and carried in the patron saint procession.

Procession of the *Madonna del Carmine* in Roseto Valfortore. The privilege of carrying the heavy statues (*macchine*) is won by auction the day before.

Traditional Life in Roseto, Pennsylvania

The Language: Italian and English

THE complex situation of Italian dialects is reflected in the Italian ethnic enclaves in the United States. Based on village or province of origin, these enclaves have long preserved their characteristics and, compared to their corresponding villages of origin in Italy, they also show the survival of archaic traits in their dialects. In Italy, increased education and the mass media have strongly exposed the dialects to the leveling influence of standard Italian, causing the gradual dropping of some archaic forms or their confinement to certain age groups. Also in Italy, besides this shift toward standard Italian, there occurred a mutual borrowing among various dialects as a result of increased physical mobility and contacts, especially in the recently developed urban areas where immigrants tend to cluster together in their exodus from the countryside.

In America, the dialects have not been exposed to the modernizing influence of Italian and the conspicuous changes that did take place resulted from contact with English—occasionally Spanish—and the creeping of words and accents from one dialect into another.[1] These two phenomena can be observed in the Italian-American press and in the current speech used by all regional groups.

Although the Italian immigrants in the United States were little influenced by standard Italian—a poor specimen was available only in the immigrant press for the few who could read—their original dialects have undergone a remarkable change in American big cities in about eighty years. As in the Italian suburbia, the groups in the United States were forced into extensive contacts, especially at work and in all aspects of public life. In spite of the natural conservatism and the in-group orientation of each dialect cluster, a certain amount of merging did take place, as when the children of a Calabrian and a Sicilian parent would have both dialect elements in their Italian-American speech. Moreover, the overwhelming southern origin—particularly Campanian and Sicilian—of Italian immigration gave a distinct southern flavor—in both intonation and morphology—to the new forms borrowed from the foreign language.

The idioms which all immigrant groups created from their American experience form one of the most intriguing aspects of immigrant culture. In the case of Italian-Americans, the morphological characteristics of their native language naturally required special types of adaptation in Italianizing foreign words. The obligatory vocalic endings to be given every word were certainly the most conspicuous of such adaptations involving a number of choices. The necessity of choosing a feminine or masculine gender for nouns and adjectives in turn called for the addition of the appropriate articles and the correct plural construction of the new nouns and adjectives according to Italian patterns. Equally important was the choice of an Italian verbal ending for the English verbs.

I noticed differences and similarities between the groups living in urban New York and Chicago and those in Roseto, Pennsylvania. They all have in common the immigrant tendency to Italianize foreign words, especially those applied to concepts or objects typical of their new life which were not familiar to them before emigration, such as check, engine, business, pound, tunnel, strike, car, quarry, elevated road, avenue, washing machine, book, picture, job, tape, loafers, truck, coats, top, nurse, boarding house, railway, cellar, ticket, streetcar, track, city hall, insurance, compensation, party, and yard, which in turn became *cecca, engìna, bisìnisse, pòndo, tònno, sdràica, carro, quarì, livetta, venùta, washa, bucco, piccio, jobba, teppe, lòffari, trocco, cotti da uomo, toppo, norso, borda, rella, sello, tacchetta, striccarro, tracca, siriòla, asciurànza, compostéscio, parì,* and *gliarda.* Equally absorbed and Italianized were some English verbs describing new actions or habits, such as to drive, to lunch, to shovel, to push, to select, which became the infinitives *driviàre, lonchiàre, shabbliàre, pushiàre, selettare,* all of them assimilated to the Italian first conjugation of verbs ending in *-are.* I also noticed the general tendency to retain in English speech the Italian words and expressions for certain concepts and objects of Italian traditional culture or coinciding with certain emotions and interests linking the speakers to the past or to their ethnic group.

Besides the Italianization of words, there were curious semantic shifts—corresponding to shifts in the speakers' cultural experience—in words phonetically similar in the two languages so that *genitore* (parent, in Italian) now means "janitor" in Italian-American, and *fattoria* (farm, in Italian) is now universally used for "factory" by the Italian-American press and by all Italian-Americans.

Also common to all immigrants—not only Italian—is the recurrent use of English words and expressions such as exclamations, interjections, and salutations: "you know," "see," "all right," "that's all," and "goodbye." Both the Italian- and American-born insert these expressions in their regional dialects. They do not seem to be aware that they are using non-Italian words and they evidently have forgotten the equivalent expressions in their original language.

While the unavoidable contacts in urban areas brought about exchanges between different dialect groups, they also contributed to diminishing the prestige of the use of Italian. In urban areas the speakers of Italian dialects were exposed to a double clash. In most of their public life they had to cope with the difficulties of an English-speaking and totally foreign society, and in their private life they were constantly criticized, often ridiculed, by fellow-Italians, who spoke and acted in a similar and yet sufficiently different way as to create uneasiness and conflict. Consequently, the use of Italian survived in the cities through most of the second generation but it was confined to private life, for basic communication between parents and children.

The Italian language among immigrants was an oral one, made up of a number of dialects.[2] By the time the immigrants' children and grandchildren went to school, very few of them studied Italian as a foreign language, and present-day Roseto is no exception in this respect. The superintendent of the High School District in Bangor told me in 1968 that no students of Italian descent—though very numerous in this area—had chosen Italian as a foreign language, while children of the other ethnic groups had. I found that the majority of Italian-Americans who do study a foreign language prefer Spanish or French to Italian. This fact may be due to a number of reasons: consideration of the little financial and political prestige of this language, inherited distrust of the Italian culture as such, and an equally inherited reluctance to be identified as Italians. Also, the older people described standard Italian to their children as a totally foreign language, completely removed from what they spoke at home, so that the youth would rather resort to another, socially more rewarding language.

In New York, I often heard the second-generation Italian-

Americans rationalize the fact that they did not teach Italian to their children by saying that they used this language as a secret means of communication among the adults—a "secret language," as they called it—to keep the children from understanding what was not proper or convenient for them. A more obvious reason may be the fact that it is well known that a strict Sicilian dialect is also the "secret" language used by the Mafia members through the second and third generations. Among my informants, Italian was usually spoken only by the Italian-born, while it was a common practice for the children to answer their parents in English, or to carry on English conversations (during meals, for example) that excluded their parents, not for the subject matter, but for the language being used.

While even this restricted use of Italian contributed to the transmission of traditional values and behavior, the tension and distrust, resulting from the need of a rapid shift to American life and language, made the immigrants soon aware of the marginality of their culture and language. Consequently, they seldom indulged in long, relaxed narrations of traditional tales and legends to entertain their children, relatives, and neighbors. Yet the memory of the Italian tradition was so strong that I could collect a large number of good traditional texts from the immigrants in New York City and in Chicago. Among the second generation, however, I found only fragments of songs and rhymes or short anecdotes and jokes, reflecting the typical language difficulties of the Italian immigrants. The following is a very popular one:

A man goes to buy nuts in a store. The clerk inquires: "Assorted?" The Italian, thinking that the clerk has insulted him by saying, '*A ssoreta*" [to your sister], shouts the stock reply, "*A mmammeta!*" [to your mother!].[3]

While most children understood and spoke their parents' dialect, they did not remember much of the formalized folklore, for which they showed little awareness or interest. The folklore that was transmitted was largely limited to the nonformalized aspects, that is, to the body of beliefs and superstitions, which did not need to be associated with the Italian language and could be transmitted through behavior rather than narration.[4]

Roseto, Pennsylvania, in spite of the many contacts with different ethnic and regional groups, has always been entirely Italian. The serious conflicts with the other groups were external problems for the community and they served to smooth old internal rivalries and to minimize the difficulties met by the few non-Rosetan clements in town.[5] The few marriages between Rosetans of different Italian origins were mostly confined to areas of Italy that were culturally related to Roseto Valfortore, such as Biccari, Campobasso or Salerno. Awareness of such different origins has always been rather strong, but it never became a conflict situation, probably because the community needed unity to survive and to succeed in spite of the external world.

In this environment the oldest Italian-born immigrants are not the only—nor necessarily the best—narrators in the community. I found informants of the second generation capable of telling better tales and songs than some Italian-born;[6] though this was not true in the majority of cases, the point is still significant. I also collected some good texts among the third generation; but, on the whole, they were not numerous and were generally restricted to magic formulas and folk prayers.

What is important to note is that the conditions were present— and to a certain extent still are—for the continuation and the transmission of the traditional lore. These conditions were: a sense of security stemming from a familiar environment, a noninterrupted cultural identity, a sense of mutual belonging due to strong and extended family ties, a continued relationship with Italy, and a fairly successful and autonomous economy of the group as a whole.[7]

All these factors not only allowed the Rosetan dialect a long survival, but they conserved its prestige in the community where it stood for a successful and independent group of people. In urban America, the speakers of different Italian dialects were struggling with their own regional differences as well as being frustrated by the overwhelmingly English-speaking society. A recent example of this process in the making is found in Toronto, Ontario, where nearly 500,000 recently immigrated Italians are undergoing this same cultural clash on several levels. The Rosetans' experience in Pennsylvania, however, was different. Although they were exposed to certain pressures for change while they were gradually becoming Americans, they had the advantage of undergoing a slow and relaxed change, constantly reassured by a common cultural identity of the group as a whole.

Storytelling in the Two Rosetos

Storytelling is still an important element—though decreasingly so—in the village life of central and southern Italy. It is found equally among men and women, while other traditional oral forms

often concern one sex group more than the other.[8] In Roseto Valfortore, as in all villages now involved in emigration to central
Europe, the absence of young and middle-aged males is obviously
restricting the tradition of storytelling to the aged and to women.
The original distribution between the sex groups is still found in
Roseto, Pennsylvania, where the population balance of the community was never disrupted by any phenomenon equal to emigration, and of 512 regular folktales recorded there, 268 were told by
women and 244 by men. In Roseto Valfortore, the fact that the
situation has changed because of emigration was confirmed by
informants, who referred to male friends and relatives in Germany
or in Switzerland as really good storytellers, and some even sug-
gested that I take a trip there to record my tales!

Though with some differences, I found that the repertoires of
folk narratives somehow follow age and social factors in both
communities. Old people in Roseto Valfortore are largely illiterate
and speak a more archaic dialect, similar to that spoken by the
American Rosetans. Many of them are—or were—good storytellers
and the narratives I recorded among them were, in order of frequency, animal tales (with the wolf, the fox, the lion, and the cock
as recurrent characters), tales of magic (mostly the Types 300,
301, 332, 403, 450, 480, 510, 567, 707), and religious and ghost
legends (mostly referring to local saints, places, and characters).

Similarly, in Roseto, Pennsylvania, I found the older Italian-
born generation inclined to tell the same animal tales and the
same long supernatural folktales and legends. In both Rosetos, they
are regarded as the most knowledgeable storytellers and the
younger people constantly refer to some deceased person's extraordinary talents in the community. In spite of similar repertoires, however, the older groups in the two communities do not
share—at least, not any more—the same audiences and the same
occasions. The old people in Italy still spend much time with the
children, who constitute most of their habitual audiences. The usual
setting for such narrations is a street corner, steps outside of the
house, or a kitchen fire. In America, this is not the case anymore.
Regarding the past, all my American-born informants tell me that
when they were children their parents used to entertain them, night
after night, with long fairytales, while neighbors and relatives
would also join in listening:

(C: Carmine)

C: We would sit and tell stories, like I told you yesterday.
B: Yes, you were telling me. Wouldn't you tell about that now?

C: Well, my father, in wintertime, we used to sit around the stove. That's when we had all our work done, and he would tell us the story. When it was about eight o'clock, he'd say, "Now, tomorrow." . . . So, we would wait—that would be the end of the story.

B: And did he know a lot of them?

C: Oh yes! He knewed a lot, a lot of stories!

B: All of them from Italy?

C: Oh, naturally. He all learned them in Italy.

B: Would he say the stories in English sometimes?

C: No, no. In Italian.

B: And did you tell them to your children?

C: I told my children in English. I told them in English. I used to tell them also when I was a boy, you know?

B: Oh, really? Tell me.

C: We didn't go to school. We would sit in the woods somewhere, and I would say the stories. I would tell the boys the story to pass time, see? That's why I keep on rememberin'.[9]

(L: Lorenza)

L: We would sit around the fire, we would say to Mom, "Ma, tell us the wolf." We didn't have anything in those days: no music, no anything, see? So then, we used to sit down and Mom used to say, "Well, we're gonna tell a tale tonight." And all of us were there, we were sewing, and the neighbors would come and they would sit and meanwhile we were telling the tales. But those were old tales, they were long and scaring, those stories.[10]

In America, grandparents are still largely present within the younger families, but there are more and more cases of old couples living alone, and while the children do visit their grandparents and spend some time with them, their visits are less often and under different conditions than they were in the past. There is still a strong regard for the old people and a deep respect for their opinions, but the actual way of being together is now changing and the mass media—televison—is the most conspicuous agent of this change.

In the smaller Italian villages, television sets are a very recent aquisition and have not entered all households, so it is a common habit to go and watch them in the public places, such as bars and osterias. In addition, the village people are not yet fully at ease with either the language or the problems on television, and although the younger generations are now quickly adapting to both, the adult part of the population has not yet been deeply influenced by the mass media in general. Storytelling is consequently still an existing feature in the interpersonal relationships.

In the American community, a situation similar to the Italian one existed until twenty years ago, and it is proved by the tales I could find among a few third-generation informants now in their mid-thirties.[11] The younger children of today, however, regardless of whether second or third generation, are almost entirely devoted to watching television in their free time from school and outdoor activities. Consequently, though their relationship with their older relatives is still a close one, it does not include any extensive listening to long traditional narratives. Today's audience for old storytellers is thus other mature people or their middle-aged relatives or friends and only occasionally the younger children. The mass media are now rapidly bringing about in Roseto, Pennsylvania, the same detachment from oral traditions that had previously occurred, for different reasons, in urban America.

In Roseto Valfortore, as in other Italian villages, children between the ages of eight and thirteen are often excellent storytellers. When their older relatives grow too old to remember—or when they die—the children still clearly remember and repeat stories they have heard, using the same archaic dialect spoken by the oldest Rosetans. Most of them now go to school up to the seventh and eighth grades and many learn folktales from their books and teachers. It is not difficult, however, to recognize the latter narratives, both from their style and structure and from the fact that the children will usually tell them in Italian rather than in the Rosetan dialect.

In both Rosetos, storytelling becomes a rare habit in the age-group between fifteen and thirty, regardless of occupation. Good narrators can be found among the middle-aged members of the two communities, but there are some differences as to repertoire, occasions, and attitudes. Few men are engaged full time in agriculture in Roseto Valfortore, and those who did not emigrate are commuting to Foggia or Lucera, where they work as unskilled construction laborers. These groups gather in the village osterias or in the square at night, and they often tell one another long series of short jokes and anecdotes about the religious orders, the returned emigrant, the stupid wife or girl, the numbskull characters from nearby villages, and the local or national political leaders. I recorded few animal tales, legends, or other kinds of folktales among the members of this group. The women, on the other hand, are nearly all engaged in agricultural and domestic work and their narratives have a clear tendency toward animal tales (especially

Types 3, 6, 9/b, 32, 122J, 130, 214*),[12] supernatural tales of considerable length, formula tales, romantic tales, and legends. I found
excellent narrators among the Rosetan women, one of whom, Lucia
Sbrocchi—aged fifty-two—was absolutely outstanding in terms of
repertory, style, and personality. Women have their usual setting
and occasions for storytelling in the open fields—during the hot
hours and break—and by the kitchen fire, during the long winter
nights.

In the American Roseto, I found the whole middle-aged group—
regardless of sex and of their being second- or third-generation
American—generally oriented toward shorter narratives, mostly
jokes and anecdotes, legends of ghosts and witches, animal tales,
and religious legends. This age group rarely told the really long
fairytales, though they were fully enjoyed whenever the older
people told them in the presence of their children. While my
middle-aged informants could not—or would not—narrate such long
folktales, they showed a certain appreciation for this kind of
narrative and participated in the narrations, sometimes suggesting
English words, names, and even episodes which were being skipped
or forgotten and which they could remember from their childhood.

(M: Mary; F: Filomena)

F: And the sister, the little girl that is, she didn't know, see?
She didn't know this thing yet.

M: Yes, she did, Ma! Yes, she did. You told us she did. Only,
she didn't want the witch to find out, remember? Papa said so,
remember?

F: Well, yes. But anyway—what was I saying?

B: The little girl knew about it.

F: Yes. Right, but *la sdreja* didn't know it!

M: The witch, Ma! She was the witch what you call *la sdreja*.

F: All right! The witch.[13]

(C: Carmine; M: Margaret)

C: So the book told her this. She said, "Well, what can I do
to take it away?" She wanted that heart. The book said, "You have
to get him go and throw up, throw it out, vomit the heart."

M: Yes. I remember, Dad, you used to say that in Italian! When
we were kids, remember? You used to say *Vomita u core*, vomit
the heart.

C: Well, I said heart in Italian, *u core*.[14]

In spite of the above interest, when the informants of this age
group tell tales, they are more inclined to tell short humorous

stories, some of which were learned in Roseto Valfortore, during a summer trip there. Although it is very difficult to generalize, it seems that the individuals who are more oriented toward, or in closer contact with, the original culture in Italy are also more inclined to appreciate storytelling as such. Some of the interviews state appreciation for the stories heard in Roseto Valfortore and for the moral benefits derived from this kind of entertainment:

(R: Rose)

B: Where was this?

R: Up there! In Roseto there, not here. When I was there, five years ago, my cousins told me lots of stories. All about those monsters, those giants there and those people who used to kill them, you know? They used to tell me about the bandits up on the mountains: they would steal the treasure from the Madonna, you know? You know the treasure of Our Lady of Mt. Carmel? And the ghosts in the Palace. Do you know that?

B: Yes. And who was there to listen to those stories?

R: Everybody! Everybody in the family and the neighbors, too. They'd all come and listen. Just like us here, when we were kids, you know? And those kids up there, they like that, see? And they like that and it's good for them, 'cause they learn and they stay more at home, I guess.[15]

The most evident difference between the Rosetans and the other Italian-Americans in terms of storytelling is the fact that in Roseto the traditional narratives are learned and repeated through the second generation. I found rich material and very good storytellers among American-born Rosetans, while this was a rare occurrence among the American-born Italians I interviewed in the large cities. This situation was partly due to such factors as language retention, family and community cohesiveness, less pressure from the society outside, and physical stability. These same factors were also responsible for a different attitude toward storytelling: not only did the second-generation Rosetans learn and still tell the folktales, but they taught their children to appreciate them, so that storytelling still has prestige in the community, even though it may be unpracticed by the younger children themselves. In the large cities, the tradition of storytelling found a powerful deterrent in the need for speedy assimilation.

Within the Rosetan tradition, while the most significant shifts are observed among the various age groups, time of immigration and place of origin are the two important variables. In the few cases where the place of origin in Italy was not Roseto Valfortore, the American-born children would either not be interested in continuing their parents' narrative traditions or they would tell the stories in English. Carmine Malpiedo, whose parents came from the province of Salerno, is an outstanding example of this attitude:

C: Yeah! What I mean is—well, Margaret, remember when that people from New York used to come and make fun of us, the way I used to talk Italian? Like same? *"Acap' a monde, A cap' abbasce"* (up hill, down hill) and *"chistu qua, quiddu dda"* (this one here, that one there). See what I mean? We talked Italian here. *I rusetane* [Rosetans] would say *"i tutere"* [corncobs]. Well, we call them *i spighe, a spiga, uranerennia*. But *i rusetane* (Rosetans) would say *i tutere*, see? Different! That's why I tell my stories in English, that's why. I told you this, didn't I?

B: Oh, yes, you did.

Although Carmine was born in Roseto, Pennsylvania, he calls Rosetans those whose parents came from Roseto Valfortore. Actually, the children of early immigrants from different Italian villages were the only storytellers who would tell their stories in English, for fear of being ridiculed by their Rosetan listeners because of their different dialects.

The time of immigration was also important for other reasons. The Rosetans who arrived in the twenty-five years after World War II, for example, brought new reinforcement of certain traditions, and narrative habits took on new interest. In particular, I found that this recent group somehow enhanced interest in the tales of magic among friends and relatives:

(M: Maria;   My: Mary)

M: Those were more—more in the art, in the old art.

B: Do you mean stories like *The Three Oranges?*

M: Yes. I think those are more beautiful. They are not jokes, they are more important.

My: Well, our folks used to tell us those. *Zi' Ndonie* [Uncle Tony] used to tell us *The Serpent*. Oh, boy! It took several nights to tell that!

B: Could you tell it?

My: Not me! But I wish I could, see? I wish I could tell *The Three Oranges*, too, like Maria, see? But I guess we couldn't do that—we are not so—we are different, oh, I don't know.[16]

Maria P. came to America in 1950 with her husband—a tailor—and they are both very good storytellers. Maria's father, who lives in Roseto Valfortore and was once a cart driver, is himself a very gifted narrator, and he warmly recommended that I go see his daughter and son-in-law in America, if I cared for really talented storytellers. He proposed to send his children a photograph and sent them this message through my tape recorder:

Hello, Maria! Did you get lost there? Always promise to come and see us and never keep your word! That's what America does to you, right? Remember what I taught you? Remember the story of the old father who wished he had been nicer to his parents? Remember that? But I was nice to my father and to you, too, wasn't I? O.K. You are busy, you seem to be all busy over there. What the hell are you busy about? Remember that life is short and we are old and we die soon. Well, this young lady here came to see me. She wanted to hear those old stories, you know? Those I used to tell you kids, you know? I filled up all her tapes, I told her *The Oranges, The Serpent, The Fisherman.* All of them. Now it's your turn and let's see if you lost all your brain in America! The hell with America! At least, I hope you are making money over there! Not like us here. I am old and your brother is ill, very. He spoke on the tape, too, but he went to bed now. The doctor doesn't know when he'll get well. The shop is not doing too well these days. We sold the old mule. Well, what can I tell you? Don't make any more babies now, 'cause food is expensive nowadays. Well, be well now. Here is this young lady, now. Be well and come to see us soon. Ciao.[17]

Among the narrative materials I recorded in Roseto, Pennsylvania, 512 tales belong to the types included in Thompson's *The Types of the Folktale*, while a large body of less formalized narratives include saints' legends, bandit stories, emigration and immigration episodes, narratives based on superstition such as ghost stories and stories of witches and werewolves. The type distribution of the material in the first group, with the limitations imposed by all distinctions of this kind, is roughly the following:

53	Types 1–299	Animal Tales
61	Types 300–749	Tales of Magic
95	Types 750–849	Religion Tales
25	Types 850–999	Novelle
13	Types 1000–1199	Tales of the Stupid Ogre
255	Types 1200–1999	Jokes and Anecdotes
10	Types 2000–2399	Formula Tales

The realistic themes contained in the jokes and anecdotes make this group of tales by far the most popular among the American-born narrators in Roseto. This preference is due to the fact that these types are evidently more easily adaptable to new settings and situations than, for example, the tales of magic. The tales of magic were largely told by the immigrants themselves or by the old members of the second generation, while the jokes and anecdotes were for the most part told by the second and third generations, who are more oriented toward seeking identification with the American society.

A comparison with the corresponding narrations collected in Roseto Valfortore shows a tendency to shorten the length of the tales of magic in the American Roseto, where they are usually ten to thirty pages long and rarely occupy sixty or eighty pages, as is often the case in the Italian village. This tendency to diminish the length can be observed even in the best narrator of the second generation, Carmine Malpiedo, whose tales are indeed very long but who repeatedly states that his father used to take several nights to finish a single tale. The abbreviations, however, rarely involve the suppression of episodes or parts that are functional to the logical structure of the tales. On the contrary, I observed in the narrators an evident respect for what was handed down to them by the previous generations, both by means of explicit statements, such as "as my Dad said" or "I wish I could say this in the proper way," and by an instinctive effort to keep faithful to what they felt had been a long-respected tradition. This respect for the expressive models consecrated by a long tradition was necessarily counteracted by the various influences exerted by the new cultural milieu. Once the setting for the action had become the cities of New York and Chicago, it was no longer easy to indulge in fantastic descriptions of the enchanted palaces and magic powers of its inhabitants. A quick mentioning of a hotel, a casino, and a café are the only realistic details that could replace the long and entertaining descriptions of those wondrous places. The narrator feels that the audience is more inclined to appreciate factual narrations and instinctively he drops whatever is not essential to the action in the plot.

The transfer to the new environment is thus more visible in jokes and anecdotes, whose scenery, setting, and actors could be altered better than those of the tales of magic. Castles and princes, towers and dukes do not exist in the American landscapes; and even the life and deeds of the American upper classes, no matter how rich and how powerful, are viewed by the workingman as earthly and material. The feudal *Signori* of Italy, on the other hand, had "blue blood" in their veins and their ancestors, the fantastic characters of the fairytales, could be imagined in the most extravagant and supernatural situations by the peasant. In America, the most recurrent characters in the Italian-American jokes and anecdotes are judges and lawyers, shopkeepers and their clients, naïve American tourists visiting Italy, astute or corrupt clergymen, Italian-American immigrants in embarrassing situations, and returned migrants in Italy. The situations in which these characters move are also more likely to stimulate the introduction of comments and opinions on the part of both the narrator and the audience.

While innovation according to the personality of the narrators is undoubtedly a universal characteristic of narrative tradition, the preference for a certain category of tales is so general in the community and so typical of the second and third generation, that it is clearly the expression of the changes which occurred in a culture which has reoriented and reorganized itself toward new models and values. It is easier to give a general evaluation of the storytelling situation in the American Roseto than it is in the Italian one. The American community, in spite of its past troubles and the cultural disruption following the massive emigration from Italy, has had the time and the opportunity to rearrange itself in a unit, with a considerable amount of stability and cohesiveness. Whatever its future might be, its present balance and stability help formulate an overall evaluation of its present culture. Roseto Valfortore, on the other hand, with the exception of the years before and during World War II, has known no regular development and stability; and its population balance has constantly been broken by subsequent migrations.

Regarding the large body of less-formalized narratives, in Roseto, Pennsylvania, the two main sections are made up of stories based on superstition and stories about emigration and immigration. The other narratives are, in order of frequency, saints' legends, bandit stories, and other "true stories" dealing with historical characters and national or ethnic groups such as *Garibaldi and the Freedom of Slaves* and *The Italians and the Invention of Music*. In spite of their recent formation, these informal narratives have had an intense circulation in the community where they are still learned and told even by twelve- or thirteen-year-old children; these accounts can thus be considered as the true historical traditions of the Rosetan people. A last observation should be mentioned in this connection. It appears that these narratives, together with the legends and the stories, are told in English more frequently than the regular folktales, because the freer structure that characterizes them makes them better suited for a new language and environment.

Magic and Religion: The Evil Eye and a New Madonna

One of the most noticeable characteristics of southern Italian magic beliefs and practices is their extraordinary relationship with the official Catholic cult. In Italy, more than in most European countries (especially those affected by the Protestant movement), problems of spiritual salvation and religious debate have been entirely confined to a restricted circle of theologians and philosophers. Outside this circle, a complex ideology of compromise between past and present, reality and divinity, official liturgy and magic ritualism has been accumulated among the masses through the centuries. As a consequence, present magic belief and practice, such as the *malocchio* or the *jettatura* (the evil eye), are not forms living in isolation or in apparent contradiction with the official religion; in the peasant milieu, such forms are intimately connected with both the external traits of the Catholic cult and the critical aspects of human life. This situation results from two main factors: the greater emphasis on magic ritualism typical of southern Catholicism itself, and the different opportunities for understanding and sharing in the dominant culture on the part of the various social classes.

The evident connections between magic and superstition and the main themes of the Catholic cult are inevitable. As De Martino says, the peasant woman performing the ritual of the evil eye or the exorcism against erysipelas ignores, due to her social condition, the conceptual distinctions of Catholic theology. She is reducing to a practical and extracanonical level the equivalent of such canonical exorcism as the benediction of the candles, wine, oil, and bells regularly performed by the priest in the church. The prayer against Satan and other evil spirits at the end of the mass or the benediction of the throat are approved and sacramental actions of the church, which follow the model of the exorcism practiced by Jesus and his apostles. The sacrifice of the mass certainly has a much wider spiritual horizon than most people can perceive, especially when the service is celebrated in Latin, as it was for centuries. Thus, peasants repeat some external traits of the ritualism of the mass for many different causes, but invariably to meet the needs of their earthly life. Folk prayers, the worship of objects and human vestiges, magic behavior patterns in pilgrimages and sanctuaries, miraculous letters and healings, the capture of witches on Christmas night are, at least potentially, mediators of Christian values. Though in a very narrow and elementary way, they are the only means of participating in the dominant and not otherwise understandable Catholic cult.[18]

At the same time, the tolerance and even the sponsoring of practices theoretically incompatible with the official cult were often a means for the dominant classes to maintain their power. As G. B. Bronzini (1964:9) says,

> Customs forming an organic unit with the life system could not be destroyed by means of a policy of prohibitions and papal anathemas. The magical ritualism of the common people actually met the indulgence of the southern educated classes, . . . and where the progressive wind of social and economic reforms did not blow, the agriculture populace was left behind, clinging to archaic forms of life. Maintaining the error was thus a means of maintaining the power for the dominant aristocracy.

Together with the other aspects of southern folklore, the magical-religious world view followed the immigrants to the new shores and stayed with them for several generations. More than folktales and songs, which needed culturally homogeneous and isolated environments—such as Roseto, Pennsylvania—in order to pass from the immigrants to their children, such a magical world view had immediate practical functions and it soon proved capable of rapid adaptations. The *munaceddi*,[19] for example, are extremely adaptable little demons which can be found even in New York's subway! From the open countryside and village alleys, similar in behavior to naughty children and in appearance to little monks (hence the name), these strange little beings now work their mischief on crowded city buses or in subway trains on tired workers. In Italy, they used to molest the flocks or harass the farmers, hiding the agricultural tools or attracting an unknowing goat to a dangerous slope. On American trains, you can find a *munaceddu* sitting on the only empty seat that you were planning to take, laughing at your disappointment and then disappearing at once, when you don't need the seat any more because you are about to get off. An informant from the island of Ponza, living in the Bronx since 1905, told me that when he goes fishing north of Manhattan on weekends, the *munaceddi* often jump into his fishing nets to deceive him with their weight, and thus make him waste time when he pulls up too soon.[20] In Roseto, Pennsylvania, several accidents were caused by the *munaceddi* in the quarries and on the highways.

S: I was at the engine, I had to run the engine to pull the men back, see? Now, I knew my job well enough, my foreman used to call me "my son." But I tell you, when those son of a bitch get there, you are in for trouble!

B: How did it happen?

S: Well, once *u munaceddu* made me pull the wrong way, see? I had to pull the men back to where I was because they were far, but they were facing me, see? So, you know, I pulled, and they went back down! They hit the slate there, two were hurt badly, and one fell into the water, right into the water! Then I saw him, the *munaceddu*, he was right there, in front of me, he was laughing. Oh, he had a dirty face!

B: A dirty face?

S: Sure! He was eating a candy bar, coconut bar, I remember, 'cause they are like kids, you know? You know kids, when they want you to get mad? But they are dressed like priests, like *i monaci* [monks], you see?[21]

The magical-religious lore followed the emigrant in the form of sacred objects and as a set of concepts and basic behavior patterns to meet the exigencies of life. Some of the objects survived and were reproduced in the new land or continued to be brought over from Italy, while others were adapted or replaced with equivalent or similar objects. Regarding the behavior patterns, each one carried with it a time-honored potential of energy and success. Whenever, in the same life situation, a traditional pattern apparently contrasted with the patterns offered by the recipient official society, the one with the greater dynamic potency was translated into action. Generally, the traditional pattern was given precedence as being the most familiar—and thus the most reliable—in moments of stress. At a time of insecurity, there was little desire for unknown procedures, and, especially if life itself was in peril, there was first a strong tendency to cling to the known, and only secondarily a timid will to translate into action whatever official concepts and procedures were at hand.

Some of the objects with magical properties brought from the village to the new land had no obvious connection with religion. I found, for example, several horseshoes, some of which were genuine, once used by the animal, and some just small reproductions—usually brass amulets—to hang on the wall or on the doors. Others of this type are horn, brass, and stone amulets representing stars, moons, horses, trees, bells, horns of various shapes and sizes, as well as small bronze mortars for witchcraft compounds.

The great majority of the objects, however, regardless of their shape, use, or material, had well-defined religious connotations; and I observed no real difference in the objects found in Roseto, Pennsylvania, and Italian neighborhoods in Chicago and in New York. Those objects I could observe—or collect—were, in order of frequency, *santini* (holy picture cards), statues of all sizes (made of plastic, metal, or clay), candles, scapulars, blessed palms, small prayer books, songbooks, rings, votive beads, medals, bottles of miraculous waters, and the cloth version of the Only True Letter of Jesus Christ. Several statues of saints and madonnas of all sizes were brought from Italy, usually bad duplications of the ones in the original villages. By means of solemn celebrations, the statue—which is occasionally produced in America—is put in the church as its patron saint or as an additional saint to be exhibited in one of the side chapels. In this way the former patron saint celebration of the village group would be restored with all possible details in the new land.

The Italian peasant had learned that, in order to secure support from a saint or a madonna and receive miracles and protection from the uncertainties of his life, he had to establish a mechanism of exchange with the divinity. He had to give all that he could and perform a definite series of acts and sacrifices in return for protection against the dangers of daily life. In particular, he could go barefoot to church or on a pilgrimage carrying a heavy stone or lighted candles, or else he could buy a wide choice of "sacred" objects each endowed with special powers. Holy picture cards (*santini*) were printed in all sizes in America and miniature statues reproducing the large ones were sold for home worship during the religious festivals. Scapulars, medals, prayer books, and broadsides celebrating the saint's life and miracles were either imported from Italy or printed in the United States. The most popular of these objects is called the *abitino* (literally "the little dress"), a scapular consisting of a square piece of fabric sewn to a miniature of a saint. The most common one among the Rosetans is the *abitino* of Our Lady of Mt. Carmel (*Madonna del Carmine*), which is made of brown wool—supposedly a piece of the Madonna's dress—and has quite complex properties. To secure the privileges offered by this scapular (mainly that of being relieved from the pains of Purgatory on the first Saturday after death), one must observe certain rules, among which are chastity and abstinence from meat on certain days.

Reproductions of "The Only True Letter of Jesus Christ" are sold in the Little Italies during patron saint festivals. The letter must be kept folded. It is often carried on the body as a defense against the evil eye.

Abitini or scapulars are worn in contact with the skin and believed to have magical powers.

A typical southern Italian iconographic display in a home in Roseto, Pennsylvania.

(P: Peppuccia)

P: That's right, but that's different.

B: How does it differ?

P: You've got to wear it, all the time, on your breast like this, see? You can't see it, but you know it. I wear it and my children all wear it, all of them! This here [she points to a holy picture card], you don't have to carry it with you. You just put it over here, over there, like my mother used to do. She had tons of saints all over the house! But me too! But *l'abitino*, no. That saves you from Purgatory on the first Saturday.

B: The first Saturday?

P: After you die. You go right to heaven if you wear this, see? Oh, I wear it! Do you want some? I have plenty, see? Take them for your family.

B: Can one wear it over their clothes?

P: Over your clothes, no! Under. It's got to be under. And it's good for your health, too, but you must not touch meat on Wednesdays and Saturdays—or on Tuesday. Well, I don't remember now. Everything is so mixed up now. Everything is changed.[22]

These objects were sold in the church or in special shops; most of them carried magical powers and had to be worn constantly to secure the expected protection or miracles. A woman in Brooklyn, from Ciociaria, had a little Statue of Liberty near that of the Madonna of Montevergine on her bureau, with a perennial lamp and artificial flowers on either side, and she referred to it as *St. Liberata*. She was an intelligent woman and she knew that it was actually the Statue of Liberty: her need for a tangible simulacre of the saint, however, was so strong that she called the statue *Santa Liberata*, convinced that the similarity of the two words (*Liberata*, Liberty) would actually annul the substantial difference. This woman was about sixty-five when I met her in 1964 and had never moved from New York in about forty-five years. She told me that *St. Liberata* had once freed her mother from the devil's possession and that she kept this devotion ever since she was fifteen. She told me several legends based on demons and witches, and her daughter described her Sicilian mother-in-law as a wicked witch.

(I: Irene)

B: Is she alive?

I: No, she died five years ago, but she used to meet the devil when she was alive. She could turn into a cat or a dog! True!

B: Really? Did you see this?

I: I saw the cat! One night she had left for her daughter's house, it was nine or ten, I believe. The door was locked and I was asleep with the baby and Tony, my husband. I heard the baby cry, and I woke up and the baby was all upside down, you know? In the bed, she was at my feet and her hair was all tied in small knots and she was all perspired! I was scared, and I got up. The minute I got up, I saw this big cat running into the kitchen. The door was locked! I had no cats, so what was it? It hissed, you know, and the eyes were red like fire! I screamed and I called Tony and the cat was gone, in a second! That was no cat, though: that was his own mother! She was a witch and she was jealous of me, that's why. She had done all sorts of dirty tricks back in Italy before she came to this country, you know? She used to go out at night: she used to turn into animals.[23]

In Roseto, Pennsylvania, the cultural cohesion of the community is such that practically the whole body of beliefs and superstitions has been kept by the members of the first generation and handed down to the second and even to part of the third. The isolation from the dominant culture was even greater here than in Italy, where the peasant life was still related to the society at large by means of various intermediate steps. This exclusion caused the maintenance of the folk world view with most of its rites, habits, and beliefs. A large number of my informants believe in the existence of werewolves, witches, ghosts, and devils, while only part of them declared that such phenomena existed in America today, many were sure that they had until twenty or thirty years ago, and nearly all believe that they still exist in Italy. Many American-born informants mention names and relatives of Italian witches and werewolves in Roseto Valfortore and repeat memorats[24] heard by the older generations about ghosts and devils living in the Saggese Palace and around such places as the old cemetery and the *Piano dei Morti* (a crossroad before entering the village, thought to be frequented by ghosts). Most of these beings appear in the form of cats, dogs, goats, horses, fire, and wind.

Several women in Roseto Valfortore are regarded as witches—*janare, streghe,* or *donne da fuora*—and a few men as *stregoni* or *stregati,* that is, capable of causing harm to people, both intentionally and unintentionally. Their unusual powers are mostly associated with midnight on Christmas Eve, either directly or indirectly. If a boy or a girl was born at the stroke of midnight on Christmas Eve, reserved for the Lord's birth, he or she is likely to possess some extrahuman power, and be a werewolf (*lupo mannaro* or *pomponaro*) or a witch (*stregone*). Some of the witch power can be learned from another witch, also at the stroke of midnight on Christmas Eve, by a normal person who was born at any other time of the year. That very special night is the only time of the year when witches are likely to be exposed to public knowledge. It is usually done by hanging a scythe, a comb, a bunch of dry wheat ears, or a little sack of rice or salt at the church doors during the celebration of the midnight mass. The witches inside the church will be unable to leave with the rest of the people at the end of the mass as they will be fatally attracted by those objects and will feel forced to count endlessly the grains of rice or wheat or the teeth of the scythe. They will be caught in this act, as they will soon be the only ones left inside the church and thus give the other people the chance to know who are the witches in town! Catching a witch, though, is far from being an act with tragic consequences and to a certain extent it was the same in the past. When I asked what peo-would do once they caught a witch in the church, the answer was that nothing would be said or done, but that people would be satisfied with knowing so that they could remember and carefully watch the witch's moves. Consequently, being considered a witch is not necessarily an upsetting element in the community, and both the person directly involved and the others seem to know how to live in complete security and tranquility with this phenomenon. I observed that the attitudes of the persons directly involved are a curious mixture of disdainful aloofness and pleased awareness of being acknowledged as gifted with extraordinary powers.

In Roseto, Pennsylvania, I was told that some witches even traveled across the ocean in a night's time:

(P: Piscianzinu)

P: Now, a girl here, a woman who came from Italy a few years ago, the daughter of "Cola Baccamorto," I mean Cola Romano, Carmela, you know her, don't you?

B: Yes, I do.

P: She told me all this now. She told us that Ciccuzzo's wife, back there in Roseto Valfortore, she learned how to do it. She said, "Hey, you know? Ciccuzzo's wife, she is one, she is a monster!"[25] So, you see? They learn on Christmas night, right at midnight, when they go to mass! Just as I told you: either they learn it or they are born like that. That happens when they are born on Christmas night.

B: I see. And what about here in America?

P: Here? A woman here, an Abruzzese, before she came here,

to stay, she came to America as a ghost! Because these witches they are devils, they are magical!

B: I see.

P: She came to America as a ghost, to check where her husband slept. Because someone back there told her that he slept with his sister-in-law, see? So, she came to see. All her relatives say that, it's not me.

B: And where was he sleeping?

P: He was where he was.

B: Where he was?

P: Sure. When she sent back to Roseto Valfortore, she said, "My husband is in such and such place, I found him there!" See? Then, she came to America and spent her life here. You could go to her, she could cure you from a bellyache, from a headache, from anything. Her name was Maria Michella. I am telling no stories now![26]

Witches have a tendency to tie things like hair, limbs, and even penises!

(P: Puttanella)

B: What would they do?

P: They used to tie up things, you know? They used to tie our kids' hair up in knots so you couldn't comb it, and the arms, too! One day I found Anna's arms all twisted up, like this, see? Oh! I was scared! And, you know? They say there was a woman here who used to tie that . . . you know? They say that. This way the poor men couldn't make love to their wives any more, see? I heard that, but it never happened to us, no. And the milk, too.

B: The milk?

P: Sure! You know when women feed the babies? Well, they've got to watch! Now, this happened to me, with my seventh baby, see? I had twelve children and one died. A witch here, her name was "*A jatta*" [she means her nickname: The Cat], she threw a spell on me and I had no more milk, no more. Oh, how the baby cried all night then! Poor kid, he couldn't suck no more.[27]

Werewolves seem to be rarer now, but stories about them were told to me by several members of the different age groups in Roseto, Pennsylvania. Here is an interview illustrating how to discover a witch and some of the werewolves' actions and weaknesses. One of the two informants, Anne, was born in America, while the other,

Angelone, came from Roseto Valfortore as a little boy about seventy years ago:

(A: Anne;   Ag: Angelone)

Ag: That woman was born on the twenty-fourth, at midnight, because Jesus didn't want anybody to be born in that moment, because that was his birth, see? And so, my father used to come home late and one night he saw her inside the church, it was midnight and the next day was Christmas, see? Because, if you want to see who is *janare* [witch], you put a scythe, you know the scythe to cut the wheat? You hang a scythe on the church door, from inside, that is, and the witch cannot go out, because, to go out she must count all the teeth of the scythe and that could never be possible, because they are too many, too many teeth, see? That's how you find out who is *janare*. That's why one says "the women who work on the night of the Annunciation," because the angels announced the Virgin on the twenty-fifth of March, and so were the witches, but Jesus didn't want this, see? See how many things I had to learn in my life?

A: People say they don't exist! But an uncle of mine told me that he had a horse, you know? My uncle was killed by the *brigande* [thieves] over there. They kept the horse downstairs, in the stable, and they used to sleep upstairs. Now, every morning he went there and he found the horse all sweaty, all wet, see? Because at night, the *janare* went there, took the horse and went running around, see? All night. Then, they took it back to the house, but the horse was all wet, all hot, see?

Ag: And the hair was all twisted and tied up in knots and braids!

A: Then he tied himself under the horse, that you couldn't see him, see? And at night, she came and went riding all night, and my uncle was there, but he could not speak, he wouldn't say anything. But he saw who she was, see? That is a true story!

Ag: They are like *le fate* [fairies], on Sunday they are beautiful, but on Saturday, no.

A: On Saturday they can become like animals, animal flesh, and so are the witches. And men, too! Men, too! Men, that are *pumpunare* [werewolves] are like this. But if you are up there, and he wants to kill you, if you step on a stair, he can't climb more than three stairs, not more than three stairs, otherwise he drops dead! See? If you are above, you're O.K.

B: Did you see any werewolves?

A: No, but I know, I was told. My mother she had a friend who went to school with her. Her father was a *pumpunare* and he had a tower, a cage in the house, that when he became like that at night, they would put him in there until he got well. But sometimes he went out at night, at midnight, and he would kill people. So, he had a friend, a shoemaker, and the wife told the shoemaker: "You know what you do? You do this and this." So he did it and he had a balcony, and the *pumpunare* had to pass under it at night. So he waited and he had a long spear in his hand, you know the spear that you cook the animals? And he waited and he hit the *pumpunare* three times, he hit him three times and that rotten blood came out, see? So the *pumpunare* got well and they became *cumbare e cumpare* [godbrothers]. Not so much here, no. Even the dead they have blessed, so they don't come out no more.

B: But this thing of the midnight, does it happen everywhere?

A: Sure, everywhere! The only thing is that here in America people aren't that smart to find out, to find out who are the witches, see? But in Italy yes. But this is why, I always tell my children, my daughters, I say: "You must watch because you can never know who people are. A woman can be an old woman, a witch, a madonna, you can't tell now." See? Because, here, there is no way to find out![28]

The evil eye, however, is the most common feature of Rosetan magic practices, thoroughly believed and performed by women and men and Protestants and Catholics of all ages. Fourteen- and eighteen-year old girls—students, clerks, and factory workers—believe in the *malocchio* (evil eye), even though they may not perform the ritual themselves.

All critical moments of human life, such as pregnancy, puberty, childhood, birth, and death, have the condition—a psychosomatic condition—for magical morbidity, that is, a disposition to be influenced by dangerous powers. This morbidity always accompanies the baby from birth to puberty and the infant has a fragile, unsafe existence, particularly exposed to the evil eye, which usually reaches it through the eyes of an envious person. When babies look very healthy that is an even more dangerous moment because they are exposed to the unrestrainable envy of the other mothers. If one pays a visit to a house where children are, one should soon say to them, "God Bless You," in order to defend them from one's unconscious impulses of envy and, at the same time, to reassure the mother about one's feelings and purposes. The possibilities of being exposed to the evil eye are nearly infiite and scattered throughout our existence. Certain individuals, usually having a physical mark—such as thick eyebrows or a scar—corresponding to an uncommon cultural or physical type, are regarded as typical *jettatori*; that is, they are capable of giving the evil eye or another magic spell, both willingly and unwillingly. Even a well-meaning, ordinary person can give the evil eye to another one, by means of a simple act of admiration. The only thing to do is to provide oneself with as much protection as possible; and the protection is acquired by not refusing any of the magical acts and concepts handed down from tradition. In other words, it is a question of acquiring as much knowledge as possible about all the risks involved in life, and to develop, for each one, magical counteraction. In Roseto Valfortore, for example, the old people say that until fifty or sixty years ago there was the habit that, after birth took place with the mother seated on a pot (an old custom no longer in existence), a nail was hammered into the floor on the spot where the pot had been. The idea was that the iron nail would firmly "hold" the baby to life, since its existence was considered weak, insecure, and full of risks.

When the evil eye strikes a victim following a person's unconscious envy, it is as if the eyes acted on their own, independently of the person's will, almost functioning as autonomous beings. One night, I happened to tell one of my informants in Roseto, Pennsylvania, that I had a bad headache. She first reacted in a typically American way:

(R: Rose)

R: Did you try an aspirin?

B: Yes, but it didn't do any good.

R: Oh, well, maybe you've got it.

B: Do you think so?

R: Sure! You may have the *occhio secco, u malocchie* like my dad used to say. Now, let me call Margaret, 'cause I don't have any oil. She can do this for you.

B: Really? Over the telephone?

R: Of course! When Vicenza was in Florida, they did it for her over the phone, too. It doesn't make any difference.[29]

I had not imagined this technological aspect of black magic, and since then I have made further inquiries which proved that the telephone was used as a means for testing the evil eye and other magic practices. I was even told that a woman cured a small child from worms by saying a long formula over the telephone, while the baby was held near the receiver. This night, however,

Margaret told Rose to wait until she made her test and that she would call again. A few minutes later, the phone rang and I learned that I had been given the evil eye, very badly, and that I was to go to rest, but without falling asleep or I would diminish my natural resistance to the evil powers. Meanwhile, she would keep on trying her formula and she would notify me as soon as I was well again, which she did around midnight. Here is a recorded description of an evil eye test performed by Margaret (third generation) the next day, at her house:

B: So, please tell me how you did it. Show me how you did the evil eye last night.

M: Well, you have to put water in a dish, cold water, and then you say these words. But, as you say the words, you bless the dish three times, like this:

> Malocchje ngenzate,
> Tre Sande m'aiutate,
> Che poss' i nt' a l'occhje
> A cchi è fatte u malocchje a Carla.

Now you say that three times. Then you take olive oil and you put a few drops of this oil in the dish, like this. Now, Carla, if you come closer, you may be able to see. See? Do you see that? Now, if you would have had the *malocchje* [evil eye], those three dots of oil would have got separated and would bubble, or, as soon as I would put more water in, the oil would spread real fast. Then, you would have it real bad!

B: I see. When your father phoned you for my headache last night, did it separate?

M: Yes! It had two or three more dots, and it just went this way, see?

B: Does it have to be olive oil?

M: Also any kind of oil.

B: I think that your mother also spoke of a *malocchje ferrate—*

[We are interrupted by R., 16, Margaret's young daughter, who drops in for a minute and, noticing the oil and the dish, says: "Anybody got a headache here?"]

M: Oh, Carla wants to learn, you know?

R: [to me] You mean, you didn't know it?

B: Well, not exactly this kind.

R: Oh, it's good to know! Well, 'Bye Ma!

M: You've got to be here when your father comes home! [to me] Now, my grandmother, my father's mother, would make it

Malocchio ferrato ritual in Roseto, Pennsylvania. The ritual was re-
quested by the ex-chief of police to cure his headache.

(1) The dish with the water and the olive oil.

(2) The woman makes the sign of the cross over the dish with the
scissors three times, reciting the magic formula each time. She repeats
these actions with the screwdriver and the knife.

(3) The three *ferri*, iron tools, crossed on the chair. The man touches
his forehead with some of the exorcised liquid, while repeating the
formula.

An American-born Rosetan curing sore
throat with Candlemas candles.

with three—irons, I mean, she would make it with a fork, a spoon, and a knife, three pieces of iron that is, see? This is—this is—

B: The *malocchje ferrate?* [*ferro* means iron]

M: Well, I don't know the word. And then, after we would do it three times this way, she would do the cross with the fork, the knife, and the spoon three times, she would spit on it [on the dish with the oil], and she'd throw it out of the door. In other words, the *malocchje* is supposed to go out of the door, or something like that. Right! But I never knew the words she said, no. I learned this other one because the children were always sick, you know? I didn't believe it, Carla, but, you know, Carmela was once six or eight months old, and she was beautiful. She got up one morning and she was all sick, and over here she was swollen, all day! Swollen, yeah! I said, "God, what the hell is that?" So, my aunt Anne, you know the one who is now on vacation in Italy? She said, "Look maybe has *u malocchjjie a pupa!* [the baby has the evil eye]. She called a lady, 'cause my mother was in bed and couldn't come. It was about ten o'clock at night, the lady was doing it, and as she was doing it, Carmela got up! This thing [the swelling] went down and she started playing. So, from that on, I said, "I'm gonna do it!" And R., you know, she was always pretty,[30] and so she was always sick, and I would go call my grandmother, or my aunt, or the lady. And then I learned, see? Priests don't believe in it, they don't believe.

B: No?

M: They say it's against religion, see?[31]

A magic outlook is a constant feature in both Rosetos. Magic and religion open escapes especially from situations of emotional stress and offer the feeling of mastering one's own human limitations. In most cases, it is hard to draw a line between religion, on the one hand, and magic and superstition, on the other. Even the common belief that an unborn baby can be heard from outside the mother's body is rationalized by means of Christian traits:

(F: Filomena)

F: She was Sicilian and she lived across the street, two blocks from here, on Roseto Street, you see that red house? There. Honestly, I heard that poor baby cry. She was crying inside her mother. I heard it from down here! The father had beaten up his wife, see? The baby got offended and cried loud, very loud! That is because Jesus Christ also cried from inside his mother. When the Lord wasn't born yet, Joseph, too, offended the Virgin, and the Christ baby cried from inside, see? Oh, I heard it, I can still hear that voice![32]

Bread, often used to mean "food" in the folk speech, is viewed as vital for subsistence; hence the numerous beliefs and superstitions connected with it, mostly permeated with some Christian coloring:[33]

(F: Filomena)

F: For the dog, we have bread.

B: For the dog?

F: Sure! Because we were good and happy once. But then we got bad, you know? So, God said he was going to take the bread away from us, 'cause we didn't deserve it, see? And the wheat ear seemed to be full from bottom to top at the beginning, but then God started to deplenish it from the bottom up, like this, see? Until there was just a little left, a little on the top. And the dog was there watching and he started crying: "Lord, don't take all out! Leave some for me!" And God left some for him, just a little on the top of the ear, like now. For the dog, we have bread, see?[34]

Bread must not be placed upside down, or the Virgin will cry. It must be crossed and kissed if it falls onto the floor. It must never be thrown away, or God will send famine. When borrowed, it must always be returned, or one will spend hundreds of years in purgatory. It should not be sold, and because it is sold, God is punishing us with earthquakes and wars.

Many American Rosetans believe that men were once able to understand animal talk and all of them rationalize the loss of this important virtue with man's evil actions and the subsequent divine punishment. It seems as if most informants tend to view present life as wrong, limited, and dangerous, in contrast to a wonderful mythical past, when men lived in complete beatitude, enjoying unlimited capabilities and virtues:

(C: Carmine)

C: Ev'ry generation is changin', changin', changin'! Before, the men were giants! Men and women *èvene gevande* [they were giants]! Tall, beautiful! My father used to say it: "*Alti, belli.*" And now they're *cookooricù*.

B: *Cookooricù?*

C: They're weaker! In other words, Pop said, it's gonna come the time when the world will get wiser and weaker, yeah! And it's comin'! Ever heard before they're gonna go to the moon? Lot of people is smart, wise, you know? They try to invent somethin' else —but weaker. My father said so.

B: I see.

C: See? At that time, the animals used to talk back. They used to talk.

B: Oh, and would the men understand?

C: Oh, yeah! Was one language here years ago, was one language![35]

The saints and madonnas invoked in cures and other magic practices were very numerous and some of them are particularly recurrent in both Rosetos: St. Blaise, St. Donato, St. Catherine, St. Philip, St. Anthony, St. Philomena, and Our Lady of Mt. Carmel (in Italy, *Madonna del Carmine*). A testimony of the popular devotion to these figures is the fact that most Rosetans have these names, regardless of religious affiliation in America. A Protestant or a Jehovah's Witness still calls his children Biagio, Donato, Carmine, or Filomena.

The following interviews are taken at random from among those dealing with cures, superstitions, and religion. The first one is an example of how vulnerable and exposed to the evil influences are the most important moments of our life. A sixteen-year-old girl has the lucky opportunity of going to America and this fact automatically puts her in a critical, weak condition. A witch receives instructions to throw a black spell on Filomena's young cousin, but the spell misses her victim and strikes Filomena because of her special receptivity at that moment.

(F: Filomena)

F: I was too weak then, see? People were envious 'cause I was coming to America. My brother had already sent me the ticket, but I got sick and my mother thought I was dying!

B: How come?

F: Because a witch there had made *a fattura* [black magic spell] to a cousin of mine and *a fattura* hit me instead of my cousin, see? It hit me because I was weaker in that moment. Oh, everybody thought I was going to die!

B: And what happened then?

F: My brother sent more money from America and my father went to this witch and paid her. But he also paid the church, see? They said so many services for me, to get me well, you understand?

So, finally, the spell went back to my cousin and she got sick and I came to America. Then she died.[36]

The following interview shows the magical-religious world view of a third-generation American Rosetan. She is so anxious to enlarge her knowledge on this subject, that, unintentionally, I happened to teach her one more belief!

(M: Menica)

M: You want to know about stomach-ache? Oh, that! You take garlic in a rag, then you close it and cross it. Then, you put the rag here on your belly and some garlic under your nose. It puts you to sleep, 'cause it's strong. It's special for worms, you know?

B: What about throat-ache?

M: That's St. Blaise, the third of February! On St. Blaise, you go to the church and the priest gets you two long candles and puts them in cross right here, against your throat and says the prayer.

B: Which prayer?

M: That I don't know. Then, you know, this priest here, he's real crook!

B: Yes?

M: Oh, imagine. You know All Soul's Day? The second, of November?

B: Yes.

M: We used to light candles here at the cemetery. Oh, it was beautiful! And the dead people need it, too. Before, Carla, you could go and put thousands, as many as you wanted candles on the graves. And when you went to the cemetery, oh, it looked beautiful! All lit up, just like daytime! Real mighty candles! He took them away, he only wants two or three candles upon a grave. If a lady has ten children, only two or three candles on a grave! He took that away from the old people and he took the singing away from the old people—all, all, Carla, all! He doesn't like our things. And, you know, no candles is bad luck.

B: I know it. But going back to diseases, do you grow herbs in the garden?

M: That's another thing. *Campomille* [camomile], that's the Italian tea. If you have a cold, a sore throat, or a cough, try the *campomille*. And *malva* [mallow], *malva*, too. You must never waste it.

B: Is it sin?

M: Oh, yes! And you must't put your shoes on the table either:

the Blessed Mother cry. The same thing when you go in the bathroom and you sing: the Blessed Mother cry. Then, when you
whistle, you know whistle? Oh, the Blessed Mother cry!

B: And can you open an umbrella in the house?

M: Bad luck! That's bad luck! If your children play and open
an umbrella in the house, you know? That's bad luck.

B: How about the bed? Are you supposed to put your hat or
other clothes on it?

M: Why? Is it bad luck? Oh, my God! My Michela, she puts
her dresses on her bed! I must warn her, God! I gotta tell her!

B: Oh, don't worry, I don't think you should worry.

M: But you never know! One must be careful. See?

B: I see. Do you know any healers?

M: My mother, she was sick. Somebody told her that there was
a lady in Easton. She would heal. So, every week, I would take my
mother to this lady. This lady in her house she had a little altar, a
little altar. She was a Catholic. A little altar. She had candles lit
and when my mother would go, she would say a few words and
then she would draw my mother down like this, double down,
yeah! Because she said, "If there's anything that bothers you, it's
gotta come out." It was gonna come out, you know? Then, I said
to this lady, "Oh," I said, "do you know what? Whenever I sit outside my house, I see bats! Around the house as if they wanna come
in the house." So I told her and she told me I would have the hospital three times. Then, Filippo got sick. Big Phil, you know, my
husband. My son was four months old, and I had to leave him and
go to the hospital because I had stones here, see? They had to
cut. I couldn't swallow 'cause I had a stone in my bend. I had
doctors all the time! So this lady said, "Do you mind if I come to
your house?" "Oh," I said, "I don't mind." So, she came.

B: Was she Italian?

M: Maybe yes, but she was Catholic! She predicted her husband's death! Yeah! He was a drunkard and she predicted that her
husband was gonna die with a bottle of beer and a candy, and he
died with a bottle of beer and a candy! And she predicted she was
gonna die: She knew when she was gonna die. So, anyway, she came
and as soon as she came in the house, she could tell where Michela
always sat! And I said, "Yeah!" Then, I brought her upstairs and
I showed the bedroom. She said, "Michela sleeps over there, doesn't
she?" And I said, "Yeah!" Then she said, "Does your Michela take
clothes from people?" At that time, yeah! At that time, I didn't
have it, and whenever somebody wanted to give my kids, I'd take it.
Then she said, "You know?—she said—You know? You have some-

body in your family that's a strict Catholic and they love to read Catholic books. They're puttin' evil on you!" Oh, Madonna, who could have been? But she wouldn't tell me, she said that would cause us more trouble! She said, "Just watch yourself, 'cause they're jealous of you!" She told me that and I watched, and from then on, I always know if there's somebody in town that doesn't like us. I watch! But now, Carla, now that you told me about throwing the hat on the bed! Michela and all my children, they throw all their clothes on the bed, their books on the bed, everything on the bed! You've got to explain to me. Is that bad? Do they say it's bad up in Italy?

B: Well, I am not sure, but I may be wrong. Don't worry.

M: Oh, but I'm gonna tell them! Oh, Madonna![37]

To concude this brief survey of attitudes toward magic and religion, I have transcribed an interview which shows some interesting exchanges on this subject with the Pennsylvania Dutch farmers near Roseto:

(P: Piscianzinu)

P: Bellyache is very easy to cure. You can cure that with Holy Tuesday, Holy Wednesday, Holy Thursday—it goes with the Holy Week, see? The *malocchje* [evil eye], too, my daughter Giovannina, she can cure it. I have a daughter-in-law, she's Catholic, she had her children sick all the time and Giovannina had to make *u malocchje*. And the priests don't believe it! *Padre Duccio*, you know, the priest before this—son of— now? Padre Duccio was good, but he didn't believe it. But if it's true, it's true! If a baby has a headache, a bellyache, see? Only yesterday Giovannina took the *malocchje* away from her sister! She had such a headache, she couldn't even stand up. But she does it for nothing. No money! They tried to teach me, too, but I've got difficulty in learning. All of this came from Italy. In Italy there are women who are healers, they know medicine better than doctors! Then, you know who is smart around here?

B: Who is?

P: The Dutch! The Dutch people! They know all herbs, they cure a lot. I took my poor wife to them several times.

B: Oh, yes? And what about English and Welsh?

P: Oh, no! They're American![38]

My data show that Protestants and Catholics share an identical world view, the same body of magic and religious practices and beliefs, and the same devotions for their only folk heroes, that is, the various saints and madonnas. Almost all Protestant informants gave me similar information about saints, prayers, beliefs, etc. The choice of a different religion was evidently not the result of any spiritual crisis, or of any theological criticism of Catholicism. More likely, it was the result of several different factors, such as dislike for the Catholic priest, opportunities of getting better employment, taking a mate's religion in case of mixed marriages, and even the fact that the Catholic church was temporarily closed at the turn of the century, while the Presbyterian one was active (Basso 1952: 30–33).

(A: Anne)

B: When the Rosetans came to this country, they were all Catholic. Why do you think many of them became Protestant or even Jehovah's Witness?

A: Well, it wasn't because of the differences in the doctrine. It wasn't because they didn't believe in certain Catholic things! It was mostly because they disagreed with that particular priest that we had at the moment. It was a rejection of the priest more than anything else.

B: Do you think economic reasons might have been also important. Maybe they wanted to get jobs with Protestant bosses?

A: Also, but it depended on the priests.

B: How about becoming nuns and priests?

A: No. We never gave much in that direction. It seems to me that we don't have that great respect for priests. Our old people here were the same. I think they came with that from Italy.[39]

Church attendance is still very high among all Rosetans and the traditional custom still followed in Roseto Valfortore—separate areas for men and women—was observed in the Church of Our Lady of Mt. Carmel until recently. The small square in front of the church usually fills up with people standing in groups before and after mass. It is evident that these informal meetings both outside and inside the church still serve the old function of social exchange and control. Unlike Italy, however, during the mass a large number of men take communion (although there is a smaller percentage among the lower-class Italian-born).

The 6:00 A.M. mass is only attended by the old people—and by the "big shots," as old Rosaria once told me, "who don't want to be seen with the other folks." The ten o'clock mass is for the "fashion show," with its profusion of flowered hats and new dresses, and it is attended by marriageable girls and newly married couples. "Normal" people go at eleven o'clock. The large, impressive stone building stands on one side of the square, right on the boundary line between Roseto and Bangor. Its location is often referred to in campanilistic language by the Rosetans, who claim the ownership of the church, the altar, whereas they are happy to leave the Bangor people the nonessential rest.

The baroque interior, with its two lines of false marble columns, has small niches in the side walls containing the "stations" of Christ's passion and, at the center of the main altar, the *Madonna del Carmine*, the statue used for the procession on the last Sunday of July. Older Rosetans often complain about Father Leone's decision to change the previous Italian writings under each "station" to the present English ones. On the left side of the main entrance, there is a large statue of the *Pietà* surrounded by votive candles, while a statue of St. Joseph is on the right side of the main altar. Farther to the right, there is St. George (on a horse), St. Donato, and Jesus Shepherd. On the left side, in order: St. Anthony from Padua, St. Philip Neri (also a patron of Roseto Valfortore), and St. Rocco, all of whom are continuously mentioned in the Rosetan folksongs, folktales, and legends both in Italy and in America. The altars are adorned with handmade laces as in Italy, where they are usually votive offerings made by the local women. Old women wear a large scarf or a veil on their heads while all other women, including little girls, wear hats and carry handbags. Unlike Italy, where children are allowed to play and run freely along the church aisles and adults talk and gossip as in a social meeting, here people observe an absolute silence. Rosetans—and most Italian-Americans—returning from their visits abroad often commented with surprise and disapproval on the Italian behavior in church.

Since mass and sermons are now in English, the older women do not follow what is being said but pray on their own, whispering some Rosetan folk prayers they have always known. This situation is not at all peculiar to the American experience as peasants had always been accustomed to being excluded from the language used in church. The Italian body of folk narratives dealing with tricks and misunderstandings caused by church Latin in peasant society is in fact exceptionally abundant. Preaching, however, had been in Italian even in their day, and so it had been in Roseto, Pennsylvania, until two or three decades ago. Now old women are unable to follow the English sermon, and the American custom of placing prayer books on each seat cannot offer them any help in joining the singing of hymns and prayers. I have collected an unusual number of beautiful religious songs from these women—many more than I could find in Roseto Valfortore—and both the length and the good quality of the texts prove their frequent use in daily life. In Italy, the church is actively enforcing the popularization of a new kind of religious songs which, though dealing with some traditional themes, have the dialect and the "pagan" elements expurgated from them. These songs are now on records and are played by loudspeakers during procession and outside the church on festive days, while priests discourage the singing of the older ballads and prayers which are defined as coarse and heretical. As a result, while many traditional songs have deteriorated in Italy, Italian-Americans have clung to their old songs as no substitutes were available for their needs.

Rosetan Catholics, Protestants, and Jehovah's Witnesses all seem to have vague and confused knowledge of the religious differences among them, probably because, following a typical Italian pattern, few of them have any deep knowledge of their own religion. The new affiliations resemble the parish allegiances common to any Italian province town, characterized by campanilistic connotations of rivalry and superiority.[40] The attitude toward religion remains a traditional mixture of natural and official religion, with little awareness and no real interest in the deepest problems of faith and salvation. Religion, like sex, medicine, and education, shows a constant interaction between the "great" and the "little traditions."

The Cycle of the Human Life

The traditional life of the southern Italian peasant is far from being a mere conglomerate of pagan survivals. Among other things, a variety of elements such as literary products, aristocratic customs, church laws and liturgy, and civil rules have been constantly filtered through the peasant culture. In some cases a custom is so thoroughly maintained and documented in written history that it is possible to trace it back as far as the Middle Ages. One example is the dowry, a custom probably imported by the Longobards. More often, however, a custom has been transformed by so many factors that it has lost all significant connection with its distant origins. In Italy and more so in the corresponding regional groups transplanted to America, there are increasing signs that the original meanings and motivations of certain customs have been totally forgotten. Sometimes, new meanings and motivations may replace the old ones or the custom is simply followed for no apparent reason by the mere force of traditional repetition.

Sterility, once attributed only to women, used to be considered by peasants as a shameful disgrace for the couple. The woman was invariably blamed for this fault, which damaged her husband's prestige in the community. The whole concept, of course, was based on the acknowledged economic necessity of having a large family for agricultural work. It was thus customary for the couple, once the marriage had been celebrated, to go in pilgrimage to some sanctuary in order to obtain healthy and numerous offspring. The most renowned places in Italy for such pilgrimages were St. Nicholas of Bari, the Incoronata of Foggia, St. Michael of the Gargano, and the Sanctuary of Montevergine, all of them not farther than fifty miles from Roseto Valfortore. Today the honeymoons, which last about fifteen days and start on the wedding day, are substituted for these devotional visits.

The extreme importance attributed to fertility helped the formation of a whole complex of beliefs, superstitions, and usages connected with pregnancy and birth. The traditional behavior surrounding these two central events of life was so strong in Italy that it continued unaltered for a long time among the immigrants and their children in America. The infamy cast upon sterility by tradition[41] is balanced by the high respect paid to the pregnant woman as an almost magical being endowed with supernatural powers. This is especially true for the first pregnancy which has the additional function of proving the husband's virility to the community. Pregnancy is one of those natural conditions full of mysterious risks and taboos. It is a condition in which the evil eye is most likely to strike its victims and a number of beliefs and precautions protects the pregnant woman and the baby from being influenced by external evil forces. The woman's behavior may influence both negatively and positively the baby and herself. Consequently a double set of prescriptions—positive and negative—regulates her behavior.

Fertility potions were once prepared by a woman in Roseto, Pennsylvania, Maria Michela, while other procedures were followed by women to enhance fertility or—more rarely—to prevent pregnancy or to stop it. Young women today say that they do not follow such practices; however, several beliefs connected with conception are still in existence, mainly those connected with the determination of sex. If a woman goes to bed before her husband, a girl will

come from the subsequent copulation and the same results are
obtained if the woman—or the man—speaks during intercourse.
Rosetan women who had babies in the years between the nineteen
twenties and the nineteen forties told me a large number of beliefs, taboos, and prescriptions regarding pregnancy and birth,
most of which I had previously heard in Roseto Valfortore. Their
attitude was sometimes skeptical, and there was an increasing trust
in official medicine. It was often stated, however, that it was always
better to play it safe and try, since it did not cost anything, "it can't
hurt." There are two common beliefs regarding the sex of the unborn baby: if the right hips hurts during pregnancy, the woman
will have a boy. If the abdomen is rounded, a girl will come.[42]
Miscarriages are to be feared in a young bride, and it is a good thing
to tie a ribbon around the waist during the months of pregnancy,
as the knot will prevent the evil forces from entering the maternal
body. In Roseto Valfortore, the ribbon is black and it must not be
measured to allow the baby an unlimited growth. Pregnant women
must eat any food they wish—in contrast with modern diets—and
everyone must be on the alert so that the mother has not even the
minimal craving, for unsatisfied cravings will leave visible marks
on the baby's skin. The birthmark will have the same color and
shape as the wanted food and will appear in the same spot touched
by the woman while she felt the desire to eat. Pregnant women must
not be offended or beaten by their husbands or the baby will cry
aloud from inside the mother.

After birth, women should nurse their babies—a statement repeated by all the old and middle-aged women—or the baby will be
similar to an animal because nonmaternal milk transmits to babies
the negative qualities of the animal from which it is taken.

(P: Puttanella)

P: I had twelve! Six girls and six boys. I was the one who made
the girls, of course! And he made the boys.

B: Is there anything a pregnant woman should not touch?

P: Her face and her neck! Because she may want to eat something, you know? I used to touch my back! My back, yes. Jenny has
a ham mark on her shoulders and Peter has a cherry mark there,
too! Because I was careful, see?

B: Is there any way by which to guess the sex of the coming
baby?

P: Yes. If he had it, he was a boy! [She laughs.]

B: I mean before birth, though.

P: I know! When my belly was round, it was always a girl.

Then, my mother used to say that if you went to bed first at night, you would make the kid like you. But my husband was so lazy that he always went to bed first, see? And yet, I made six girls! Oh, there must be a trick somewhere!

B: Are there any other ways in which the unborn baby may be affected?

P: My babies used to cry when my husband hit me, see? They cried. You could hear them cry. *A cummare* [godmother] heard.

B: You mean from inside?

P: Inside my body. The kids cried, "Ah! Ah!" [She imitates the voices.]

B: Where did you have the babies?

P: Right here! And I didn't do like those girls nowadays! I nursed all my babies, twelve, fifteen months each! They never got sick because they took my milk. No milk can be as mamma's milk. That's why these American kids are like animals: they are like animals because they drink the milk of the animals. They take that milk and they become animals. No respect, nothing! They don't care, they tell you, "I don't care!", see? When the baby takes my milk, he looks at me, and by looking at me, he becomes like me, like his mother. And then, he cares for his mother! Not now, no!

B: How about your daughters? Did they nurse their babies?

P: Yes, but not my daughter-in law! No, no. She's Dutch. She goes like this! [She makes the gesture of shaking bottle.]⁴³

Many of these beliefs are based on the magic principle that a defect or a characteristic can pass from one organism or object to another just by way of contact. A pregnant woman will thus avoid crossing her hands on her abdomen or in front of her or on a table, or else her baby will be born with the umbilical cord tied around its neck as many times as she crossed her hands. Such an unfortunate occurrence, however, could be counteracted by making the opposite gesture as many times as necessary.⁴⁴

On the twenty-fifth of March—Annunciation Day—abstinence from sexual intercourse must be observed for fear of having a baby on Christmas night, in which case the baby would be either a witch or a werewolf, according to the sex. A baby born between the seventeenth and the twenty-fifth of January will be immune from serpent poison and shall be able to catch snakes by merely calling them.

The afterbirth is very important. It must be buried under a fig tree so that the mother will have abundant milk to feed the baby. It must be buried very deep, too, to prevent animals from eating it or the person's life will be in serious danger. The umbilical cord, on the other hand, must be dried up and kept with special care.

(C: Connie)

C: Yeah, it was Easter when I was born, and my godmother she was a midwife, too! Oh, nearly all the babies here passed through her hands. Mothers always sent for her, even at night, all the time. She was a midwife, but she didn't go to school, of course, still she was good.

B: Oh, yes? And by the way, do you know if she kept the funiculus of the baby?

C: Well, of course, that's human flesh! You don't throw away that! You put that in some—cotton, maybe, or something. You keep it and then, when one of your people pass away, see, you put that in the coffin. That's human flesh, see? [45]

When the baby is born still enwrapped in the amniotic veil (called *camicia*, shirt), he is considered very lucky as the veil is a sign that he is already protected from the dangers of life. The veil is dried and kept in a little sack and often worn by the baby around his neck or offered to some saints as a devotion. All women in the American Roseto now have their babies at the hospital, but until the outbreak of World War II, most women delivered their babies at home with a midwife—or a doctor—and always with neighbor women and godmothers acting as nurses. The midwives (*mammane, levatrici*) delivered the babies and did other jobs in the room; they washed the mother and the child and they took care of the after-birth and the funiculus in the traditional way. They neither weighed nor measured the baby as this action would limit the growth to the original weight and height. In this whole phase, the future godmother had an important role. She became a family member who would soon take over the most important decisions regarding the child. This pattern is still followed today. During child-birth, doors and drawers were open and all knots in the house were untied in order to facilitate an easy birth. There was a time when one of the father's garments was placed on the wife's bed to help her delivery with his virile strength, and the baby had to be washed in a special basin (*catino*), which came to the bride with her wedding trousseau.[46] A. Z. Falcone, the first American-born boy in Roseto, Pennsylvania, and now a Protestant, says that after baptism he was soon dressed in a brown woolen votive dress, similar to that of St. Anthony of Padua. He wore that dress continuously until he was thirteen months old; then the little dress was burned and the ashes were put in a small scapular and hung around his neck, to stay there until puberty. After his thirteenth year of age the scapular was put in the coffin of a relative of his.[47] Ernesto de Martino (*Sud e Magia*, 1959:71) says that this usage is to be considered as equivalent to that of the amniotic veil: a protective container to be cherished and worn constantly for a magic number of years and then returned to the other world by putting it in a coffin.

The birth of a girl is not cause for great joy, while a boy is always welcomed by everybody. The practical origin of this attitude is quite obvious in Italy where boys were needed to help the household economy. In America the same attitude seems to survive today among Italian-Americans and the new psychological motivation may be the fact that having a boy increases the sense of virility of the father and thus his prestige in the society.[48]

"It's better a lame husband than an emperor father" is the Italian proverb reflecting the enormous importance for the girl to find herself a husband in a peasant society. Forming one's own family is the only solid anchor capable of securing social acknowledgment even to the humblest members of a society. The wedding day is the most crucial event in a peasant woman's life, while her husband has the additional memories of the years spent in distant places during his military service. One's own wedding as well as marriage problems and community events are the favorite topics of conversation in both Rosetos and among peasants in general. Although marriage customs have changed more than others both in Italy and in America, a great amount of time and energy are still devoted to a detailed planning of the wedding day, from the banns and the invitations to the banquet and the honeymoon. Girls very early begin their anxious expectations of the event that will mark their passage to a more respected role in society. In Roseto Valfortore and to a lesser extent in the American Roseto, various means are used to predict the identity of the future husband and the date of the wedding: melting wax and then observing the shape it acquires when resolidified, watching a falling star in order to enhance a revealing dream in the following night, and asking a number of a friend and then guessing a boy's name from the corresponding letter of the alphabet.

(J: Judith)

J: Well, it's a joke more than a serious thing, see? In other words, we don't believe it's true. We just do it.

B: Did women believe it in the past? Your mother?

J: Oh, yeah! She did! She knew she was going to marry Pap

even before they were engaged: she knew the initials and his job, see? My girl friend believes it now. She says there's something, see? I don't believe there's anything sure about it. It's fun, though.[49]

The period of engagement, *fidanzamento*, is still quite long in Roseto Valfortore where it can last from two to five years, although longer periods are not at all infrequent. In America, the circumstances of immigration changed the traditional behavior. If a girl came from Italy for a wedding which had already been arranged, she would be wed immediately. Otherwise, under normal family conditions, courting could take quite a long time and would be subject to all traditional sanctions. Today, things are changing rapidly for the young people: engagements are easily ended without much fear that the girl will not find another suitor and girls are allowed to go out with their boy friends without chaperonage. Some of the old sanctions, however, are still enforced even by American-born parents:

(R: Rose)

R: Oh, yes, oh, yes! I don't mind if she picks up somebody, see? She's young and she's got to have her own family one day. But she must watch! See? She's a woman and, you know, women bring home things, see? She must watch! Her father told her, "Ten o'clock, ten thirty, you must be home." She has to be here, with all of us, and if there is a boy friend, all right! He can come here—two, three days a week—eat supper, and all that—that's fine. But we won't let her run around like some girls up here! Not her father—he's strict! And he'd better be Italian!

B: Yes?

R: Oh, sure! Things don't turn up right otherwise—he'll tell her dirty things—he'll call her "Wop," and all that, see? Oh, I know that! And she'll be sorry, then, see?

B: I see. Did you see any such cases before?

R: All the time, all the time! In Bangor, you know? And other people I know—that's bad, you know? See, for example, my son? Phil, you know him. Well, he goes out with a girl from Bangor! But he's not serious, see? He's only kiddin'. Those are girls that will stay out all night and Phil knows that. He says, "I'll never marry one of those gals, never." Then, you see, once a girl had to be a virgin.

B: And now?

R: Well—sure! If she's a decent girl, from a good family, she'll be a virgin. But who can tell? And men want that—our Italian men here—they won't take a girl that isn't an honest girl, see? Anyway, things are gettin' mixed up, now.

Once the wedding day is chosen, the girl and her family are very busy with the final preparations. The custom of the bride's trousseau (*biancheria*) is still followed, but it no longer includes all the items once required by tradition. Until the early nineteen forties, the girl was supposed to provide a fixed number of items for the house, such as six (sometimes twelve or twenty-four) bed linens, towels, and pillowcases, and for personal use, such as nightgowns and other underwear for both herself and her husband. Nowadays she usually provides the basic items for the house and for herself, plus most of the furniture, while the groom is supposed to provide the house if he can. In both Rosetos, the transportation of the trousseau to the new house used to be an important ceremony. On a given day of the week preceding the wedding, the women of both families would all go to the new house, each carrying a large basket of *biancheria* on her head. The little party would also include the godrelatives, who had a special prominence in the ceremony. Then, the bed would be prepared by the groom's mother and sister, and the *biancheria* was put on display near the bed, while refreshments were offered to the party and to the visitors. All sorts of precautions were taken in order to protect the nuptial bed from the evil spirits to which it was particularly vulnerable in those critical days preceding the wedding.

The village custom of getting married in the months which are less occupied with agricultural work faded away quickly in America, where the people had no reason to observe such a rule. There are days, months, and periods, however, in which people do not get married in Roseto, Pennsylvania. For example, Tuesdays and Fridays are avoided for weddings (as well as for departures and beginning a new activity), and Sundays are preferred by most people in both Rosetos, while Mondays are reserved for widows to remarry. There is a proverb known in both Rosetos that says, "Don't get married in May or the bed will be widowed," because May is regarded as the month of the Virgin and thus improper for human weddings. To this day, meeting another party—wedding or funeral—is considered a bad omen for the nuptial procession. Some brides still wear a scapular of Our Lady of Mt. Carmel as a particular protection for that day; and until thirty years ago, brides would also carry a little sack full of salt and metal nails to ward off the devil. Occasionally, in order to secure fertility, the couple may choose to get married during the first or the second quarter of the moon, or the bride can step into the church with her right foot first. The ceremony inside the church is regulated by official liturgy, and several Rosetans say that, as St. John's Gospel is regarded as lucky, the priest will often pretend to be reading that particular gospel, even though the gospel of that day may be a different one. Up to ten or fifteen years ago, the nuptial procession used to move—it still does in Roseto Valfortore—to and from the church, preceded and followed by a crowd of children and other villagers. Now it moves in a long line of noisy cars, even when the church is but two or three blocks away from the bride's home. The *comare* (godmother) and the *compare* (godfather) are still the most important guests during the ceremony and the subsequent banquet, which used to take place in the Marconi Social Club or in the Roseto Hotel, both on Garibaldi Avenue. Recently, however, with the abundance of cars, it became fashionable to go to quite distant motels and restaurants for the banquet, where crowds of three to four hundred guests and a musical band enjoy hours and hours of refreshments and dancing. I once attended one of these banquets where all the 565 guests lined up in several circles around the huge room, awaiting their turn to kiss the bride, while a photographer took pictures to distribute to each guest as a lucky piece. At a certain point, before opening the dances, the bride threw her little bouquet of flowers up in the air and the unmarried girls all tried to catch it first, as this showed who would be the next bride. Then, while the bride sat down, the groom took off the fancy garter she was wearing for this purpose and threw it up in the air for the unmarried men in the room to catch it; this, in turn, showed who was going to be the next groom. Late in the evening, the couple usually leaves the banquet which often goes on till dawn, and either leaves immediately for the honeymoon or goes home for that night to leave the next morning. The old custom of the groom's friends singing the wedding serenade at night outside the house is disappearing fast in Roseto Valfortore, and in Roseto, Pennsylvania, it is only occasionally done as a joke for a widower's wedding.

(A. Z.: Anthony Zilio')

A. Z.: You want to know that? Who made the bed for the bride? [He laughs.] The bride's mother and big sister! Yeah! And they had so many baskets, you know? *I canestri.* They used to put the pillowcases there, the linens there, everything. Then, they would hang them on a side, like this, you know? And you bring one basket, I bring another—with the *biancheria* [trousseau], see?

B: Do you mean that each person used to carry some?

A. Z.: Yeah! Yeah! They used to take twenty, thirty girls, for this, see? Eighteen, nineteen years old? Well, they used to carry a basket each on their head! With the *biancheria*, up to the bride's home. But not the old home, the new one, where she was going to live, see?

B: Did they do this in America?

A. Z.: It was done for my wedding, sure! Yeah!

B: And how was this ceremony called?

A. Z.: It's called—it's called—"to bring the *biancheria*—to make the bed," or something like that. But when I got married, they made the bed, two or three days head, you know? I used to live down here. You know where Mike Zito is?

B: Yes.

A. Z.: There! But then I went to live here, near the church, the Presbyterian church, see? And that day my mother-in-law she cooked supper for everybody. She gave food to twenty, forty people! And when I came from work, they had just finished making the bed. The first thing my sister-in-law told me when she saw me was, "A. Z., be happy now, the bed is ready! I watched. You've got the bed ready and all the *biancheria*, too, it's all there! That's what she told me the first thing when I got in the house. I remember. Then, you know what they used to do? My friends put a rope under the bed, a rope with a bell, and the rope went outside the window! Then, we ate, you know; and then, we went to bed. At that time, we had no electricity, just oil, and we put it off. Then, they played the bell![50] Oh, what a noise, oh!

B: Was that a custom?

A. Z.: For good luck, sure! Your friends would do it, but not now any more, no, no! Not that I know anyhow. Then, we went to Canada for the honeymoon.

B: Did you live with your family?

A. Z.: Oh, yes, yes! Father and mother moved right in with me! Until they died.[51]

Love potions were used not long ago in New York as well as in Roseto, Pennsylvania. Their dialect names are *fattura* (charm) and *legatura* (from the verb *legare* meaning to tie), which symbolize the intention of attaching two persons. In all cases parts of the girl's body—usually hair from the armpits, or from the pubis, and menstrual blood—are mixed to sugar, coffee, wine, or liquor and are taken secretly to mass for blessing during the elevation while reciting special words. The mixture is then given to the man to drink without his knowing. Sexual and sacred elements thus combined are viewed as powerful love vehicles, capable of producing irresistible attraction by means of transferring part of one body into another. Saints, especially St. Anthony of Padua, are also invoked as mediators—as a sort of sorcerers in heaven—in these practices.

As it often happens, none of the persons who told me about such practices admitted to having personally done them, but many mentioned names and relatives of the persons involved. All the cases concerned girls trying to attract men and not vice versa. This may be due to the fact that, traditionally, a girl is only considered young until she is about twenty-five, while a man has all the initiative and time he wants to start a family and he is often envied and admired by the other men if he is able to keep his "freedom" as long as possible. Providing he gives other proofs of his virility, he is allowed an unlimited time of liberty during which he can enjoy the attention of women without committing himself or diminishing his status.

In the early days of immigration, several boys went back to Italy to marry a girl they knew, or one they were introduced to by proxy. Just as often, after the turn of the century, very young girls would arrive by themselves to America, where men they had never seen before were waiting to marry them. The attitude now toward these arranged marriages is a mixture of justification and rejection of matchmaking:

(C: Carmine)

B: Is it still done?

C: At times, yeah! But when you fix marriages like that, the bed stinks. It stinks because there's no love, no affection. Oh, I think so. Those days, of course, our people was poor, they was ignorant, so, they *had* to do it. But now, no. Not my children, anyhow![52]

Death, viewed as a transitional event that connects human life to the other world, is also surrounded by a whole complex of beliefs and superstitions that concern the few days preceding and following the fatal moment. This whole set of ritual behaviors handed down by tradition tends to one main purpose: providing the living with a sort of "scientific" knowledge concerning the handling of death and its nature. Ritualizing death means acquiring some control over it and thus affording some reassurance and peace in the face of this fatal event. The fear of returning souls—which stems from their belonging to the underworld—for example, can be overcome by establishing regular relationships with the deceased

The Malpiedo family in Roseto, Pennsylvania, in 1909. Carmine sits beside his oldest sister who is holding the baby.

Funeral wake of a returned emigrant in Roseto Valfortore in 1909.

by means of periodical masses and recurrent wakes, offerings, mourning, and flowers taken to the cemetery. The whole funeral period is thus viewed as a gradual passage from one cycle to another which must be carefully guarded and observed, in order both to secure the dying a person a peaceful rest in the other world and to make the departure less painful and frightening for the living.

Recent innovations—mostly imposed by modern laws—have changed some of the oldest funeral customs of the community in Roseto, Pennsylvania, as among other Italian-American groups. One of these innovations, imposing the early removal of the body to the funeral home, has strongly weakened the ancient southern Italian custom of night wakes and funeral lamentations. This habit was long held by southern Italians in all parts of the United States,[53] and in Roseto it continued until not long ago, leaving fresh memories in all Rosetans.

When it became known that I was collecting old pictures showing traditional customs, a woman gave me permission to copy a very interesting and quite unique photograph. It represented her father's death in Roseto Valfortore, after she had left the village as a young girl to come to America at the beginning of this century. The picture is a precious documentation of funeral rites as it shows the bed with the body, publicly displayed in the little square in front of the house. The man traditionally dressed in his black wedding suit with his hat on his knees, rests on beautifully embroidered linens and quilts. The widow sits by the bed, while a little crowd of fellow-villagers circle all around in the square, praying, lamenting, watching the departure of one of them from the community life. The wake being held in the public square testifies to the participation of the group in the death of a member of the community, where death is not regarded as a solely private event.

In America the body was, until recently, waked at home, continuously for several days, until the moment of its transportation to the cemetery. The whole development of the wake was a sort of drama, staged in the home during that intermediate state in which the dead was considered as suspended between the realm of the living and that of the dead. The house filled up with relatives and friends who would come in and out continuously for several days. The closest relatives—and, in absence of these, godrelatives or neighbors—would actually take over the direction of the household to allow the mourning persons a total attention to the body. All relatives were expected to come, even from a distance, for a brief visit to the family. Funeral lamentations were sung on the life and virtues of the deceased person, in which the women of the family (but also some especially trained ones from the neighborhood) would join in a rhythmic monotone chant.

These and a number of other ritualized actions were performed by most Rosetans until World War II. Many of my informants say that they do not like the new custom, which seems to them to endanger the journey of the dead to the other world, and that they keep their wakes at home as if the body were still there.

Once the imminence of death is ascertained, this fact automatically determines a certain number of actions, some of which tend to facilitate the passing away and the shortening of the agony. To this purpose, the relatives take away from the body all the amulets that previously tended to defend and keep life—such as medals and scapulars—as these would painfully lengthen the passage. The closest relatives are also supposed to leave the room as their presence there would prevent the dying person from expiring. A second set of actions, which could be called "positive" actions, tend to publicize the event once it has occurred. In the American Roseto, these actions include the traditional tolling of the bells in a given way and the posting of death announcements on the church walls. Another set of "negative" actions is usually made up of taboos and prohibitions of various kinds. All start at the moment of death and some last for a few days, others for a few weeks, and some even for a year and more. The most common prohibitions are halting of nonessential activities in the house, refraining from going to rest, lighting the kitchen fire, cooking as long as the dead is unburied, and wearing colored garments. In the past, it was customary to cover mirrors and decorative paintings. Along with these taboos, more traditional behavior takes place, such as the *recuonzolo* (consolation), that is, food brought by relatives and friends to the mourning family and wearing black clothes for fixed periods of time, according to the degree of relationship.

There is undoubtedly a large number of customs and beliefs connected with death still observed in the community. Instinctively and by force of tradition the community clings to this rite of passage as to something that helps to accept and overcome an inevitable event. Compared to the corresponding behavior in Roseto Valfortore, however, an important change is now occurring in this as well as in other rites of passage. Individual life is becoming more and more private and the participation of, as well as the dependence on, the immediate circle of relatives and trusted friends is becoming less essential. Consequently, while the various aspects of human life are still surrounded by traditional beliefs and customs, they are becoming more and more the concern of the individual rather than being a part of the community life, as it was in the past.

The Cycle of the Year

The observance of calendar and agricultural festivities is rigorously followed in Roseto Valfortore, where some of the behavior connected with these rites of passage still has traces of its original motivations. Roseto, Pennsylvania, as a homogeneous and isolated community, also kept some of its traditional festivities and has absorbed relatively little from the official American calendar. More than in the Italian Roseto, however, the rites and beliefs relative to the yearly cycle gradually lost their original strength and communal function and now are restricted to mere entertainment or oddities. The drastically changed environment, as well as new laws and regulations—both from the church and from other authorities—caused the disappearance of many community customs and the gradual impoverishment and fragmentation of those still carried on. Second-generation Rosetans speak of times when Carnival was celebrated collectively by the community, and Christmas and New Year's celebrations did not really differ from those of their parents back in Italy. The community organized a theatre with periodical performances, which closely recalled the folk plays still used in southern Italy. Rosetans often traveled all the way to New York to see "Farfariello"—an Italian immigrant character sketch also called "Macchietta Coloniale"—and the Sicilian puppets of Elizabeth Street, at the Italian theatres on Mulberry Street and on Grand Street, and then they tried to recreate similar productions for their own theatre in Roseto.[54] They made their annual religious festival in honor of Roseto's patron saint, Our Lady of Mt. Carmel (*Festa del Carmine*),[55] one of the most important events in Northampton County, and they now complain about the relative impoverishment of this festival—which they call "our big time"—and blame their present priest for this situation. They also repeated, during the Holy Week, the pageants and the processions representing the traditional religious plays of their Italian village.

(D: Donato)

D: Big times, see? You get together, play games, have fun. Then, the big, big time, *a fest' u Carmine* [Our Lady of Mt. Carmel], you know? That's *our* Big Time! Everybody look forward to that. You know how the kids look for Christmas? That's the way we used to look for the Big Time. But now it's less. It's still fun, because—because you git company, people come from outta town, forty, sixty people home! And we always had a lot of drink and a good time, you know? All weekend, night and day. Now, too, but it's different. It's the last week of July, I don't know why. Oh, we used to have such a big festa up here, Carla! A huge—four, five o'clock in the morning people was still walking and dancing in the street! The fireworks were crowded and the streets, too. Oh, the fireworks! Thousands came from outta town, from Canada, from Florida, from California! He—[the priest] grabbed all the money, he has no carnival! He has our Sodality—The Men Sodality—the Women Sodality—and that's all. He doesn't want other people to know that we have festas.[56]

B: No? Why?

D: Ah, see? You know Martin's Creek down here? They are Abruzzese, they have all their festas and we don't any more—well, not as it used to be. No, no! Oh, I love festas, people go crazy![57]

All communal celebrations took place on the dates and in the ways prescribed by tradition for the ancient rites of passage. Now, however, the communal aspects of life are disappearing more and more and, to the disappointment of old Rosetans, people are orienting themselves toward privacy—once totally unknown—and individual behavior.

V

The Community and the World

I N many areas of southern Italy, where contact with modern mass
culture has not yet caused many radical changes, it is still relatively simple to examine the relationship of the peasant culture to
that of the dominant classes. With a correct evaluation of the socioeconomic structure of the Italian South and of Italian society in
general, one can identify the causes and functions of certain themes
and values traditionally transmitted from generation to generation.[1]
In studying the folklore of Italian immigrants in America, a similar
method should be followed, though the problem is far more complex, especially in urban areas. An investigation in depth, concentrating on one or two urban groups, would be needed for any
meaningful study of traditional culture in relationship to American
culture at large.[2]

The situation in Roseto, Pennsylvania, however, offered several
advantages. An obvious advantage was the opportunity to compare
the culture of the American Roseto with that of the Italian namesake. Another advantage was the relative isolation and homogeneity
of the group, which offered a stable situation with the possibility of
collecting the local traditions in the context of the total Rosetan culture and to consider it in the larger context of American society.[3]

Family and Society

Casa sua non mena guerra (home yields no war) is one of the
many Italian proverbs stressing the concept that only at home can
one be safe from enemies and perils. From birth on, each member of
a southern Italian peasant community is warned of the dangers

coming from the "others," that is, from the persons who are not related to him either by blood or by proven friendship. The long lullabies that peasant mothers sing to their babies contain very clear references to this painful state of things, both by means of direct statements and by symbolic imagery:

> The love of your mother is the only love,
> The love of the other people is but words.

> Your own people love you truly,
> The other people's love is like nothing.

> You're like a little lamb that's growing,
> Your curly hair is like wool.

> Oh, little lamb of mine, how did you do,
> When you found yourself in the wolf's mouth?

> Your mother's house is warm, is safe, is gold,
> Outside is dark, is black, the wolf is there.[4]

The wolves are the "others," all the other people, the powerful ones, who live a different life, and the poor ones, who are but potential rivals in the sharing of the limited "pie."

In Roseto, Pennsylvania, the community experienced a period of reinforcement of mutual trust and cohesion at the time of immigration. The cultural isolation of the group also facilitated the survival and the reinforcement of those elements of traditional culture that helped to give the community a sense of security and self-appreciation. In the absence of an understanding of and identification with the American society, the group could overcome insecurity and isolation by strengthening their traditional value system. At least among the immigrants themselves—both of old and recent immigration—there is a definite antagonism toward the chief values and symbols of American society and a strongly traditional attitude toward family, education of the children, work, law, and authority. The family, in particular, has retained most of its traditional importance. In spite of the changes which occurred in the status of women and in the conception of parental control, the fundamental role of the family in relationship to society has remained almost unchanged for the individual.

Most women stayed at home before World War II, as available jobs implied heavy work in the slate quarries, and this fact helped the survival of the traditional family with its internal and external codes and functions. Now most young women go to work; but, as they are generally employed in the village blouse mills, often just around the corner from home, their detachment from the family

almost never happens. In the same blouse mill, they often work side
by side with close relatives, godrelatives, and neighbors, so that
even when they work they continue their roles as wives, mothers,
and sisters and are seldom viewed independently from such roles.
Often a woman is called by a nickname, which, being common to
all her family, only serves to identify her as a member of her kinship. The superficial changes that did occur in her status came
from her economic contribution to the family subsistence and
from the models offered by the mass media in general. For the most
part, however, her role in the family circle is still characterized by
traditional attributes and duties, and the following proverbs illustrate some of the typical virtues of a good woman and wife:

The silent woman increases honor [in the household].

The husband must be wise; the wife patient.

He fills the sack and she ties it with a string [thrifty].

Miserable is the home where the hen sings and the cock is
    quiet.

Never buy women and cloth in the dark.

When the husband speaks, the wife must lose her voice.

The thrifty woman makes her house rich.

The speedy woman vacations always.[5]

Most proverbs, songs, and folktales repeat the above picture
firmly based on southern Italian patterns. A woman's duties are un-
counted: she is to be obedient, patient, fast in her work, thrifty,
quiet in front of her husband, capable of good housework. She can
be bought like any object and is trained to a discipline by which
she learns her duties and limitations and not to question the authority and traditional rights of both her father and her husband. Her
role is not unimportant, however, as from her behavior stems much
of her own husband's and children's reputation and fortune. She is
weak and incapable of resisting outside temptations, thus she must
stay in the house and limit her contacts with the rest of the world.
As the proverbs say:

The woman at the window and the man on the road.

Don't put straw next to fire and women next to men.[5]

The education of the children is almost totally entrusted to the
mother, while the father supervises disciplinary matters both inside
and outside the family. In contrast to urban areas in America, the
father in Roseto seems to have retained more of his authority over

his children's behavior in society, and both the wife and the community support his retention of this role. The father's main concern is to watch over his family's reputation in the community, and only to a small extent does he look any further, that is, at American society. The people to whom one's behavior is to be related are still the town-fellows and the ethnic groups in nearby towns, who are usually identified as *the* Americans. Recently, however, with the children going to college and acquiring professions that will eventually take them to distant places, the situation has slowly been changing. The conditions are probably being created to establish a deeper relationship of the community with the rest of American society.

The following interview, besides emphasizing the importance of the family in Roseto, Pennsylvania, shows how the family is changing from older times and how a third-generation Rosetan views the American family in general.

(A: Anne)

B: And what do you think of the kids today?

A: I think they're spoiled.

B: Spoiled by what?

A: We are giving them too much, and that's American. Our grandfathers and fathers they had to work real hard, see? They had to carry water, stones, wood, everything. I mean, they were living in shanties. When my grandmother came here, she was twenty years old, she was the mother of my mother. She was a real strong-willed woman. She used to gather wood for the stove and for that she had to go to prison for ten days once. Because the people, the English people that owned that land, denounced her to the police. So, as she didn't have the money, she had to go to prison. We have always been so proud of her! Her husband was only making a dollar a day, see? But our future will be—who knows? Like the rest of America, we'll be selfish, we'll only love ourselves and money, and God knows what will happen to the family. It may be destroyed completely, ruined! Who can tell? Too bad! And this is the way those kids are now. We were used to call every old woman in town *zia*, that is, aunt. Out of respect, you see? But these kids they don't, no! The oldest people used to be almost the owners of the town, see? This is the way my grandmother was.

B: I see, but I had heard that the man was the head of the family——

A: Oh, yes, sure! Because the wife respects her husband. They make him feel like he were a king. Women teach children how to respect and fear their father and so on. Sure, the father is the real head of the family. There is no family without a father! But the wife takes care of the money, she spends it, that is. The rent, the food. She gives the children the moral values, religion, see?

B: In other words. If you did something wrong——

A: It depends! If I wanted an extra candy, my father was the easiest one. But if I didn't behave at school or in the street or if I was home late, then I would have a treat by my father! On the whole, though, I think that wives and husbands agreed more than they do now. Now men are becoming more and more feminine, I think. And this, too, isn't Italian. It comes from our becoming American! Yes.

B: Oh, really?

A: Definite. I don't like seeing men helping in the house, doing dishes and this and that. It's not for a man! But some do this nowadays. But their wives all work now, though they wouldn't need it, I mean, they don't need it as they used to before, when we were all poor! But now they work to send their children to college, that is the question, see? And the family breaks, see?[6]

Girls and boys are soon taught in both Rosetos how to differentiate their roles and relative duties, privileges, and limitations, and they are often reminded of the good qualities respectively attached to womanliness and manliness. They are encouraged from the very beginning to imitate the adult members of the same sex, and girls are actually expected to behave like miniature mothers. The children learn the subtleties of the power distribution in their nuclear family very soon, so that if they need their father's permission for something really important or uncommon, they will use their mother as an intermediary, who in turn will know what policy to follow in the procedure.

Outside the nuclear family, the relatives are almost the only persons to be trusted, though a whole range of differentiated behaviors exists to deal with them from time to time, according to a large series of variables. The child is gradually taught how to behave with the different members of his extended family, which, in both Rosetos, as elsewhere in southern Italy, usually includes the godrelatives. He will learn about the duplicity of the in-laws and the maliciousness of some cousins and godrelatives:

> *Sorelle come cani non se vollero mai male, cognate come miele non se vollero mai bene* [sisters like dogs never hate each other, sisters-in-law like honey never love each other].

Tre sono le c pericolose: cognata, compare e cugino [The dangerous "c's" are three: sister-in-law, godfather, and cousin].

Life taught the Italian peasant that law and state authority exist only to punish and to exploit him. Reality showed him how useless it was to fight with the powerful and to hope for any kind of legal justice. Anecdotes and proverbs especially contain a clear knowledge of this state of things, together with the traditional wisdom that teaches the poor how to survive *in spite of* laws and governments.

After so many years of life in America, Rosetans have modified somewhat their concepts and behavior regarding the nation's law and authority. From the mass media especially, they have absorbed a confidence in governmental efficiency and learned to expect a certain attention and care on the part of the government for the needs of the citizens. As most of their personal experience has only been with the local Italian reality, the Rosetans' notions of state, government, and national laws are almost alien to their daily life. It is as if the concepts they have acquired have no place in nor reason to be applied to their own reality. In the community, life is culturally self-sufficient, while the connections that exist with the "outside world" arise from the mass media and practical needs.

Politics is also viewed in local terms and not so much on a national or even international level, and while there is a lively participation in the Republican and Democratic Rosetan administrations, the competition is always among Rosetans and for Roseto's welfare. Actually most people in Roseto consider politics and politicians with suspicion and even contempt, while local political life does not appear to them as a part of politics at all. In this, they are following the traditional distrust of central authority, and the equally traditional confidence in all that is known personally, by means of family or friendly relationship.

Rosetans often make use of proverbs to express in a condensed and efficient way their traditional wisdom and world view. Proverbs reflecting traditional warnings about law and state are still heard among Italian speakers, and they are often repeated in either an informal conversation or the telling of a traditional narrative. Here are some self-explanatory ones:

Obey the law and shove it up your ass.

With the powerful there is no choice: either die or be their slave.

There's nothing the lamb can do against the wolf.

With bosses and lawyers there's no escape.

He who is born poor, will die poor.

Tie your donkey where your master says to.

He who rules does not sweat.

The just man must pay for the bad one.[7]

In the numerous folktales about the ordinary man who has been offended and goes to court, it is seldom through the official legal channels that he obtains any just protection but only thanks to his own shrewdness and bribery, without which he might even be punished by the judge. As the proverb says:

> With money and brains, you fuck the justice and the villains.

(A: Antonio)

B: And what about politics?

A: The Italians have the upper hand in the whole area.

B: You mean in Roseto?

A: No! All over. In Northampton County and in Roseto, sure. The others have the law, the politics, and all that, but we have everything. We have doctors and business now, 'cause we are serious people, see? Not like some drunkards down there! All they do is talking. They talk. They say we've got no power, but we do have power! Years ago, they used to say, "Oh, Italians will never own a quarry!" Well, when we opened this quarry here, we were the first Italians to open a quarry. And we never needed them in the Town Hall! Thank God, no. They didn't want us in the area, they wouldn't sell no land to us! You could never buy next to an American, never! When the Italians would buy a house down in Bangor, they would move down further, see? But we are well off, we're well off by being nice and by minding our own business, see? Not like those politicians! That's all politics.[8]

Antonio was born about fifty years ago in Roseto, where he now owns a quarry. The real meaning of his apparently confused interview is found mostly in the continued repetition of the personal pronouns *they* and *we*, which reflects the strong dichotomy between the local, familiar, trustworthy environment and the outside, alien, and official authority. The latter constitutes the "others," vaguely identified as non-Italians or as abstract entities called "politics" and "law." Antonio expresses the same attitude when he tells some traditional narratives. Here is the beginning of one:

They say that in Trenton there was a dishonest lawyer. He was not an Italian lawyer, he was always trying to fool poor workers. He would never help any Italians, he was always against them. A real crook. So, one day, they say that this young man went to see him. He came from Roseto, I think.[9]

During one of my trips to Roseto, Pennsylvania, I once found that some of my most affectionate friends seemed worried about me, but for some time none of them would tell me what the problem was, instinctively following the traditional inclination to silence. As the proverb says: *Bocca chiusa non c'entra mosca* (keep your mouth shut and no flies will go in). Finally, but with some reluctance, my good friend A. Z. Falcone told me what it was all about. The local priest had expressed some suspicions about me and had even warned the people that I might be a Russian spy. To their comments that I was a learned person and seemingly a nice woman, he had replied that those are the kinds of people that are usually chosen for such jobs. The charming conclusion of this episode—which had no consequences whatsoever on the attitude of the Rosetans toward me—was that A. Z. burst out with the following passionate defense: "Well, Carla, do you know what I told him? I said, 'Look, we all like her here and she seems a nice person to me! Then, if she's a spy of some kind, well, too bad! I don't care! I'll go to prison with her!' Oh, I told him, Carla, oh, I did, too!"

Old and New Attitudes toward Work, Wealth, Waste, and Necessity

Old Rosetans still remember the work songs they used to sing at harvest time in Roseto Valfortore, even though they have had no occasions to sing them while working in America. These long and highly lyrical tunes, which the farmers used to sing very loudly in the open fields, now sound rather strange in the closed space of a kitchen or in a living room. The memory of singing in the fields is very strong in old immigrants who enjoy talking about that custom of their youth. The different world of their origin, which can never be understood by their own children, is characteristically confused in their memory with their youth, which naturally coincided with the best time of life. Consequently, they tend to explain the old singing habits with the fact that they were happier, "poorer, but happier."

(C: Consolata)

C: What we have here, the work we have here, is not like what we had in Italy! In Italy it was far better! If I had a lot of money, I would go to Italy. I would go there, because the air and the people there are not like the air and the people here! The old people here —we are in prison! In Italy, we used to walk four, five miles a day, morning and evening, and we always had to carry heavy things with us. And yet, we used to sing all the time, all the way to work! And loud! They used to hear me from here to down in the valley. It's true! Oh, it was beautiful!

B: Why don't you people sing any more?

C: Why should we? We used to work and be happy, then, see? Poor, but happy. Now, look at me here. I work, but I am not happy. No, we don't sing any more those nice tunes! And then, our children they don't like us to sing. They say, "Ma, be quiet now. Don't make noise, it isn't nice." They say it isn't nice, they like silence. But they're animals, because animals don't sing![10]

The work songs these people knew were not suitable for the new environment, nor could they be welcomed by fellow-workers or bosses of other nationalities in the slate quarries or in the mills. Rosetans thus learned to keep their singing within their family and community life and, in this environment, work songs lost their function and soon became mere remembrances of the past.

Work is considered a necessary physical effort to provide subsistence and security. From their parents, the second-generation Rosetans learned to accept this daily effort obediently and with good will, but they were never taught any fanatical attitude toward work. No emotional involvement or moral implications in relationship to work were ever transmitted by the immigrants to their children, but only a clear acknowledgment of the necessity of work. This attitude seems to have continued through most of the third generation who still hold moderate ambitions in terms of career and wealth. All Rosetans are proud of their town and like to talk about the past work and sacrifices that brought about the present achievements. Their work, however, related them to their own group and hardly at all to the rest of society, even when they did not work in town and depended on the outside world for their jobs. While there is no fanatical attachment to money and the rich are often ridiculed in the traditional lore, waste is generally disapproved of and, characteristically, attributed to Americans. The following Wellerism illustrates the attitude toward waste:

> *Disse la robba all'omo: Non me jettà ca non te jette*
> [Said the thing to the man: Keep me and I'll keep you].

Following the traditional belief that ostentation of wealth attracts envy, and thus the evil eye, the older people tend to blame the younger ones for spending too much:

(M. A.:Maria Antonia)

M. A.: We used to wash our clothes in the canal. Now it's all luxury, all botton, bottons! We used to bake our own bread, which is a blessing; we used to save and work hard. Our kids, now, our grandchildren, they only want cars and college. That's all they look for. And guess who goes to work? Papa and mamma! We work our gardens, we make tomatoes, peppers, onion, fruit, anything. We store food, we save. The kids shout at me, they say, "We can buy that! You don't have to do it!" See? They say we don't have to do it, but we make wine and they like to drink it all right. Now, when we'll be dead, they'll buy the wine, they'll buy anything! They don't understand. They want graduation parties, American parties! But we say, "If you want your house to last, even water must be saved!" [Proverb.][11]

B: Do they [parties] cost much?

M: Much? Of course they cost much! They cost a fortune, and the people think you're rich and they envy you. So, you catch the evil eye, see, what I mean? Envy is powerful! We say, "If envy were fever, the whole world would be in bed." [Proverb.][11]

In spite of the traditional attitude toward work inherited by the second generation from their elders, a substantial shift has occurred in conceiving of their relationship to money. During my visits to both Rosetos, I observed a curious phenomenon which indicated two opposite evaluations of that relationship. While informants in Roseto Valfortore often asked me to reward them with money for the information they were giving me, more than one American Rosetan asked me if *he* had to pay me for being interviewed, once he heard that I came from an American university! The Italian peasant is now beginning to learn that even his culture is of some value to the dominant classes in addition to the hard work of his hands, but the Italian-American has no such awareness. In spite of his heavy contribution to the construction of American cities, he still feels he must pay if he wants his voice to be worth listening to.

Although the above phenomenon might be viewed as a reflection of Americanization and—better—as an acceptance of capitalistic values, the very fact that this attitude coexists with a strong sense of ethnic consciousness and differentiation needs further consideration. If integration of the immigrant means losing the uneasiness of feeling alone and different from the host society, it should also mean the achievement of a new consciousness. The immigrant—and even more his children—should consider himself a part of the larger mass of immigrant labor—regardless of ethnic groups—which is there to satisfy a need that would otherwise not be satisfied. This knowledge would permit him a full understanding of his own position, in relation to the needs and problems of the host society, and of the impact of his own work and culture on the socioeconomic dynamics of that society. There is evidence, however, that the marginality originally caused by immigration tends to crystallize itself in ethnic marginality, where all problems, faults, suspicions, and misunderstandings are explained in terms of ethnic differences, and one fails to see that the ethnic barrier is a false one, which only conceals the real social contradictions of the whole society. The same situation is found in Italy, where the awareness of ancient divisions and regional differences tends to explain all the persisting injustices and contrasts and does not permit a broader evaluation of the problems of Italian society.

Medical Care and Folk Medicine: Education and the American Way of Life

The traditional trust in healers and home remedies has survived among the American Rosetans. While this trust was in the past their only guide against diseases, most old and middle-aged Rosetans have now modified their attitudes toward official medicine. Education, the mass media, and the expansion of public medical care have turned Rosetans into regular clients of doctors and hospitals. Minor ailments are still treated with home remedies, while hospitals and doctors are consulted for more serious problems. There is an ambivalent attitude toward doctors that clearly stems from the traditional concept of folk medicine. While doctors possess a potentially unlimited, quasi-magical power of curing anything—for which they are to be respected and even feared, they are also humanly limited, subject to being dishonest, careless, and even unwilling to help. Rosetans will cautiously ask for the doctor's help and at the same time follow traditional folk practices that might help in case of the doctor's failure. A woman said that while her husband was in the hospital in Easton for a hernia operation, she went to see a godrelative in Philadelphia every other day. Together they tried the evil eye test for the patient; they recited traditional rhymes until he got well and went home. She also said that while he was ill she avoided mentioning the name of the disease, as this could "offend" the disease itself and cause the husband more suffering. The woman was clearly continuing the traditional personification of diseases and, furthermore, it was not clear whether she attributed her husband's recovery entirely to the doctor's skill, or partly—or even mainly—to her magical precautions.

Traditional life also taught Rosetans certain healthy habits which they still carry on and try, unsuccessfully, to teach their children and grandchildren.

(C: Capozzolo)

C: Our old people knew how to live. They used to go to bed early. They didn't drink much, they stayed home. Now is too much late hours and night life is what kills. It's true that our old people here didn't die from heart attacks. Dr. Stewart is right.[12] But I don't go for that for our own generation or for the next! Now, my mother, she came here as a little girl. Or even my uncle Louis, he had his way of doing it. Early to bed and early to rise, you know what I mean? As soon as it would get dark, after he had done his work, he used to say a couple of stories and he'd go to bed, and as soon as it got light, he'd be up. He's dead now and our young kids didn't even know him. That's bad![13]

Traditional lore is particularly rich in "medical" advice:

Sun through the glass and draft through the door bring death for sure.

Diseases come horseback and leave on foot.

Hot hand, sick hand; cold hand, hand in love.

Hot feet and cool head.

In April don't shed your heavy garb.

Make clear piss and screw the doctor.

If you don't shit now, you'll shit later; if you don't piss now, you'll die.

Three dangerous "c's" for the old ones: catarrh, fall, diarrhea.

Better warm than well fed.

Milk and wine make the baby fine.[14]

Food habits in Roseto are still largely traditional Rosetan or southern Italian in general. Apart from the changes caused by mass-produced—and heavily advertised—items and by the different quality of food available in America (scarcity of olive oil, lack of goat cheese and goat milk, etc.), an important change is evident in the Rosetan diet. The same traditional dishes are becoming richer and richer, because of the increasing affluence of the consumers. This is by no means a unique trait of the Rosetan cuisine, and the same trend may be observed in other Italian-American homes. A traditional *pizza*, for example, used to be just a flat, thin bread, with salt and oil on it. Its variations, from place to place, consisted only in the addition of some fresh tomatoes, onions, or anchovies, while in Roseto Valfortore it is still made with bread dough, fresh tomatoes, and *papinedda* (dialect for *origano*). The Italian *pizza* now served in America has an incredible variety of rich ingredients, such as sausage, green pepper, pepperoni, salami, ham, and even eggs. The same is true for the traditional *pasta*. Homemade or not, this dish originally consisted just of boiled pasta with very simple ingredients, such as fresh tomatoes, or cheese, or fried garlic and parsley, and other similar variations according to the regional area. The traditional food of the peasant was quite simple, as it reflected a frugal economy and culture. A moderate quantity of food consumption—as well as of anything else—was a celebrated "virtue" of the peasant and traditional sayings tended to reinforce this moderation:

> *Poco magnà, poco dolore* [Little food, little pain].
>
> *Lo poco abbasta e lu troppe faci murì* [A bit is enough and a lot makes you die].
>
> *Chi magna assai scatte e chi fatìa mitte a parte* [If you stuff yourself, you'll burst; if you work, you'll get rich].

After some time in America and with the affluence now available to him, the immigrant found that his traditional food could be "improved" by adding more and more ingredients to his preferred dishes. This fact gratified him as a tangible proof of his achievements, besides still offering him the reassuring continuity with familiar flavors. In addition, these tasty "improved" dishes turned out to be a successful means of introduction into the host society and a profitable device for economic advancement with the spread of *ristoranti italiani*. Most dishes went through this process, including sweets, which used to be strictly festive fare and not as rich as they are now. While I observed this phenomenon in every Italian-American home, I could see it much better in Roseto, because of the advantageous conditions of observation that I had there, and because I had the Italian Roseto to use as a comparison. I collected recipes of traditional dishes both in Italy and in America and this gave me the opportunity of following the changes in some dishes in America. Food habits remained quite simple for a long time in Roseto—possibly longer than elsewhere—and it was after the end of World War II that the diet became more and more elaborate. Some older women cook as they always did in the past, like Filomena Pagano, for example, who still makes her simple, delicious *biscotti* and *taralli* with very little or no sugar at all. The only change is that now she can make them whenever she likes, whereas before they were strictly reserved for Easter and Christmas. *Ravioli, cecateddi, fusidda, cannelloni,* and any other kind of *pasta* are now dressed with a much richer sauce than before, certainly richer than the one still used by the peasants in Roseto Valfortore. Curiously enough, most Rosetans are not consistent in their evaluation of this phenomenon, so that, at one time, they will say that the *pasta* you are eating at their table is "really *Rosetana,* like we always had up here," and, at another time, they will proudly remark how much tastier their food is now:

(M. A.: Maria Antonia)

M. A.: Before it was not like now! With all this food here—all this eating stuff—not before. We eat well now, see? Look at this *lasagne:* We couldn't make them before!

And, of course, they didn't have them before because, among other things, *lasagne* is not a Rosetan dish to begin with, but one borrowed from the pan-Italian-American cuisine now popular even on TV. The obvious, richer quality of Italian-American food, in contrast to its original frugality, reminds me of an analogous phenomenon presented by the archaeological objects found in the Greek excavations in southern Italy. The vases, jewels, and similar items produced by the Greek pre-Roman colonies greatly exceed their Greek originals both in size and quantity, though not always in artistic value.

Urban Italy is also witnessing a similar increasing complexity of such dishes as *pizza, pasta,* sweets, and other traditional food. The phenomenon, however, is not merely due to an increased abundance of means. Tourism and a growing upper- and middle-class interest in exotic tastes and looks are pushing cooks' creativity and imagination toward an "amelioration" and variation of traditional dishes. Eating peasant food, with colorful dialect names, is becoming fashionable among the rich—who thus make their safe excursion into the "poor but genuine" peasant world—which is being rejected by the peasants, who are living the opposite illusion of becoming part of the upper society.

With a richer diet often came obesity, previously unknown in peasant Italy. For a long time, this characteristic was not conceived of as either an esthetic or hygienic problem and everybody kept his own roundness cheerfully. When I was in Roseto, Pennsylvania, however, many women explained to me that they were following a "five-pounds diet" and proudly showed me a special card with rules and instructions. This is how the "diet" was viewed by Filomena, an old Italian-born lady:

F: I think it's crazy! It's not a good thing. They even spend money on that stupid diet—oh, it makes me laugh: that one should pay just to starve? We never did that, see? We had other things on our mind—getting fat? Well, maybe we weren't fat, but—why? What's wrong with that? Do we have to be all skin and bones like those ladies on TV? Eh, Carla, did you see the President's wife? Ah, ah! [she laughs.] I'm skinny because I'm old, but I don't do anything—just normal. A man wouldn't find any fun in hugging me! Ah, ah! [Laughs.]

Traditionally the southern Italian peasant always attributed great importance to the education of the young. As the world is so cruel, it is necessary to give the children an adequate means of facing life as soon as possible. Several proverbs and songs state this necessity of early training, based on strict discipline and with the aim of assimilating the new generation to the previous ones.

The branch must be straightened while it's still tender.

Bread and blows make children grow.

The good day must be secured at dawn.

Kiss your children when they're asleep [meaning, "when they don't see you"].[15]

Education, conceived as early correction of deviant behavior and attained by means of example and punishment, has acculturative purposes, and the traditional lore helps the educational process in the transmission of time-honored values from one generation to the other. This pattern of family education was strictly followed in the new land until school education gradually took over the greater part of the work. Older Rosetans complain that school education is now estranging children from parents and blame modern education and wealth for what they view as disastrous changes in the community life. Some of them are particularly bitter because the main purpose of traditional education—securing cultural continuity —could not be realized beyond a certain point in America. Here is an example of parental ambivalence about the usefulness of school education:

(C: Consolata)

C: We don't want to say that school isn't good! It's good. But now it's too much and it's different. Children come out different from school. These new kids here, they don't like us too much, they even spit at us and throw stones. They don't understand us talking, they're like strangers! I have a grandchild here, I don't even know his name: Jefren—Jefron—Jeferne—who knows? Who can pronounce it? I can't say his name! I ask him, I say, "Come, sweetheart, what is your name? Teach me." He yells at me, "Oh, shut up!" But what do they teach him at school? Not to respect old people? Maybe they know too much, maybe—maybe they're American. But you know how the old man said? [Meaning a Wellerism.]

B: How?

C: The old man said, "I wish I were a priest, who is called 'father' but has no children to raise." [Laughs.][16]

American-born Rosetans are convinced of the benefits of school education and do their best to send their children to college. Yet they, too, hold some doubts as to the educational methods used in school and complain about the lack of authority and discipline.

(P: Peter)

P: My son graduated from Fordham University. He has a tremendous ability in sport, which is good, although it's not sport like in our days, it's all school teams and such! Everything changed now. In our days, there was more of a system to punish, you know? The teachers at school would use their hands, or a stick. Now, you take, for example, our public school system here in Bangor, they wouldn't dare touch you!

B: And is it better or worse?

P: My theory is, that if a boy or a girl, but especially a boy, a boy especially, would be given a corporal punishment, at the proper time and in the proper place, I think he'd be more respectful at home and at school. But, of course, they have the law, they can't touch them now. Among the Italian people it's still better than the others. But, I say, my feeling is that we're losing ground, we're losing out, gradually.[17]

The traditional wisdom warned the peasant that "He who makes his child better than himself shall cry one day," and this fear of the gap widening between parents and educated children remained in America. The drastic and urgent adaptations that confronted the immigrants upon their arrival made them eager to provide their children with all those privileges that were once forbidden to their social class. In Roseto today all children go to high school and many of them—but especially boys—are attending college. In spite of the uncertainties as to school methods and moral results, the community as a whole actually follows the general trend of modern society toward getting more school education.

I tried, during my field work, to test the levels of personal interest, readings, and taste in the community, both through participant observation and by direct questioning. I found that, with the exception of a few books—mostly school texts—occasional magazines and local newspapers, reading is a rather rare habit, while TV-watching receives the greatest part of the free time, especially among the second and the third generation. As for preferences, the following interview with an American-born couple in their early forties is sufficiently typical to illustrate the situation. Filomena, the wife's mother, also joins in part of the discussion.

(R: Rose;   D: Donato;   F: Filomena)

B: And so, what do you like to read? Novels, magazines——

R: I like the True Story magazine. I used to buy that. But now, who reads now?

D: I used to look through these mechanical science books, you know? I used to like to read those.

F: We didn't read, we used to say things. We told tales and other things. Even now, we don't read much, see? Like in church, now. They want us to read all those books and papers there. But I don't do it, I pray better by heart, with the things I already know.

B: What about TV? What's good to see here?

R: I like the musicals, the comedy, you know? Entertainment. Then, I like true stories. Then, if there's something goin' on, you know? Like when the Gemini go up? I watch. Then, I feel I gotta watch, but I don't like war stories.

D: I like western and war stories.

R: Oh, I can't see that shootin'!

D: War stories. I like to watch a good story, not real war, though.

B: How about politicians, their speeches——

D: The only one I enjoyed was when President Kennedy was campaigning for—you know? When those debates with Dewey—not Dewey—the other guy—Nixon! That I enjoyed! I wouldn't miss one of that. I would sit and watch more and more.

B: And then, when he died——

R: Oh, everybody was crying! We stopped——

D: Everything stopped, stopped dead. I was over Mary Birth, you know? In the luncheonette there. And over there, young kids, even kids, you know? Teen-agers, when this thing came—everything went solid! Like one of us. That's just the way it was. This one here [Johnson] is no good, no good for nothing, nothing!

B: Well, and what about people like, say, Perry Como?

R: Oh, yeah! Perry Como, Dean Martin, Eddy Williams——

D: Oh, sure! We all go for them, 'cause they're all on top. I mean they're like the—the top ten. Best performers, you know? They call them the Top Ten. They have them on top.

R: I like Dean Martin, I love him!

D: Dean Martin, yeah! And Perry Como! See? They're natural actors, natural! In other words, when they come on TV, that they're on a show, they act as they're natural. The other, they act as they knock theirself, you know? All that movement? But not Perry Como or Dean Martin, they're just nice and calm, they don't—they don't overact! They're natural.

B: What about movies?

D: We don't go there.

B: Do you buy records?

D: We don't buy no records, they [the children] do! But I like those records—Mario Lanza, Al Martino—they sing opera songs, like *Torna a Sorrento*, see? We have those albums. We have Claudio Villa, Mario Lanza——

B: If you decide to take a trip, a long trip——

R: I wanna go to Lourdes! That's where! I mean, beside Italy and things like that, of course.

D: Well, I don't think I wanna go abroad. In the States, some-where—I was on the West Coast when I was in the service.

B: Do you like planes?

D: Nope! I mean, I rode both, both trains and planes, but I like trains better. and I don't like the sea either.

R: And that's why he doesn't want to go abroad, see?

B: What about music?

D: Well, you know my great-grandfather? You must have heard about him!

B: Yes, of course, in Italy, too.

D: Well. All of our folks were great musicians, great! Oh, this Roseto Cornet Band now in town! They're just trying to get somethin' done! This is—this is just a li'le shuffling thing, yeah! They learn at school, it's mostly school music, it's not—not natural! Before, oh, before they had big concert bands, two, three at the same time. They had national contests in Philadelphia and all around! My grandfather, every time he was seen, he always had that cornet under his arm, wherever he'd go! And he played and played all the time. American bands went to Philadelphia from all over the country to compete with our bands, you know? You've heard of Maestro Ungaro?

B: Yes.

D: He could play! But see? These people used to go play for fun, for drink. They used to bring the wine and the *presutto* [ham], they used to git together, see? Now, the young generation, they like to have these three or four-piece bands, orchestras, and they go play for—oh, for night clubs—things modern. They go for money, for money. It's the American way. In America they don't do it for the fun, or for drinks, they all go for money, money! And that's ruining music. The older folks, they used to do it to enjoy themselves and they had more touch, more passion, see? They liked to get together, but not now! Not these young people. But some of the older folks still do it occasionally, and they play *a morra* [to decide who would buy the drinks].[18]

Donato's two daughters are in high school and also help him and his wife Rose in the small blouse factory they have just opened in Bangor. His little boy, Donato, Jr., has already joined the school band and plays clarinet there. Before opening the blouse factory, Donato, from early adolescence, had been a street fruit vendor, as his father, who came to America at the age of eight, had been. Donato reveals the common attitude of appreciation for traditional entertainments and a definitely poor opinion of whatever is modern and American. In a country like the United States, where youth and modernity are venerated and age is fought strenuously by everybody, this is a community for the most part past-oriented. While all adult members love their children dearly and do their best to give them the maximum support, the departure from the old patterns hurts them and appears to them as a decline in humanity which they blame on America.

"Who Will Take Over Our Town?"

The future development of this Italian-American community is rather uncertain. Hostile neighbors and other difficulties in the life of the community generated, in the first decade of the settlement, forces which strengthened the internal cohesiveness of the group. In this respect, the American Rosetan group enjoyed a greater community spirit than Roseto Valfortore and most other southern Italian villages. The Rosetans who grew up between 1915 and 1940 lived in a totally homogeneous, traditionally oriented society, which transmitted traditional lore from one generation to the next. The introduction of mass media and other technological innovations in the last twenty-five years and the influence exerted by school education have visibly transformed much of the community life and weakened one of its traditional pillars, the family. Increasingly, the community expanded its experience to include other places and other people, both in America and abroad. Many Rosetans—especially the younger people—quickly dropped many aspects of the traditional culture and substituted new patterns that are not approved by other Rosetans. This younger group tends to move away from the Italian group and to seek identification with American society, aiming mostly at middle-class values and positions. Other Rosetans started new contacts with Italy—both by traveling and by correspondence—and seem to find gratification in relating themselves, culturally, to Italian village life. This last group, mostly in the late middle age, shows a conflict attitude toward American society at large and a strong criticism of the way the younger generation lives today.

It is impossible now to judge the future outcome of this combination of acceptance and rejection of the American way of life in Roseto. Apart from the relationships with Italy, the community is now facing a number of conflict situations, some of which are common to most small towns in industrial societies: family and society, old traditions and modern ways, old people and young people, Catholics and Protestants, folk religion and church religion, Rosetan and non-Rosetan, Italian and non-Italian, thrift and waste, community life and outside life.

The most conspicuous problem will be the exodus of the younger generation. While Roseto Valfortore in Italy has always witnessed successive waves of departures, mostly of its young people, Roseto,

Pennsylvania, has maintained a rather stable population balance throughout its history. Now, however, with many children attaining college education, the community becomes poor in resources for them and is unable to meet their new wants and needs. Parents tend to hope that their own children will not go far, but most people in Roseto realize that emigration may be once again the necessary experience for this community of ex-emigrants. Neither the slate quarries nor the familiar blouse factories in town will offer suitable positions to college graduates. The questions often heard among worried Rosetans are "Will there be a Roseto in Pennsylvania?" and "Who will take over our town?"

Notes

Preface

1. The author used folklore data from Giuseppe Pitrè's famous collection, *Biblioteca delle tradizioni popolari siciliane*, 25 volumes, published between 1870 and 1913.

2. The need for these kinds of studies was deeply felt as early as 1911 when the First National Congress of Italian Ethnography approved the following research proposal submitted by Professor Lamberto Loria: "Having considered the report by Miss Bernardy and Dr. Baldasseroni, this Congress is urging the Italian Ethnography Society to sponsor and organize specific research studies on the folklore of Italian emigrants and is asking that the Regio Commissariato di Emigrazione give its valid help to the best realization of such studies." In spite of such an early incitation, however, specialized studies on Italian immigrant folklore are still lacking.

3. This area, once an immense marsh heavily infested by malaria, is now agricultural and, after so many years of Venetian farming, strongly resembles the northeastern Po valley and the Venetian countryside. It is called the Agro Pontino, from the name of Pontius Pilate.

4. These are the groups I visited:

New York: Immigrants from Sicily, Calabria, Puglia, Lucania, Sardinia, Lazio, Veneto.

New Jersey: Immigrants from Abruzzi and Molise.

Chicago: Immigrants from Tuscany, Emilia-Romagna, Piedmont.

5. In 1968 I was able to add further data to my immigrant studies with folklore research among the Italians in Toronto, Ontario, in behalf of the National Museums of Man, Ottawa.

6. F. A. J. Ianni (1958) has a detailed proposal for a similar study.

7. S. Wolf 1964:845.

8. The term "second generation" is used in this book to indicate the children of the immigrants, both those who were born in America and those who arrived here at a very young age (under 10).

9. R. Redfield, *The Little Community* and *Peasant Society and Culture* (Chicago: 1956), pp. 40–59.

I. *The Rosetan Emigration to America*

1. *Contadini* literally means "farmer," but it is usually applied to a poor farmer (e.g., a landless farmer or a very small proprietor).

The concept of the peasant has evoked considerable scholarly discussion. I use the terms "peasant" and "peasantry" broadly to cover rural agricultural workers, without attempting to refine the definitions according to such anthropologists as Redfield (1960:20), Firth (1956:87), and Kroeber (1948:284). The most useful statement for my purposes is probably that of Joseph Lopreato, who defines the peasant as "any worker engaged in direct agriculture as his major occupation or way of making a living" (1967:40). His concept of a landless farmer is applicable to the situation of most *contadini* in Italy up to the land reform after World War II, and it therefore applies to most of the Italian peasants who emigrated to America at the turn of the century.

The word "peasant," however, is a loose generic term covering a variety of types, from the different kinds of peasants existing in the countryside to those who live in semi-urban environments. It is also important for the purposes of this book to remember that many of the cultural characteristics of inland villages in Italy are similar to those of villages along the coast, even though the former villagers are farmers exclusively and the latter are usually a combination of farmer-fishermen. In addition, because they actually belong to the same cultural levels and subordinate classes, minor landlords, artisans, and other categories of workers living in agricultural and urban areas exhibit cultural traits and patterns associated with peasants. Accordingly, Kroeber's definition of peasants as "a class segment of a larger population, which usually contains urban centers also," has some value for most Italian emigrants past and present.

2. Original text: "Tu vui sapé la storia di quisti mane? Mé: au sembe fatiàte e ffatiàte, propie accùme a Madonna accummanna! Ma i cunde po', n'anne arrremenùte cchiù appàre!" (Taped interview).

3. 1861: Comitato per l'Emigrazione Italiana, Istituto Centrale di Statistica, Roma.

4. The official number of returned migrants is not known, however, as records were only started in the first decade of the twentieth century. See L. Monticelli, 1967:10.

5. *La Legge* 1901: n.31, n.23.

6. First Quota Act, approved in May 1921; Second Immigration Quota Act, 1924.

7. Annual Report of the United States Immigration and Naturalization Service, Table 13, 1961.

8. 1960 Census Data, Department of Commerce, Bureau of the Census, "Country of Origin of the Foreign Stock in the U. S. and Figures of their Urban Settlement: 1960."

9. (Taped interview.) Italian words and expressions intermixed with English by informants are italicized in the transcribed texts throughout this book.

10. McCarran Act, Public Law 414, 82nd Congress, 1952.

11. October 3, 1965, Public Law, 89–236, fully in force on July 1, 1968.

II. *The Two Rosetos: Two Related Communities*

1. All these nearby villages are mentioned in Rosetan folklore, both in Italy and in the United States.

2. The Tavoliere is practically the only arable land of considerable size in the South. Its name is equal to "plains."

3. *St. Filippo Neri:* an ancient mansion successively adapted to a church. Philip is a widely recurrent name in both Rosetos because St. Philip Neri is one of Roseto's patron saints. Two legends exist among the Rosetans about this saint.

San Nicola da Bari (St. Nicholas of Bari). He is also a major figure in legends, songs, and folktales of both Rosetos.

Santa Maria Lauretana: a small church named after the Madonna of Loreto. This Madonna recurs in religious songs and tales.

Cappella della Croce: The Chapel of the Cross at the very edge of the oldest section of the village.

San Francesco Saverio: formerly a private chapel, now open to the public cult.

Cappella del Calvario: a small chapel on the hillside where the Easter procession terminates in the annual performance of the Passion and Crucifixion.

San Rocco is the chapel of the old cemetery. Now the cemetery has been moved to a higher part of the town and the old one has become the site of numerous ghost stories widely told in America. San Rocco recurs in the folklore of the community.

Oratorio del cimitero: chapel of the new cemetery.

4. For good studies on social stratification in southern Italian villages, see Moss and Thomson (1959), Lopreato (1961), Friedman (1962), Lopreato (1962), MacDonald (1963), Moss and Cappannari (1964), and Silverman (1966).

Because of factors such as continuous emigration, politicization of all social strata, and technological "explosion," life has been changing very fast in the past decade and the above studies are obviously to be taken as strictly referring to definite places and times.

5. By semi-illiterate, I refer to persons who can sign their names and read simple headings such as prices or shop-signs. In the cultural context described in this book, such persons have often attended the third grade.

6. Rather than mere lists of the baptized Rosetans as their name suggests, these impressively large books, which are in the possession of the Church of Mt. Carmel, Roseto Valfortore, contain all sorts of details on the community's history. I even found a stanza from a folk ballad written there by the local archpriest in 1711.

7. Good sources for the cultural and social history of the province of Foggia are Sacco (1795), Cirella (1853–60), *Foggia e la Capitanata* (1933), Vochting (1955), Saba (1956), and Villani (1962).

8. Northampton County, Assessment Office, Assessment Records, Easton, Pa., County Archives. It gives information about the beginnings of the various settlements.

9. Roseto City Hall: "Feasibility Report, Sewerage System and Storm Sewers for the Borough of Roseto, Northampton County, Pennsylvania" (Autumn 1965, unpublished paper).

10. From the Town Hall records.

11. Rosetans will remember for a long time the visit of the Michigan State University Concert Band and its director, Leonardo Falcone, on March 21, 1966. It was one of the major events in the past two decades and Rosetans came from all parts of the nation to attend the concerts.

12. Roseto, Pennsylvania, Golden Jubilee, 1912–1962.

III. *The Rosetan Migration and the Myth of America*

1. A. C. (taped interview).
2. Lucia S. (taped interview).
3. Mimma De Angelis (taped interview). Original text: Chi s'ha fatto mericano magna e beve da cristiano.
4. Ibid. Original text: Chi l'America po' vedé se fa ricco comme un re.
5. Elisa del Grosso (taped interview). Original texts: Non se truva femmena bella senza farina nta tiella. Si va cercà n'ùcche de pane, sì cacciate cumm'a nu cane. Tristo chi ha fame.
6. Filomena Pagona (taped interview). Original text:

> "Mamma, mamma, dammi cento lire
> che in America voglio andà."
> "Cento lire non telle dò,
> e in America, no, no, no!"

"Se in America non mi manda,
Ala finestra mi butterò."
"All'America non ti mando,
meglio morta che in disonò!"

Il fratelle de la finestre,
"Mamma mia, lascela andà."
"Mamma mia, dammi cento lire
che in America voglio andà."

"Vacci pure, figlia maldetta,
mezzo al mare pozzi nfonnà!"
Quanno fu ala metà del mare
bastimente ca s'infonnò.

"Bastimende, ca vai al fondo,
mai nel mondo ritornnerai.
Pescatore che peschi i pesci,
pesca puri la bella Gi."

Li capelli della bella Gina
pesci al mare se li mangiò.
Li bell'occhi dela bella Gina
pesci al mare se li mangiò.

Le manucce della bella Gina
pesci al mare se li mangiò,
la vituccia della bella Gina
pesci al mare se li mangiò.

"Queste sono le maledizioni ⎫
che la mamma mi manderà." ⎬ repeated twice
                      ⎭

7. Nigra 1888:172,n.23: *La maledizione materna.*

8. The American equivalent of today's 100 lire is fifteen cents, but at the turn of the century it was quite a realistic price for the sea passage.

9. Mariantonia Casciano (taped interviews).

10. For a recent collection and analysis of *Mamma mia, dammi cento lire*, see Paola Tabet, *Quattordici canzoni narrative* (Milano, 1967).

11. Regina Baldi (taped interview). Original text:

Io me ne vo all'America,
col lungo bastimento,
parto col mio tormento
che non ti vedrò più.

Ma prima di partire,
io me ne vo giù in piazza,
chissà qualche ragazza,
la porterò con me.

Ragazze non si trova,
ci sta la mia sorella:
addio terra mia bella,
non tornerò mai più.

12. Filomena Gruppo (taped interview). Original text:

(NOTE: *the first line of each stanza
is repeated three times.*)

Che cosa vol dire l'Amereca?
Nu mazzettino de fior.

Lu bastimende è pronto
e è pronti per partì.

Ariva a Gibbleterra,
scure lu sole e scure la terra.

Ariva a la battaria,
e tutte parlavene e je nen capìa.

Arive a Neve Yorke,
acqua pa sotte e ttrene pa ngoppe.

Arive su marceppede,
e tutte le donne da berzaglier'.

Ma quand'è fessa l'Amereca,
pur' u cafone co la sciammereca.

Lu povare arteggiane
e tocca zappà che le picche ammàne!

This is how informants explain this song: The Gibraltar Straits
were so narrow that the sunlight could not go through and the air
became dark. New York women looked like soldiers to the immigrant because they often wore hats, while Italian peasant women
only wore shawls. The Italian immigrant viewed the artisan's status
in America as lowered to that of a peculiar type of farmer: a frustrated plowman tilling the asphalt instead of his field.

13. Giovanni Giannini, nicknamed "Garibaldi barbuto," or just
"Barbuto" (taped interview). Original text:

Mamma, dammi la dota,
in America voglio andà.

Saluti a la namurata,
non gi vedremo più.

Te lascio la bonanotta,
e nen gi vedremo più.

Rumane mene parte
e a la Mereca e Nova Yorke.

Che cosa vol dire l'Amereca?
Nu mazzettine di fior.

Lu vastimend' è pronda,
ma è pronda pe partì.

Rivati a Gibblitera,
Scur'è lu sole e scur'è la terr'.

14. Consiglia Bozzelli (taped interview).

15. Recently I found that this song is better known in the countryside of Molise and Abruzzi, where it circulated in broadside form
not many years ago.

16. The following text was sung by a second-generation informant in Roseto, Pa.: Costanza Falcone (taped interview). Original text:

> Maritem' è gghiute a l'Amereca e nen mè scritte,
> nen sacce qua manganze l'agge fatte.
>
> REFRAIN: tirirullalléro e tirirullallà.
>
> De tre fangiulle n'à truvate quatta
> e quest'è la manganze c'agge fatta.
>
> Nen mporta, marite mie, ca sì curnute,
> abbaste ca magne e bbivi e bai vistute.
>
> Cendecinguanda lire me sì mannate,
> de coppole e nfasciande l'ai cumbrate.
>
> E mò ce l'ai fatte na cuppulella
> e sotta ce li mettìme li curnutella.
>
> Nen ha da iesse cchiù lu chiante amara
> me quann' s'accocchie cu n'amerecana.
>
> Ma ià da iesse mò lu chiand' e rise
> ma quanne ca me manne li turniese.
>
> E queste iè lu cchiù dulore forta
> la meglie giovendù l'Amereche le porta.

17. (Taped interview.) Original text: *Si lu cafòne lo sapà, a l'Amereca nen ci jiéa.*

18. Annina B. (taped interview).

19. Maria Antonia Falcone (taped interview).

20. Luisa Strippone (taped interview).

21. Giovannina Martino (taped interview).

22. Domenica Sabbatino (taped interview).

23. Giovanni Antonio Micheli (taped interview). See folklore texts in Part Two for more songs, tales, and interviews on emigration.

24. I was told that a girl was the first American Rosetan child but, evidently, the birth of the first male was to be considered as the real beginning of the new generation.

25. Anthony Zilio' Falcone (taped interview). Dr. Stewart G. Wolf, Jr., the former head of the department of medicine, University of Oklahoma, and now at the University of Texas medical branch at Galveston, conducted a research study on the heart diseases in this area. During one of my stays in Roseto, it often happened that in visiting one of my informants he would say, "You are coming and the doctors just left!"

26. Carmine Malpiedo, also called "Armie" (taped interview).

27. A. R. (taped interview).

28. Leonardo Castellucci (taped interview).

29. Gilda Giovane, from San Marco Argentano, Calabria (taped interview).

30. Luisa Strippone (taped interview).

31. Pasquale Bozzelli (taped interview).

IV. *Traditional Life in Roseto, Pennsylvania*

1. On this subject, see Livingston, "La Merica Sinemagogna" (1918), Buscemi, "The Sicilian Immigrant and His Language Problems" (1927), and Gisolfi, "Italo-American: What It Has Borrowed from American English and What It Is Contributing to the American Language" (1939).

2. The language in Italy and in the United States was made up of dialects because standard Italian was never a spoken language in either place. For over six centuries in Italy, from Dante's time through the first three decades of this century, the Italian language remained almost unchanged for the simple reason that only poets used it, and only in written form. For oral communication, everybody, including the Italian king Vittorio Emanuele II and his dignitaries, spoke in dialect.

3. Maria Trantino (taped interview).

4. On this subject and on the relationship between folklore and language, see Christiansen, *European Folklore in America* (1962).

5. For interethnic conflicts and Rosetan solidarity, see the interviews with Anne Ruggero, Carmine Malpiedo, and A. Z. Falcone in chapter 3.

6. Carmine Malpiedo is one of the most striking examples of this storytelling ability among the second-generation Rosetans.

7. These past and present conditions and attitudes appear in the interviews with my informants, and they are also clearly expressed in the locally printed materials, such as the poems, *The Progress of the Town* and *Letter to America*, and Ralph Basso's *History of Roseto, Pa.*

8. Approximate distribution of oral traditions among the sex and age groups in central and southern Italy is as follows:

> Traditional ballads — mostly women (all ages)
> Street ballads — mostly men (all ages)
> Lullabies — women (all ages)
> Worksongs — women and men
> Serenades — men
> Folk prayers — women
> Religious songs — mostly women
> Nursery rhymes — women and children
> Songs of local color — men and women
> Funeral lamentations — women (old)
> Magic — mostly women
> Storytelling — men, women, and children
> Proverbs and riddles — men, women, and children

9. Carmine Malpiedo (taped interview).

10. Lorenza Spagnolo, American-born (taped interview).

11. I recorded the most extensive, well-told folktales from informants of the first and the second generations, above the age of sixty.

12. Type 3   — Ricotta cheese as brains.
    Type 6   — Animal captor persuaded to talk.
    Type 9/B — Division of crop.
    Type 32   — The wolf rescues the fox from the well.
    Type 122J — Lion (donkey) has thorn in foot.
    Type 130   — Animal concert.
    Type 214* — Ass envies horse in fine trappings.

13. Filomena and Mary P. (taped interview). Mary is over forty, Filomena's eldest child, American-born.

14. Carmine Malpiedo, American-born, and his daughter Margaret (taped interview).

15. Rose A., American-born (taped interview).

16. Maria P., about thirty-five, housewife, Italian-born, and Mary F., factory worker, American-born (taped interview).

17. A. D. (taped interview).

18. See De Martino, *Sud e Magia* (1959:350 passism), and the chapter entitled "Magia Lucana e cattolicesimo meridionale."

19. These demonic characters are called by names with a very unstable spelling in the South. Sometimes, even in the same group, they are *munaceddi, munacelli, monacelli, monachelli, monachieddi*, etc.

20. Raffaele Vitellio (taped interview).

21. S. D. (taped interview).

22. Peppuccia Basso (taped interview).

23. Irene G. (taped interview).

24. Memorat is a folklore term, coined by Von Sydow, which means a very short narrative, based on a folk belief, and referring to a personal "experience."

25. Ciccuzzo C., shoemaker. He was one of my informants in Italy, where I heard that his wife was considered a witch. She is not from Roseto, but from a nearby village.

26. "Piscianzinu," a nickname for Leonardo Castellucci (taped interview).

27. Maria Antonia Casciano, "Puttanella" (taped interview). "Puttanella," is a nickname affectionately used by Rosetans without the slightest offensive intention.

28. Anne P. and Angelone R. (taped interview).

29. R. R. (taped interview).

30. Being pretty is a dangerous condition because it attracts the evil eye.

31. Margaret Farole Malpiedo (taped interview).

32. Filomena Pagano (taped interview). On the distinction between magic and religion see Malinowski, *Magic, Science and Religion* (1925:88).

33. A number of beliefs and ritual behaviors exist concerning food in general: bread and olive oil, however, receive the most

careful attention. Here is a belief about oil: it should not be spilled and, if it happens, one must throw salt (a powerful magical ingredient) on it or God will send troubles.

34. Filomena Pagano (taped interview).

35. Carmine Malpiedo (taped interview).

36. Filomena Pagano (taped interview).

37. Menica S. (taped interview).

38. Leonardo Castellucci (taped interview).

39. Anne Ruggero (taped interview).

40. For the history of Roseto's Presbyterian Church, see Scarpellati (1948).

41. Mussolini, for example, gave a money prize for each new pregnancy.

42. Carmela Romano.

43. Maria Antonia Casciano (taped interview).

44. Costanza Z.

45. Connie F. (taped interview).

46. Maria Antonia Capobianco (taped interview).

47. Anthony Zilio' Falcone (taped interview).

48. Both the Record of the Wills and the informants' interviews show that sons inherit two thirds of the family estate, while one third goes to the daughters.

49. Judith L., nineteen years old (taped interview).

50. The bell is a fertility symbol.

51. A. Z. Falcone (taped interview).

52. Carmine Malpiedo (taped interview).

53. See Williams (1938:207) and Grieco (1953).

54. On Italian-American folk theatre, see Cautela, "The Italian Theatre in New York" (1927), and Irving, "When the Players Are Marionettes and the Age of Chivalry Is Born Again in a Little Italian Theatre on Mulberry Street" (1907) .

55. Calendars assign this feast to July 16, but from remote times Rosetans, as well as other southern Italians, have celebrated it on the last weekend of July, as most of the community is engaged in harvesting earlier in the month. American Rosetans still observe the later date, and most of them do not know why their own calendar, printed by the Roseto Catholic Church, indicates a different one.

56. The present priest is particularly disliked by Rosetan Catholics, who devotedly remember past priests, such as Father Ducci.

57. D. M., in his forties, once a fruit vendor, now a blouse mill-owner, a third-generation American (taped interview).

V. *The Community and the World*

1. For recent studies on the different levels of culture in Italy and the relationships between mass society and folk traditions, see

the valuable works of Alberto M. Cirese (1970 and 1972). See also Luigi Lombardi (1968 and 1972) for a brilliant study of Calabrian folklore.

2. My field work among urban Italian-Americans was more a pilot survey of all the regional groups represented in certain metropolitan areas than a study in depth of any group in particular—even though the Sicilians and the Ponzese are extensively represented in my field collection. That survey aimed more at breadth than at depth and was more concerned with collecting folklore texts than with the other aspects of culture. Consequently, the material could be of much value for a study of oral traditions; in this book I have used it only as background material for the Roseto study.

3. For the cultural absorption of immigrants, I received some theoretical inspiration from Eisenstadt (1955) and Redfield, Linton, and Herskovits (1935).

4. Original text sung by Lucia Sbrocchi:

> L'amore di la matri iè une sule,
> L'amora di la genda sò parule.
>
> Lu bbena ca ti vole veramenda,
> lu bbena di la genda nenn'è nènde.
>
> Sì cumma n'agnedduzze quanni crisce,
> comma li picure la lana ti crisce.
>
> O picurella me' cumma facista,
> quannu mmucca lu lupe te vedista.
>
> La casa di la mamma iè tutta d'ora,
> la vie iè scur'i u lupe sorti fora.

5. Original texts from Costanza C.:

> Fimmene muta cresce onore.
>
> Al marito prudenza; a la donna pazienza.
>
> Isse u sacche e jésse a zoca.
>
> Trista la casa se la jaddína canta e iàdde è mute.
>
> Nez'accatta femmena e tela al lume di candela.
>
> Quanne parla l'omo, la femmena ha d'esse muta.
>
> Femmena avara, ricchezza de la casa.
>
> A femmena lesta fa sembre festa.
>
> A femmena nda finestra e l'omo nda via.
>
> No pagghia ucine u foche e no femmena ucine l'omo.

6. Anne Ruggero (taped interview).

7. Original texts:

> Rispetta la legge e ficcatela 'nculo.
>
> Col padrone non c'è scampo: o la morte o la catena.
>
> Le pecore se l'ha de magnà il lupe.
>
> Cu padroni e cu avocati, non ci furono mai scampati.
>
> Nasci povere e more curnute.

> Attacca l'asino dove vole l'padrone.
>
> Chi cumanna non suda.
>
> Paga il povero pel peccatore.

8. Antonio C. (taped interview).

9. Type 831. Antonio C. (taped interview).

10. Consolata De Lessio (taped interview).

11. Maria Antonia Ronca, Protestant (taped interview). Original texts:

> Si vo' ca la casa dura, puru l'acqua ce vo la mesura.
>
> Se la mmídia fusse frebbe, tutt'il mondo ce l'avrebbe.

12. The informant refers to one of the cardiologists from the University of Oklahoma medical school, who studied the low incidence of heart attacks among Rosetans in 1964–66. Recently, however, heart attacks seem to have reached the normal American average.

13. Antonio Capozzolo (taped interview).

14. Original texts:

> Sule di vetre e fessúre di porte danno la morte.
>
> Il male vene a cavadde e senne va a pede.
>
> Mane cauda, malata; mane frisca, nnammurate.
>
> Pedi caldi e cape fresche.
>
> Aprile, nen te scuprire.
>
> Piscia chiare e fa' la fica u miediche.
>
> Si nen caca, cacherà, se nen piscia scatterà.
>
> Le tre c peridolose dei vecchi: catarro, caduta e cacarella.
>
> Megghie caude ca pasciute.
>
> Vine e pane fa u cristiane.

15. Original texts:

> Tocca ndrizza a rama quann'iè verde.
>
> Mazze e pane fa crisce i cristiane.
>
> La bona juornata s'accumenza a matina.
>
> Ndànne s'anne a vasà i figghij, quanne se vanne a cuccà.

16. At the same time, however, being parents improves human qualities: gende senza figghi, lundame milla miglie (childless people: keep them a thousand miles away from you). Consolata Restucci (taped interview).

17. Peter R. (taped interview).

18. Rose and Donato Martino (taped interview).

Works Cited

Ascoli, Max. "The Italians in America," *Group Relations and Group Antagonisms*. New York, 1944.

Basso, Ralph. *History of Roseto, Pa.: 1882–1952*. Easton, Pa., 1952.

Blegen, Theodore. "America Letters" and "Early America Letters" in *Norwegian Migration to America: 1825–1860*. Northfield, Minn., 1931.

Bronzini, Giovanbattista. *Vita Tradizionale in Basilicata*. Matera, 1964.

Buscemi, Philip A. "The Sicilian Immigrant and His Language Problems," *Sociology and Social Research*, XII (Nov.–Dec., 1927), 137–143.

Carnevali, Emanuel. *A Hurried Man*. Paris, 1925.

Carpitella, Diego. *Musica e tradizione orale*. Palermo, 1972.

Cautela, Giuseppe. "The Italian Theatre in New York," *American Mercury*, XII, n.45 (Sept., 1927), 106–112.

Christiansen, Reidar Th. *European Folklore in America*. Oslo, 1962.

Cirelli, Filippo. *Il Regno delle due Sicilie descritto ed illustrato*. Napoli, 1853–1860.

Cirese, Alberto M. *Tradizione popolari e società dei consumi*. Roma-Pordenone, 1970.

——. *Cultura egemonica e culture subalterne*. 2nd expanded edition. Palermo, 1973.

Cronin, Constance. *The Sting of Change*. Chicago, 1971.

Cunningham, George E., "The Italian: A Hindrance to White Solidarity in Louisiana, 1890–1898," *The Journal of Negro History*, L (Jan., 1965), 22–37.

Dégh, Linda. "Approaches to Folklore Research among Immigrant Groups," *Journal of American Folklore*, LXXIX (1966), 551–552.

——. "Two Old World Narrators in Urban Setting," *Kontakte und Grenzen*. Göttingen, 1969.

Del Re, G. *Cronisti e scrittori napoletani*. Napoli, 1845.

De Martino, Ernesto. *Sud e Magia*. Milano, 1959.

De Mauro, Tullio. *Storia linguistica dell'Italia unita*. Bari, 1963.

Dore, Grazia. *La democrazia italiana e l'emigrazione in America.* Brescia, 1964.

Dorson, Richard M. "Immigrant Folklore," in *American Folklore.* Chicago, 1959.

——. "Ethnohistory and Ethnic Folklore," *Ethnohistory,* VIII, No. 1 (1961), 12–30.

Eisenstadt, Samuel N. *The Absorption of Immigrants.* Glencoe, Ill., 1955.

Facchiano, Annibale. *Roseto Valfortore.* Sant'Agata di Puglia, 1971.

Firth, Raymond. *Two Studies of Kinship in London.* London, 1956.

"Foggia e la Capitanata," a special issue of *Ospitalità italiana.* Foggia, 1933.

Förster, Robert F. *The Italian Emigration of Our Times.* Cambridge, Mass., 1919.

Gans, Herbert. *The Urban Villagers: Group and Class in the Life of Italian-Americans.* New York, 1962.

Gisolfi, Anthony M. "Italo-American: What It Has Borrowed from American English and What It Is Contributing to the American Language," *Commonweal,* XXX (July 21, 1939), 311–313.

Glazer, Nathan, and Daniel Patrick Moynihan. *Beyond the Melting Pot.* Cambridge, Mass., 1963.

Goldstein, Kenneth. *A Guide for Fieldworkers in Folklore.* Hatboro, Pa., 1964.

Gottschalk, Louis R., Robert Angell, and Clyde Kluckhohn. *The Use of Personal Documents in History, Anthropology, and Sociology.* New York, 1945.

Grant, Madison. *The Passing of the Great Race.* New York, 1922.

——, and Charles Stewart Davison. *The Founders of the Republic on Immigration, Naturalization, and Aliens.* New York, 1928.

Grieco, Rose. "They Who Mourn: Italian-American Wakes," *Commonweal,* LVII (March 27, 1953), 628–630.

Grifo, Richard D., and Anthony F. Noto. *A History of Italian Immigration to the Easton Area.* Easton, Pa., 1964.

Handlin, Oscar. *The Uprooted.* Boston, 1951.

——. *Immigration As a Factor in American History.* Englewood Cliffs, N. J., 1959.

——. "Historical Perspectives on the American Ethnic Groups," *Daedalus,* XC (1961), 220–232.

——. *The Americans: A New History of the People of the United States.* Boston, 1963.

Hansen, Marcus Lee. *The Immigrant in American History.* Cambridge, Mass., 1940.

Herskovits, Melville. *Acculturation: The Study of Culture Contact.* New York, 1938.

Ianni, Francis A. J. "Time and Place as Variables in Acculturation Research," *American Anthropologist,* LX (1958), 39–46.

Irving, Elizabeth. "When the Players Are Marionettes and the Age of Chivalry Is Born Again in a Little Italian Theatre on Mulberry Street," *Craftsman*, XII (1907), 667–669.

Jones, Maldwyn Allen. *American Immigration*. Chicago, 1960.

Kroeber, Alfred L. *Anthropology*. New York, 1949.

La Legge, n. 31, n. 23, 1901. Torino, 1861–1912.

Levi, Carlo. *Christ Stopped at Eboli*, trans. Frances Frenaye. New York, 1947.

Lewis, Oscar. *Life in a Mexican Village: Tepozlàn Restudied*. Urbana, Ill., 1951.

——. *Five Families*. New York, 1959.

Livi-Bacci, Massimo. *L'immigrazione e l'assimilazione degli italiani negli Stati Uniti e le statistiche americane*. Milano, 1961.

Livingston, Arthur. "La Merica Sinemagogna," *The Romantic Review*, IX (1918), 206–227.

Lombardi-Satriani, Luigi. *Contenuti ambivalenti del folklore calabrese*. Messina, 1968.

——. *Antropologia culturale e analisi della cultura scebalterna*. Messina, 1971.

Lopreato, Joseph. "Social Stratification and Mobility in a South Italian Town," *American Sociological Review*, XXVI, n.4 (Aug., 1961).

——. "Interpersonal Relations in Peasant Society: The Peasant's View," *Human Organization*, XXI (Spring, 1962).

——. *Peasants No More: Social Class and Social Change in an Underdeveloped Society*. San Francisco, 1967.

MacDonald, John S. "Agricultural Organization, Migration, and Labor Militancy in Rural Italy," *The Economic History Review*, XVI, No. 1 (1963), 236–255.

Malinowski, Bronislaw. *Magic, Science and Religion*. New York, 1925.

Marcantonio, Michele. *La Superstizione nell'Alta Valle del Fortore*. Sant'Agata di Puglia, 1968.

Monticelli, Lucrezio. "Italian Emigration: Basic Characteristics and Trends," *International Migration Review*, I (Summer, 1967).

Moss, Leonard, and Walter H. Thomson. "The South Italian Family: Literature and Observation," *Human Organization*, XVIII, No. 1 (Summer, 1959), 35–41.

Mussolini, Benito. *Scritti e discorsi*, X:163–164. Milano, 1936.

Nigra, Costantino. *Canti popolari del Piemonte*. Torino, 1888.

Pitré, Giuseppe. *Biblioteca delle tradizioni popolari siciliane*. 25 vols. Palermo, 1870–1913.

Redfield, Robert, Robert Linton, and Melville J. Herskovits. "Memorandum for the Study of Acculturation," *American Journal of Sociology*, XLI (1935), 366–370.

Romano, Jennie. "Letter to America," *Roseto Columbus Day*. Roseto, Pa., 1952.

Roseto, Pennsylvania, Golden Jubilee: 1912–1962. Roseto, Pa., 1962.

Saba, A. *Storia della chiesa.* Torino, 1956.

Scarpellati, C. J. *History of the Presbyterian Church of Roseto.* Bangor, Pa., 1948.

Silverman, Sydel F. "An Ethnographic Approach to Social Stratification: Prestige in a Central Italian Community," *Ethnology,* IV (1966), 172–189.

"This Is Our Country in War or Peace," *The Indianapolis Star,* Dec. 12, 1941.

Thomas, William, and Florian Znaniecki. *The Polish Peasant in Europe and in America.* Boston, 1918.

Thompson, Stith, and Antti Aarne. *The Types of the Folktale.* Helsinki, 1961.

Toschi, Paolo. *Guida per lo studio delle tradizioni popolari.* Torino, 1962.

U. S. Department of Commerce, Bureau of the Census. "Country of the Foreign Stock in the U. S. and Figures on Their Urban Settlement: 1960," *1960 Census Data.* Washington, D. C.

U. S. Immigration and Naturalization Service. Annual Reports, Table 13. *Historical Statistics of the United States, 1960,* C 88–100, pp. 56–57. Washington, D. C., 1961.

Vario, Peter. "The Progress of the Town," *Celebrations for the Opening of the Roseto City Hall.* Roseto, Pa., 1935.

Velikonja, Joseph. "Italian Immigrants in the United States in the Mid-Sixties," *The International Migration Review,* I (Summer, 1967), 25–34.

Villani, Pasquale. *Il Mezzogiorno tra riforma e rivoluzione.* Bari, 1962.

Vochting, F. *La questione meridionale.* Napoli, 1955.

Williams, Phyllis H. *South Italian Folkways in Europe and America: A Handbook for Social Workers, Visiting Nurses, School Teachers, and Physicians.* New York, 1938.

Wittke, Carl Frederick. *We Who Built America: The Saga of the Immigrant.* New York, 1939.

Wolf, Stewart. "Unusually Low Incidence of Death from Myocardial Infarction: Study of an Italian-American Community in Pennsylvania," *Journal of the American Medical Association,* CLXXXVIII (1964), 845–849.

PART TWO

Rosetan Folklore

The texts in Part Two are a small sampling of the genres in the Roseto folklore collection. They were selected to show the distribution of the folklore traditions among the various age and social groups by choosing informants of different generations and socioeconomic conditions.

V I

Folktales

1: *The Bird and the Magic Liver*

Tale Types: Th 567 and Th 567/A (The Magic Bird-Heart, The Magic Bird-Heart and the Separated Brothers). Parts: Th 567: I (b,c), II, III; Th 567/A: II (a,b,c), III (a,d).

Motifs: B113.1. Treasure-producing bird-heart brings riches when eaten.

M312.3. Magic bird-heart (when eaten) makes man become king.

D861.5. Magic object stolen by hero's wife.

D661. Transformation as punishment.

Bibliography of Italian texts: S. Lo Nigro, *Racconti popolari siciliana*, p.120, n.567. G. Pitrè, *Fiabe, novelle e racconti*, I:221, n.25.

Informant: Carmine Malpiedo.

Text obtained in English.

(B: Bianco;   C: Carmine;   M: Margaret, Carmine's daughter)

B: You mentioned that story about the liver and the bird.

C: *U fatte du pecciune* [the story of the pigeon]?

B: I think so, yes.

C: Well, that hunter had killed a pigeon and the pigeon said, "Whoever eats my heart, will become a king, a king of a town! Will be the king of France. And whoever eats . . ." What's near the heart that you mentioned?

B: The liver?

C: The liver! ". . . will become the king or the prince of another *regno* [kingdom], *un'ato regno* [another kingdom]." Well. So, when the king's son sawed this, which he would have been the king if his father dies, . . . because, if the father dies, the son becomes a king, see?

B: Sure.

C: Well. He wanted to be the king of the other countries, do you understand?

B: Yes.

C: He wanted to be the only king of the three other countries. Now, he had married the daughter of the *giardinere*, of the gardener, see? She went wrong and he had to marry her. But he mistreated her and she used to work in the kitchen. So, he told his wife, "I've killed this pigeon, I don't want you to take the feathers off. Cook it as it is!" Now, this girl had two small brothers and when they see put this pigeon to cook and she was turning, these two boys were crying, always around that kitchen, see? So, she has *u caccicarne* [dialect for *spiedo*, a roasting spit], you know? To turn the pigeon. Then two . . . things got fasten on there when she pulled it out. So, she pulled one and gave it to one boy, to one brother. The heart to one brother and the liver to the other brother. See now? And the brothers kept quiet: didn't cry no more. So, when the prince came, the son of the king, he started to clean this thing to get the parts. He opens and he was looking for the heart and the liver. But it wasn't there! Wasn't there, it came out, some way or the other, it came out of that pigeon, see? And he whipped his wife, he mistreated, he kicked them out of the palace, you know? Kicked 'em out of *u palazzo!* Because she didn't take orders. He said, "I told you not to." He noticed that the pigeon wasn't cut, but still the things wasn't in there! Wasn't in there. Like Pap said, "It wasn't meant for him." See? He wanted to be a powerful man, he wanted to be the king of the three kingdoms, *i tre regni*, that's right, *i tre regni* [the three kingdoms]! And so these boys they grow up, they got kicked outta there, and they go by the mother and the mother would whip them. "On account of you, we got kicked out! We got kicked out *u palazzo!*" So these boys they got disgusted and they left home. They left home. They kept on traveling together, and they came to a place. They didn't know that one of them, every morning he'd wake up, he would find a hundred dollars under the pillow!

B: One of the brothers?

C: Yeah! One of the two brothers. Dad said the name, but I don't remember. One was gonna become a king and the other one was gonna become—oh, a wealthy man. Ev'ry morning he would find a hundred dollars. So, finally, they traveled together, they gotten into a wood and slept under the tree and they took leaves in their pillow, you know? So, one woke up and he found like something hard. He found *una borsa* [a bag] with—with well, was silver, you know? With . . .

B: Coins? *Ducati* [ducats]?

C: *I ducati.* Yeah! He counted and, "Whaw!" he said. "Now we don't have to sleep in the wood no more. We go to the hotels!" The next mornin', he found another hundred dollars. Whenever he slept on his pillow, he'd find a hundred dollars. *I ducati,* but Pap used to say that he'd find a hundred dollars, a hundred dollars. He mentioned in Italian, *i ducati,* you know? Because they were hard, they were silver, see? Well. He said, "What's matter? last night I put leaves in my cushion, it was soft, now it's hard!" And there'd be a bag with—*i marenghi* [napoleons], *i marenghi, i marenghi,* that's it! So, they were big shots. Now, the other brother he didn't know his destiny: he was to become a king! So they separate and so one brother said, "Any time you need me . . . in other words, I'm gonna go to New York City." And the other one said, "Well, I'm gonna go to Chickako [Chicago]. So, in case, we would get in touch." So the fellow that went to Chickako, he landed in Chickako at night, see? At night. And he couldn't enter the city, 'cause, at that time, the city they had gates that you couldn't enter. Italians they call them "a fence," *il cangelle* (the gate), *i barre* [the bars], you know?

B: Yes.

C: So, nobody wanted to be a king over there because they always used to be in war, and they always used to lose! *Chillu regno* [that kingdom], that county or that—state, nobody wanted to be the king! The king and the children of the king were all killed, killed in war. Because kings then used to go like the headman. So, these kings were always killed. Well, the kings used to fight then, in other words, they'd have a general like they have now, but they used to go out! The kings first and then his regiment would follow, see? That's how it was.

B: I see.

C: Well. So, they made a law. At night they'd close the gates and they made a law that the first one that would be at the gate when they open was gonna be the king. The first one! Well, the people in that town, around that town, knew it but nobody would go! But this boy—he had grown up a young man—he was gonna enter in Chickako and he couldn't enter unless they open the gates. So he said, "Well, what am I gonna do? I'll sit by the gate." So, he lay down. When they open the gate he was the king! He was, yeah! He was the king. See, now it's comin' back to me, see? I knew that there was somethin' there, see? He became a king. Now, we'll forget about the other brother that was gettin' the hundred dollars, O.K.?

B: O.K.

C: We'll forget about him. This boy, this young fellow, he became a king. But they attacked that country: another—another kingdom attacked them. So, he had a horse, he had everything, you know? And he went. He went to fight with the rest of the men and they won the battle! And then he was more than a king in that town! Every time another kingdom would put war against him, he'd always win. This new king, you know? But they didn't know who he was, they didn't know where he came from—but he was good. He would lead his men to battle and the other kingdoms had to run away! Before, they used to kill the king, they always used to get defeated. It was, maybe, you know, a smaller kingdom and they always used to get defeated. But this one: he always won. Well. This went for, say, a couple o' years. Now, while he was a king over there, batting and doing, other nationalities or other countries didn't declare war no more, because they were gettin' defeated. So, he got married and then he had peace in that territory, you know what I mean? Peace.

B: Sure.

C: Now we go back to this other, this other man that was gettin' the hundred dollars. He went to New York City. To New York City, yes. He had so much money he had to a gambling house. And—gamble, gamble, gamble, gamble! And the owner of this gambling house was a lady and lot of rich men used to go there. They'd go for the weekend, they'd go broke, they would go no more. But this young man he continued to go there, continued to go there. Rich people would go, everybody. All millionaires would go there and gamble and they would lose. After they'd go there for a week, they'd lose, they wouldn't go back there no more. But this young fellow continued to go. So, this lady had a magic book.

B: A magic book?

C: *Libri di comando* [a book that can be commanded to respond to questions and demands]! So, this went on for two, three months and he was a nice-looking boy, too, you know? So, she took *u libre di comande* [the magic book], she open the book and the book said, *"Comanda, padrone!"* [at your orders!]. So, she went like this, "I'd like to know . . ." Dad would put in the name—you will have to put a name that would set that character, you know what I mean? You're smarter than I am, you wanna pick up a name to resemble the man that happened that story before! See?

B: The one in Chicago?

C: That's it! So you'll have to put a name to it. But they *had* the names, but I don't remember. It would be like Giuseppe—Pasquale—Alberto—Donato—Martino—or Silvestro—that kinda names,

yes. Like Silvestro became the king and Donato—Don Donato, Don
Donato became the guy with the money, O.K.?

B: O.K.

C: So, when she opened the book, the book said, *"Comanda,
padrone!"* She says, *"Voglio sape* Don Donato [I want to know Don
Donato], where does he get all this money?" So that book said,
"He lucky. He ate a heart, a lucky heart, that as long as he has
that heart in his body . . ." Because you see? He didn't chew it.
It was real thin, you know? It stayed there and, as long as it stayed
there, he would always get these hundred dollars. Yes! And the
other one it stayed there, too, the liver! He became a king. By
havin' this liver in his heart, he would always win, just like Don
Donato, he would win. See now?

B: I see.

C: So the book told her this. She said, "Well, what can I do
to take it away?" She wanted that heart. The book said, "You have
to get him go and throw up. Throw it out, vomit the heart."

M: Yes. I remember, Dad, you used to say that in Italian. When
we were kids, remember? You used to say, *"Vomita u core* [vomit
the heart]."

C: Well, I said heart in Italian, *u core*. But I didn't say really
u core because *i rusetane* [Rosetans] say so! Not us. My father he
said different—*il cuore*, or somethin' more—more in the body! More
good! The Rosetans say *u core*, we say different. For example, we
say *a capa* [head] and Rosetans say *a coccia*, see? See what a
difference?

M: Right! And we say *a furcine* [the fork] and Dad says—what
do you say, Dad?

C: *A furchetta.*

M: *A furchetta,* right!

C: Yeah! What I mean is—well, Margaret, remember when that
people from New York used to come and make fun of us, the way
I used to talk Italian? Like Sam? *"A cap'a monde, a cap' abbasce*
[up hill, down hill]" and *"chistu qua, quiddu dda* [this one here,
that one there]." See what I mean? We talked Italian here. *I
rusetane* would say *i tutere* [corncobs]. Well, we call them *i spighe,
a spiga, u ranerennia* [corncobs in the various dialects near Salerno,
where Carmine's parents came from]. Mamma used to say, *"Mas-
sera, faceme i ranerennia* [tonight we shall have corncobs]." But
i rusetane say *i tutere*, see? Different! That's why I tell my stories
in English, that's why! I told you this, didn't I?

B: Oh yes, you did. So, what did the book tell her?

C: The book told her, "He has to throw out that heart and you swallow it. Then you'll be gettin' the hundred dollars." So, they got acquainted, you know? Because he had been going there for a year, they were like—not in love, but—— So, when he got drunk, the next morning he didn't find no hundred dollars! And he started to worry. Because he didn't have no money, he used to gamble all the time, you know. A hundred dollars a day, a hundred dollars a day, he lost a lot of money! So he realized that there was something fishy. He borrowed some money to go and gamble. He had to borrow money, but he was well known in town, he was well known in New York City! In other words, he had become a big guy, you know? Well known. So he go and borrowed—two thousand dollars, and he went and while he were playing on that table, a card felled. It got outta his hands. So, as he stooped down, he saw a strange book under the table! It was a round table and where the legs were, that's where the book was! So, instead to pick up the card, he picked up that book and he picked up the card and he put the book in his pocket. He played, he lost. Then he went back to the hotel and then he opened the book and the book said, "*Comanda, padrone!*" He said, "*Voglio sape* [I want to know] why I don't receive that hundred dollars no more!" The book said, "Donna Filomena—Donna Filomena was the lady—Donna Filomena done this, this, and this. Remember that day over the garden? You threw up. Well, she got your heart!" And then the book explained, said, "You know, when you was a kid, you was crying around your sister?" And the book told him the whole story. He said, "Well, no wonder we got hit. No wonder we was kicked out! That's why we was kicked out. Because he wanted to be a king, and he wanted the hundred dollars. Now, what am I gonna do to get them back?" The book said, "You must do the same thing. Now you got so friendly and you got broke. So, tell her that tomorrow you're not gonna go because you're all outta money. You wanna go back to your town and get money. Give a big celebration, but you must put a certain thing in the wine, that she gotta throw up right away." So he did. He went there, and he said, "I'll be missing for about a week." And she had a servant there and everything, see? Anyway, he made the lady throw up and he watched the heart as she threw up and he swallowed it. He swallowed. See? Then he stood away for three, four days. But she didn't notice that the book was missing, 'cause she used to get it when she'd get at tight things. So, finally, after three days, he went back and he started to win. And she said, "Well, I guess you're lucky." But he continued to win, so before she was gettin' wise, this man opened the book and the book said, "*Comanda, padrone!*" And he said, "*Voglio un carrozzino e*

doje jummende [I want a buggy and two mares], *una Donna Filomena e una Maria Pasquala* [one must be Donna Filomena and the
other Maria Pasquala].".—Maria Pasquala was the servant— So
he got up in that morning and there would be the buggy and the
two horses ready for him! So he'd get on there, and he whipped
those horses! He went buggy riding. But he made a date, like "Tomorrow afternoon I'll come and play cards." So, the first day she
didn't complain. The second day this man asked, "Well, what
happened?" And she said, "Oh, I'm black and blue!" But he knew,
see? He made them turn to horses!

B: Yes.

C: So, he used to whip 'em. Then, when he'd go and play
cards, they were so sore! She was sore, see? Well, this went on for
about a week and she couldn't stand no more, she was gettin' black
and blue—she went to reach for the book. She wanna know why she
was black and blue, but the book wasn't there, the book wasn't
there! So, she couldn't figure out what happened. Don Donato went
over there and he told her the story. He said, "Now, if you promise
me that you run this house honestly, I let you go. *I* am the one
that you is a horse, and I whipped you! But you won't get the book
back." So they remained like that. Well, a couple of years went by,
he became a millionaire again and he was the owner of Donna
Filomena's Casino, or Caffe, or whatever you wanna call it, but
where they go and gamble. He was the boss, she was the slave, and
she had to take orders from him. So, it came to his mind that he
was gonna go and see his brother, and he started to go. They were
writing to each other, you know? So he said, "Well, now I'm well-
to-do, I own half of New York: I wanna see my brother." And he
went to his brother to Chickako. His brother was well liked there,
all the battles were won, and he said, "Nobody bothers me." So the
two brothers they got together. He was married, the one who became a king, and the other wasn't married because he wanted
the daughter of the king where he had been kicked out. Because
they were raised together, one of the sisters married the prince and
the prince had a sister. So, the one that was a king, he said, "You
know? You know what we're gonna do? We're gonna declare war to
so and so!" So this king was a powerful king where they got kicked
out, and all at once the king of France—or anything—declared war
on the king of Italy, or so. The king of Italy said, "What's the
matter? I'm not botherin' that guy! All right, years ago we battled—
but." Well, so they declared war, but the king of Italy was pretty
powerful, and he said, "O.K.," he said. So when they went to battle,
the two brothers were together: Don Donato was with his brother

Pasquale and, boy! They laced that king! Donato had that book, and he had a white horse, and he would take the lead. Everybody followed him and everybody liked him because he never went back, in other words, he would take the lead and the other soldiers they would follow him, they wouldn't back out. So, finally, he got defeated: the one in Italy got defeated, yes. And they had to sign papers, so this king of Italy wanted to know why he declared war and that one said, "Well, you know why? I'm the son of Don Nicola. Nicola was your *giardiniere* and Don Nicola is my father. Now, you kicked my father out, and my sister is your sister-in-law," he said. "Now, I am the king over there and Don Donato owns New York City. Now, either you take my sister back, or I'll take the whole thing out!" So, naturally, he was defeated! He was defeated. Because one of the brothers had control of all the stocks, like now the Stock Market! So Donato controlled the money from all over the country: He was well-to-do and he had the book *di comando* [the magic book], see? And, naturally, then the son had to take back the wife and the other brother married his daughter. In other words, then they made—like three weddings together. Oh, yes, because a few years went by and the prince then had a wife. And what a feast they had! Oh, Gee! Like over here, you know, when they have a weddin': you have to have an invitation, see?

B: Sure.

C: But I didn't have any! So, I sneaked there. I sneaked there, and I was under the table, you know? And when they threw crumbs or something, and I'd go and pick it up. And I bumped on a man's leg, and this man thought there was a dog under there, and he took a bone, you know, and he'd go like this! Oh, boy! He cracked me in the eye and what a black eye I had! Oh, my, what a black eye I had! And that was the end of the story.

B: But how was it called?

C: Oh, the story of the liver—and the bird—*The Bird and the Magic Liver*, or *The Hunter*, but, no: *The Bird and the Magic Liver*. That's it.

2: *The Fisherman*

Tale Type: Th 303 (The Twins or Blood-Brothers). Parts: I (a), II (b), III (d), VI (a,b,c), V (a,b,c).

Motifs: T511.5.1. Conception from eating fish.

T589.7.1. Simultaneous birth of animal and child.

F577.2. Brothers identical in appearance.

T685.1. Twin adventurers.

N772. Parting at crossroads.

E761. Life token.

R111.1.3. Rescue of princess from dragon.

L161. Hero marries princess.

D321. Transformation of man to stone.

K1311.1. Husband's twin brother mistaken by wife for her husband.

T351. Sword of chastity.

D700. Disenchantment.

N342.3. Jealous and overhasty man kills his rescuing twin brother.

The motifs relating to the imposter and the tongues removed from the dragon's head are missing here, while they are present in most of the texts collected in Roseto, Pennsylvania (six) and in Roseto Valfortore (five). The audience to this tale consisted of the informant's wife, his two children, and his grandchildren.

Informant: Carmine Malpiedo.

Text obtained in English.

(B: Bianco;   C: Carmine)

C: Well, I'll start with "once upon a time."

B: The way you want, the way you feel like.

C: Well, my father told me a story in Italian, but then I've been repeatin' it in English. Some of the words I get stuck. . . . And he told us that once upon a time there was a fisherman. He used to go fishing and he used to make a livin'. They really wanted a family, but they could get no children. Oh, he was getting disgusted! So one day he was fishing, and he didn't get no fish. He went home; he was mad. When he came, the woman wanted some fish. He said, "I didn't catch no fish." So one day he went to his wife and he said, "When the sun goes down, ——" of course, that was all in Italian, "*quannu cala lu sole* [when the sun goes down], and I'm not home, that means I threw myself in the ocean!" Because the wife she wanted a child and she was after him, and he was gettin' disgusted! So, the sun was ready to go where the mountain is. My Dad said, "Like over here." You know when the sun goes over the mountain?

B. Yes. *Dietro la montagna* [behind the mountain].

C: And he felt something. He pulled up and took a big fish and the fish spoke to him, said, "Throw me back, and you'll be a rich man." The man said, "For a week I ain't catch no fish." He said, "I'm gonna take you home, and I'm gonna eat you!" And the fish begged him, "Throw me back and you'll become a rich man!" "I don't wanna be rich. I've had no money for the last week, my wife and I are trying to get a child, so," he said, "I don't wanna be rich." So the fish said, "Well, if that's what is in your mind." He said, "If you do what I tell you, O.K., you don't have to throw me back. You're gonna kill me anyhow!" The fisherman said, "Oh, yes." So the fish said, "All right. You go home, and you tell your wife just what I'm telling you. Skin me, put the bones——" See? The fish knew that they had, like ayardsman, an old trunk, and the fish knew he had a dog, too. So, he said, "You cook me. The water you give it to the dog, and some marrow——" The man had a horse, a female, a *jummenda* [mare], do you understand a *jummenda?*

B: Yes, a mare, a horse.

C: Oh, you knew that! O.K.! ". . . and forget about it!" So the man went home and told the wife, "Kill the fish, we're gonna eat it. The broth, the water that you wash it, you give it to the dog, and the bones . . ." Because that was a big fish, and he had a big back bone, you know? ". . . you put it in the—the trunk." There was an o-o-old trunk. This trunk was made outta steel years ago. So, that's what she did and then, all at once, nine, ten months went by and she got a twin boy: two boys! The dog got twins and also the horse, so the children and the dogs and the horses they were raised together. Well, when they became around nineteen, they were well smart and they sent to college. After that time, the father used to get lots of fish, and he became well-to-do and he sent the boys to college. So, while these boys were playin' with the dogs and the horses, they were ridin' the horses, and they noticed this old trunk! So one of them said, "Let's look what's in there," and he asked the mother for the key. But the mother said, "We threw the key away, so we don't know." She had forgotten that she had put the back-bone of the fish in there! See?

B: Right.

C: Well, so the boys they broke that up. When they open the trunk, there was two beautiful suits of *cavaliere* [knight]. It was out of the world! They never saw a thing like that! There was a sword in there, a helmet, that no one had it in that country. It was something out—of the country—

B: Like an *armatura* [armor]?

C: Yeah, *armatura!* They both put it on and had it fit just like tailor-made. Well, on vacation day—they were over twenty-one then. They were over twenty-one and they were gonna go out there, discovering—venture, like we say here in America. So, they each have a dog—and every dog follows the master. So, one day they started to pull out, told the parents that they were gonna go out and try the fortune and see what's——. One said, "We know this town, we're well known, we're well-to-do, we wanna go out." So they did. They kept on traveling for a couple of days and, finally, they came to a crossroad. It was more like a "Y." One road went one way, and another road went another way. One of the boys said,

"You know what we're gonna do?" He said, "We traveled together."
Because they used to stop in hotels, motels, you know? And there
the people couldn't tell the difference, 'cause they were twins! See?

B: Right.

C: The horses were twins, the dogs were twins! So, when they
came to the crossroad, one of the two boys said, "You know what
we're gonna do? You go this way, I go this way." And Dad used to
say, "You know, Armie [Carmine], our American Bangor Junction
down here? Like this." I explained you the other night.

B: Yes, you did.

C: One way would go straight and one would turn to go to
Pen Argyl. He [dad] said it was like this [he makes the sign of a
"V"]. Like a "V," like a "Y"! See? A road come together and
then, when it gets here, it would split: one go one way, one go
the other way. Well. So the other brother said, "There's a tree
here." It was a willow tree; in Italian they call it *l'arbele chican-
gente*, the crying tree. That's right, the crying tree. So they made a
nick on there, on the crying tree. He said, "After one year we're
separate, whoever comes here first, if this is healed, that means I'm
O.K. If this does not heal . . ." The bark, you know? You cut the
bark of the tree—the bark.

B: Yes.

C: ". . . then, we go and find out who is in trouble." Well, they
separate. So one of the boys traveled maybe a couple of days—they
lost track of each other. So, one of the boys landed into a city and
it was a sad city. Everybody was downhearted and he started in-
quiring why everybody was sad. The people said, "Well, here it is
an animal——" they called it the dragon, or something that has seven
heads. ". . . and every day the king has to send a person, otherwise
he would come in town and destroy the town!" So, the king figured
that it wasn't fair that he had to pick this and that and he made
like a lottery: the number that'd come out—'cause everybody had
a number in that town—whichever number would come out would
have to go! So, finally, the number of a prince [*sic*] came out: the
daughter of the king!

B: The princess?

C: Well, yes. The people didn't want to see her—everybody
would volunteer, they wanted to take the queen's place, the princess' place, rather! And they, well—no. So, finally, there was a big
field where this animal would come. They would leave the girl
there, and they would leave the town. They had to leave town
because the animal would eat them up. So, this young fellow now,
with the horse and with the dog, he followed the crowd, because

everybody was like a procession to take this lady to the slaughter house, 'cause she was gonna get killed! So everybody left and this *cavaliere* remained and he sawed this big animal comin', you know, with seven heads! Seven heads. So he figured, "Well, now, she's a pretty girl." He said, "I'm gonna try to do something!" So he pull out his sword and he was cuttin' the heads off. The heads would come off, because he was so powerful—he chopped the heads off, but then they would jump right back again! Right back! See?

B: I see.

C: So the prince, the *cavaliere* turned around and he saw the dog was sittin'. He called him by name. ——He had a name, right? But I don't remember the name of the dog, see? The dog *had* a name, though—— And he said, "What're you doin' there? You see that I'm fightin' and——" He was mad. So the dog said, "Well, Master——" He spoke, the dog spoke, see?

B: He spoke?

C: Oh sure, animals used to speak then. He said, "If you don't tell me, I don't know what you want." The fellow said, "When I cut the heads off, you take 'em, take 'em out!" And he said, "Shake 'em up, get them dizzy, so they won't connect it." Well, finally, the dog said, "O.K." As his master kept on cuttin' them heads off, he'd take them away, see? And finally, by cuttin' all the heads off, and the dog would take them away, the animal died. So, he picked that girl, put her on the horse with the dog, and brought her back to the king's house. When the king sawed her daughter, they rejoiced themselves! They were happy, you know? And they invited him to stay there. Finally they felled in love. When they got married, he stayed there a while, but at the same time the year had gone by. Well, being that he married the prince [*sic*] and she was well-to-do, he told his wife that he was wanna go out to meet his brother, "That I have a brother, a twin brother!" So, he left the town and he went back to the road, to this "Y." It took maybe a week to get there, and when he got there that thing wasn't healed! The way they cut it, that's the way it remained. That was the sign that the brother was in danger. Otherwise, they would have met there that same day, see?

B: I see.

C: Well! Then, he started following the road that the brother took. He traveled another four, five days and he came to the city. When they sawed him, "Hee! *Cavaliere Alberto* is back!" This other brother had got married to another wealthy family, see? Everybody was yellin', "He's back, he's back, he's back!" They made like a procession with the band and this and that. They were happy because he was missin' for about a week, the other brother. Then he knew that his brother was in very danger. But the wife, which he didn't know, said, "Alberto," said, "where were you? you were away, and it's a week!" So he figured, "Well, she's my sister-in-law." Then they had a big time and when they went to bed, he had to sleep with her, but he said, "She's my sister-in-law!" So, he took the—the spade and he put it in the center of the bed. And the wife said, "Well, you've been away a week and why this now?" He said, "Well, I made a wish. In Italian, *nu vote*, that for one week this must be in the center of the bed. You stay on your side, and I stay on my side." Then he got up in the morning, he went to the bathroom, and he noticed a beautiful garden! It was like on a little hill, it was beautiful! With nice statues and everything. So, he asked his wife, which was his sister-in-law, he said, "What's that big beautiful? Who lives in it?" And she said, "But I told you last week what it was." She said, "That's a cemetery, that's *ingandeseme* [an enchanted cemetery]: once you enter in there, you'll never come out! Now, I told you to stay away from there!" Of course, she told the brother. See?

B: I see.

C: So, the brother said, "That's where my brother is." He imagined, "He went out there to discover something, and so he got stuck in there." Well, finally, he got up that morning, and he started to go towards over there. But he had to put two and two together. He said, "That's a place of *ingandeseme* [enchanted]. I've got to watch. I must study." So, as he walked in through there, they called him by name! And my father told me that when they call you by name and you turn, you remain as a statue, you—you couldn't move no more! A statue, see?

B: I see!

C: But in the center of the place there was a tree, a bird, and a spring. *L'acqua* [the water] was dancing, boiling, you know? The bird was singin' and—and a whisperin' tree!

B: A whispering tree?

C: The tree would whisper, see? So they called him by name. It was like in a cemetery, there is a road that you go up and there is a cross up there. Now they were callin', but he wouldn't turn, no. He went right up to this cross, and when he got there, a voice said, "Well, you got this far," said, "you're wise." See? Someone whispered, and this was the tree that whispered. He said, "Be careful!" The whisperin' tree said this, and the water was dancing 'cause it was happy that he would twist and he would remain there! The bird was singin' and whistlin' from one place to another so

that he would turn! But the whisperin' tree told him. He said,
"You made it this far, don't turn now!" This was the whisperin'
tree, you see? Then, there was other things in there, too. Finally,
he said, "Well, I'm this far." He said, "What am I supposed to do to
save all these people?" And the whispering tree says, "Go so many
feet, turn, go where the water is dancing." He said, "You will find a
buchette, a bucket. Don't turn, don't twist your eyes! Get this
bucket full of water, there is . . ." How do you say a brush?

B: *Pennello* [brush]?

C: *U pennello!* ". . . go to your brother there, dip the brush in
this water, and paint, like you paint a statue, so that he'll awaken!"
He said, "But what about the rest?" The tree said, "After you
awaken one, then you leave the bucket, then everyone will paint the
next one!" See? Oh, finally, that's what he did. And the brother
woke up! And the dog also . . .

B: The dog?

C: Well, the dog remained as a statue, too, the horse, everything! So, he painted the dog and the dog came to life. See? His
dog was with him, and the dog paid no attention, or the horse.
Because, when they called, they all turned their head, my Dad said,
you know? The dog, the horse, any of them! And then they remained like that. There were lots of rich people over in that cemetery. They went there for—for—how do you say? Curio—curio—

B: Curiosity?

C: That's right! That's why they used to go! Just for that.
So, after he embraced his brother and the dog, and the horse, they
started to awake up another party and they said, "Now you do the
same to this one." Then, they would do it and then it became a big
procession! And everybody started to go back home and now the
two brothers they started to go back to the city and the one who
saved the brother that was a statue told the other that he had slept
one night with his wife. So the brother got jealous! As they were
walkin', he pulled his sword and killed his brother. When he had
killed his brother, the horse and the dog remained where he threw
them, on the side of the road. So, the horse and the dog would move
no more, they stood there with their master, see?

B: Yes.

C: So he went back home and she said, "Oh, I see you came
back early tonight!" Then they had supper and then it was time
to go to bed and they went to bed. But he didn't put the sword
there! He didn't! So, the wife said, "Alberto, last night you told
me that you would put the sword in the middle for one week, and
I had to stay on this side and——" So he started to realize, and he

said, "Oh, I misjudged my brother!" See? So, he was worried! He went back over there and the cemetery was almost empty: everybody was goin' home. So he took that water with the brush and he went back to the road. He hit his brother with the brush and the water and he got healed again! See? He was O.K.!

B: I see.

C: He got healed up again and they both went into town. Then the wife and the people were surprised: there were two Umberto— two Alberto, rather! Dad would mention the name: the horse had the name, the dog had the name—but I don't remember the names. And so they both entered the town and the people said, "But—there is two Alberto." And when they went to the house, the wife said, "Which is my husband?" But she made up her mind and she said, "The one that comes to bed with me that one must be my husband!" So, finally, that night they had a big feast and he introduced him. "That's my brother." Like that, he said it was his brother, but that doesn't mean that separated they could tell the difference! See?

B: Right.

C: So, like I said, she said, "The one that comes to bed with me is my husband." Then, she realized that the one that put the sword in the middle that was the brother-in-law, and the one that'd come to bed now, like he did last night, he must be the husband. They went to bed and then he confessed and he told his wife what had happened. She said, "See? Your brother was honest 'cause I didn't know the difference! He put that sword for one week." He said, "Yes, and I was jealous and I killed him." Well, then they got together and they had a big feast. Then the one that married that king's daughter said, "You know? I am a king of so and so." And he was a big deal, too, at that time. I don't remember what title.

B: Do you remember the country? France? Spain?

C: Was—was some king, you'll have to name, 'cause I don't remember what king. I don't know just what king it was but it was a king! Married a king's daughter but different territory, see? Because—like Italy or—France, or whatever goes, I don't know. But different. Well, then they got together and they said, "Now I married so and so, I am from—we'll say from Germany and—they were from Italy. So, they got together and they said, "Before I go home, I go pick my wife and we go home and see how Dad's makin' out in—in Italy," or we say in Rome, somewhere! So, they got back and when they saw the two horses, you know, and the girls! They were on horseback, too, see? And they had a big celebration and the father was so tickled! He said, "You know? It's over a year that you's went away!" Because they didn't write him nothin'! They don't know. Like I said, the father was well-to-do, he was well liked in the town—and boy! What a feast! They invited the whole town, yeah! So there happened to be a dirty guy in that crowd. They were eatin', but he didn't wanna leave the bones in his dish. I wasn't invited, but I sneaked in and I got under the table. So that when this guy was eatin', he threw the bones under the table and he hit me on the nose, yeah! And that was the end of the story because I started to get bloody nose and they kicked me out because I wasn't invited! That was the end of the story.

B: Very good!

C: Now Rose can tell you a story, 'cause I've got to think. I've got to remember.

3: *The Fox and the Ricotta*

Tale Types: Th 41 (The Wolf Overeats in the Cellar), Th 3 (Sham Blood and Brains), Th 4 (Carrying the Sham-Sick Trickster).

This is the most recurrent combination of types to be found among Italian animal tales. In Roseto, Pennsylvania, there was hardly an informant of any age group who had never heard this folktale several times.

Informant: Anthony Joseph C., American-born.

Text obtained in the Rosetan dialect, with many words and sentences in English.

(B: Bianco;   A: Anthony;   W: his wife)

A: Shall I sing now?

B: No, tell me the story first.

A: The Madonna, when she was a young lady?

B: The other one.

A: The Fox and the Ricotta [a soft cottage cheese]? But, you see? I'm not so educated now. We talk Rosetan up here and my mother used to tell us the stories in the dialect. It should be printed in English, I imagine, but it needs some—some thinking, see?

B: Say it in the dialect or in the way you like.

A: And then, will you print it in English in here? [He points at the tape recorder.] All right. Well, listen then, you too [to his wife], I'm going to tell the fox now, the story of the fox when she went to eat in the cellar. To tell the truth, men should look at the animals and learn. But we are too stupid, we don't learn a thing! Well, this fox she was hungry. Do you know the fox? She's smart. But she's hungry all the time, and she cheats. She could cheat me, you, anybody. Now, the fox had her house in the woods, and every morning, when she went shopping in town, she had to pass in front of a rich house that was the house of a rich man. He was one of those rich industrialists, a rich house. So, she passed there and she used to smell and to look through the windows, see? Like dogs do, you know, when they go smelling for food and things? So she did, too. She used to stop by the basement window and, oh Madonna! What a perfume! A smell of heaven, of good things like salami, *presutte* [ham], ricotta, sausages! I'm getting hungry myself, see? Well, so this fox was hungry and she was hungry because she was poor. She didn't work or anything and she was poor. So, she passed today and she passed tomorrow and she passed the day after tomorrow and her belly was empty and painful because there was nothing in there and she was starving. So, she thought, "I've got to eat, I've got to get in there and eat. But what if that son-of-a-bitch catches me? What am I going to do? Oh, how can I go? I can't go there by myself, all alone." See, the rascal? She wanted to eat, but she was looking for a scapegoat! Well, you know what? She went visiting. She went to see her *cumpare* [godfather] which was the wolf. Because, in the woods, she lived across the street from the wolf and so she went to see him. But the wolf is another one like the fox, another good one! He's a robber, too, only he's dumb, he isn't smart, no! And they were *cumpare* and *cummare*, see? [They were godfather and godmother] because, like the proverb says, "First, God makes them, and then he puts them together." If you know what I mean . . .

B: Sure.

A: Good. So she said to him, the fox said to him, "Hi, *cumpa'* [godfather]." And the wolf said, "Hi, *cumma'* [godmother]." And she said, "Well, *cumpa'*, what the hell are you doing here? Starving to death? Can't you go eat some place? You, good-for-nothing idiot!" And he, of course, he was her *cumpare*; but he was a man and he didn't want to look idiot, see? So, he said, "Of course, I'll go, just show me the way. Let's run!" And so she goes ahead and he went behind and when they get at that place, they stop there. Now, you know how the city buildings are. They have those iron fences on the windows that are near the street, right? And you can't get in there. But there was a hole in there that an animal could go in, see? A horse couldn't go, but a small animal could go, see? Have you ever seen a fox?

B: Yes.

A: Well, I haven't, but she's small. And she's like a cat. She can stretch and get thin as much as she wants, see? Well, then, a *cummare* she went in there and she called *u compare*, she said,

"Cumpa! Hurry, get in! Hurry!" And he went in and *Mamma mia belle!* [Oh, mother!]. What a paradise in there! What a magnificent feast they started having! You don't know how good those things were: ham and salami and thousands of different cheeses, and olives, and nuts and this and that! And they were eating fast; they ate fast, see? Oh, they ate a lot, but you don't imagine what *la cummare* did, though. Sure, women know more than the devil himself! Do you know what she did?

B: What did she do?

A: What did she do? She ate, all right, but every now and then she stopped eating and went to measure herself through that hole, see? That hole in the fence! Because she figured, "If I eat too much, then I get too big to fit in there." See how smart?

B: I see.

A: So she figured, "I keep on trying and then I'll stop eating." Now, wait and listen to what happened. The *cumpare*, the wolf, you know, he was strong and all that, but he didn't have enough brain to see that he was getting too big, bigger than that hole, see?

B: I see.

A: You see, now? Well, the idiot wolf kept on eating and *a cummare* kept on going back and forth, back and forth, back and forth, and this way she kept slim, see? But now comes the best. That rich man at that moment was upstairs, he was there, writing a check, I believe, or a bill, I don't quite remember that, and he heard a noise from the basement! So, he ran downstairs with a big heavy stick, see? To catch the robbers and beat them up. Now, *a cummare and a cumpare* heard him, too, see? And they ran, they ran for the hole! But, of course, *a cummare* was slim and she could fit in the hole and run away, but *u cumpare*, that stupid pig, he had got this large, see? Like a big drum. And he tried to pass through the hole, but he couldn't make it. He didn't fit in there! So, he got beaten up real good by that gentleman. He got for two, see? Then—well, then, of course, my mother could tell you more details about this story, like she would add more artistic touches to it and all that. Now, you could make it last for an hour or two. You could make a book and sell it, even!

W: But you didn't finish it! You left the ricotta.

A: Oh, yeah! How was that now?

W: Well, the wolf was half dead from the beating and he was aching all over, see? And he was trying to go home and——

A: [Interrupts her] Oh, yeah! And then——

W: —let me finish now! The wolf was mad at the *cummare* fox, because she had run away first, see? And guess what? He met the fox in the woods! Your mother used to say—because I remember when she used to tell this story to our kids, see? She used to say that the fox cheated. She moved as if she had been beaten up, too, see? But she hadn't! And she limped and she coughed and she had spreaded all that ricotta cheese on her head and shoulders! So, she had the nerve to ask the wolf to carry her home because she wasn't able to walk, see? She said, *"Cumpa'!* See what she did to me? You've got nothing, but look at me! My legs are broken and my brains [the ricotta] are all over my body. Won't you help me? I tried to defend you, and I got more blows! Take your *cummare* home, won't you?" And *u cumpare*, he thought, "Well, she worse off than me!" And he said, "All right." So the broken body was carrying the healthy one and to top all that, *a cummare* was singing, too! She was singing, *"Terlentano, terlentano, u ruttu port' usano!"* [Terlentano, terlentano, the broken one carries the healthy one.] So the wolf said, *"Cumma',* are you singing?" And the fox said, "Are you kidding? I'm crying and I'm saying that my head is going to pieces, oh, poor me! Oh, poor me!" [To her husband] Don't you remember that?

A: Not so well, not so well. Yeah! Well, as I said, you can stretch it and fix it the way you like, see? Then, of course, you know how.

4: *The Man Who Went to Church*

Tale Type: Th 805 (Joseph and Mary Threaten To Leave Heaven).

Bibliography of Italian texts: Giuseppe Pitrè, *Fiabe e leggende,* p.247, n.61. G. Tammi, *Il devoto di S. Giuseppe nella leggenda popolare* (Roma, 1955).

Well known in both Rosetos. Compared to the Thompson tale type, the tale gives a greater importance to the legal aspect and to the family connections.

Informant: Anthony Zilio' Falcone, American-born.

Text obtained in English but with a large number of Italian words and sentences.

(B: Bianco; A. Z.: Anthony Zilio')

B: What's the title of that story?

A. Z.: *The Man Who Went to Church.* Shall I tell that one?

B: Yes, that one.

A. Z.: Well, like they told me, there was a fellow who finally went to church one day and the priest was preaching. He was saying that sinners had to turn to religion and pick up a saint as a patron saint, you know? As a defender, as a lawyer! That was needed to go to heaven, that is. Well, this fellow chose St. Joseph as his patron saint and every morning he said his prayers to St. Joseph that was his lawyer now. Finally, this fellow died and when he died he reported to heaven. But when he got there, St. Peter wouldn't let him enter! He said, "What the hell are you looking for, here?" And this fellow said, "Well, I died and now I want to get in heaven, I want to get in." St. Peter said, "But you need the Eternal Father's permit, you need a pass from him 'cause you've not been a good believer; you didn't go to church. You didn't do anything!" And the dead fellow said, "But I've got a lawyer out here! A defender of my rights! I got myself a patron saint when I was still alive, see?" "And who is this lawyer?" The fellow said, "It's St. Joseph, the defender of the 'Good Death.' Now I'll go call him and I'll show you!" Because, you see, this fellow was pretty sure his saint would work for him up in heaven.

B: I see.

A. Z.: So he went to St. Joseph and St. Joseph said, "What do you want?" This soul said, "You mean you don't recognize me? I'm the one who paid respect to you every morning, and you're my lawyer, my defender in heaven!" Then, St. Joseph said, "Oh, I see." And he went to St. Peter and he said, "Peter, let him in!" But that Peter wouldn't listen to him, he wouldn't. He said, "What? Let him in? Thank God that *you* are in heaven! No, sir, here we need the Eternal Father's permit!" "All right," said Joseph; and he went to his wife *la Madonna* and he says, "Hi, Mary, I'm quitting. I'm leaving this place." His wife says, "What? Why would you quit now?" "Well," he says, "there is a soul out here. He chose me as his defender when he was alive. He was smart; he chose me and I am his lawyer now, and I've got to defend him anyway, see? But Peter won't let him in! So, I've got to leave. I've got to quit, see?" Then, his wife says, "Wait, I'll go and see what's happening." So, *la Madonna* went to speak to St. Peter, but he wouldn't listen to her either, see? He still wanted that damn permit from the Father, from the Great Father. See what was happening? No kidding!

B: Yes!

A. Z.: Well. So, she said, "Wait a minute, now. Let me go find my son over there." And they say that she went to the Nazarene and said, "Well," she said, "Nazarene, listen. Here is a fellow from the world. He died and now he is out here and wants to get in heaven. But St. Peter won't let him in. He wants a permit from the Eternal Father, see? Now, that fellow, when he was still in the world, he picked up your Daddy as his lawyer. That is he wanted your Father as a defender, to come up here, see? What are we going to do now?"

So, her son says, "Well, so what? What's happening?" "How do you mean, what's happening? Your Daddy is leaving! He's quitting Heaven because he didn't make it, he—well, he flunked as a lawyer, see? And if he leaves, I leave too. Because where the husband goes, there goes the wife, right?" And, of course, what do you think? The Nazarene said, "Well, you know what? Where the parents go the son goes, too! So, if my parents quit, I quit, too, now!" Ain't that awful? The whole family getting out of there? "Well," he said, "Let me try my Father now. I mean my other one, the Eternal Father. Let me see what I can do there for our family." So he went to the Eternal Father up there, and he found him in. He spoke to his Father. He said, "Daddy, Eternal Father. Here's a soul from the world. He came from the world and wants to enter, but Peter won't let him in." "Well," says God, "Maybe, he doesn't have no business here!" The Nazarene said, "But, you see, when he was alive, he chose my Daddy, that is Joseph, as his lawyer, because he wanted him to defend him, see? He figured my Daddy would help him in this." And God said, "So? What's happening?" "It's happening that all our family is quitting your Heaven! See? None of us could make it, and since Daddy is his lawyer and Peter won't respect his authority, we've got to quit! Daddy is losing his job, see? And Mammy is supposed to follow her husband, right? And can I let my poor parents go lost in the world like that? Can a son do this? You tell me. I must quit, too!" See? The fellow was smart. He knew that all this would happen in the Holy Family, you know?

B: I see.

A. Z.: The Holy Family's reputation! Poor Joseph, what could a man do without a job? What could my own father do in America without a job? Go back to Italy, right? So was Joseph! Well, that fellow won.

B: Did he?

A. Z.: But sure! The Eternal Father had to fix that business. He had to give His permission. He said, "Son Jesus, it's O.K. Go tell Peter he can open that damn door and let that fellow come in!" He had to face it; God had to fix it that way, see? Well, that's how I've heard the story and I wouldn't know if the story is true or not. That I don't know, 'cause, you see? No one ever came back here to tell us what's really going on up there so we don't know, see?

B: I see. How often did you tell this story?

A. Z.: Of course, many times. My poor woman, my wife, she used to like this story, yeah! She like it. But I think I heard it at the Marconi Club, you know? Around the corner? Oh! Those days! You should have come here long ago, when we used to get together every night there, every night! And the stories, the jokes, the things we did! It's all over now.

B: Really? I saw the club is open.

A. Z.: Yeah! But—well, it's not the same any more, it's not the same anyhow.

5: *What Is the World Doing?*

I was not able to find any specific tale type for this religious anecdote (Th 750–849). I decided to include it as I found it extremely common among all my informants who use it to indicate that a variety of human conditions is the ideal requirement to have a happy and well-balanced world.

Informant: Anthony Zilio' Falcone, American-born.

Text obtained in English with a large number of Italian words.

(B: Bianco;   A. Z.: Anthony Zilio')

B: What about Jesus Christ, when he went——

A. Z.: Oh, you mean when he used to walk around the world with his Apostles? Oh, I know that.

B: Good, tell me that.

A. Z.: Oh, boy! Well, he went wandering and his Apostles were with him all the time, right? Well, they say that he called on St. Peter because he used to call on him all the time, see? Says, "Peter, go to that window over there and give a look at the world below. See what the world is doing and then come right here and tell me what is that you saw. Hurry!" They say that Peter went, you know? And he looked and he came back to Jesus Christ. He says, "*Maestro!* They're all ugly down there, all ugly! They're all crying, and one cries here and one there. It's all like that, it's a mess!" Are you following [to me]?

B: Oh, yes!

A. Z.: Well. So the Lord says, "That's not right; that's wrong. They shouldn't all be ugly!" See? Then he said, "Peter, go again now and look at the world. See what's going on now and then come right back!" So, Peter went and he look and he come right back where the Lord was. He says, "*Maestro!* They're all laughing; they're all having a ball down there!" Well, they say that the Lord didn't like that either. He didn't like that business at all. He says, "No good, no good!" Then, after a few days, Jesus Christ calls on Peter. He says, "Go, Peter, go now and look again." So, Peter went to the window and looked at the world below, and then he came right back where the Lord was, saying, "*Maestro!* Some are laughing and some are crying. It's a mixture!" And then the Lord said,

"Oh, now the world is fixed up all right! Some are ugly and some are beautiful; some cry and some laugh. That's the way it should be, see? And, the ugly one is to go with the beautiful, and the beautiful is to take the ugly one. Now the world is O.K.!" And, Carla, believe me. That's how it really is! Honestly, I tell you!

B: Yes?

A. Z.: But sure! It's mixed! It's got to be like that!

6. *The New Crucifix*

Tale Type: Th 1347 (Living Crucifix Chosen).
Informant: Giannina Castellucci.
Text obtained in the Rosetan dialect.

(G: Giannina)

G: This one is different. This one is about Roseto, but it is way back, way back! They had collected much money to build a new church, after the earthquake, see? And, with the new church, the peasants wanted new marbles, new things, right? Like they wanted new statues, they wanted new candles, and they wanted a new crucifix because they had an old one which wasn't so good any more. A new church and an old crucifix? It doesn't look good, right? So they collected that money and they decided to buy a new good crucifix. But they didn't sell any in town and the only thing to do was to go to San Bartolomeo and buy it there. Now, there was a market day in San Bartolomeo, you know? A big fair, a big, big market, huge, big! They used to sell lots of things, different things there. You could buy a pig, a horse, a mule, or a blanket, anything, anything! And they sold all the things that were needed in the churches, like —well, like, you know? Things—sacred! Candles, big, huge candles. And statues, saints, madonnas, see? You should see the statues they sell there! Many, oh! Like—like hundreds of saints and other things. So, these peasants thought: "Let's send *u cumpare* [godfather] Michele. He's honest. We give him our money, and we tell him to buy us a new crucifix for the new church." So they did it. And *u cumpa'* Michele took the money and took his mule that morning and he went to the fair. When he got there, there was a big crowd, and he was confused. Like he didn't know where to go. He asked here, and he asked there and finally a woman told him to go there and turn there. He went there and turned there, and he found a long line of stands all full of these statues! It was Jesus Christ, see? In so many colors and in so many shapes. *Cumpa'* Michele went up and down, up and down, up and down; and he didn't know which crucifix he was supposed to take. There was too much of a choice, see? So, they call him, those men that were selling, you know? They called him, and they yelled at him, "Man! Man, come here! Look. It's nice. It's dead, see? Do you want it dead or alive? I have it young and old, big and small, look! This one is still alive, see?" Now, you understand what happened? Poor Michele he was confused, see? He was all mixed up in his head because he figured, "Damn! They didn't tell me how they wanted it! What the hell do I know?" And he was getting mad, see? Then, he thought, "Tough! I know what I'm going to do now! I get one that's alive; then, if they want it dead, *they* kill it!"

7: *The Nervous Wife*

Tale Type: Th 1378 B* (Wife's Temporary Success).

This tale was told several times, mostly in Italian, by first- and second-generation Rosetans. The few changes from the texts found in Roseto Valfortore consist only of changes in the setting (i.e., the social Marconi Club instead of the tavern), or of names (some texts have English names!).

Informant: Anthony Zilio' Falcone, American-born.

Text obtained in English with frequent Italian words and sentences.

(B: Bianco; A. Z.: Anthony Zilio')

A. Z.: I have another story that I used to tell my mother-in-law when I was engaged to Maria, my poor wife. It's called *The Nervous Wife*. Would that do?

B: Of course, it would do!

A. Z.: Good. Well, there was a guy up here in Pen Argyl. He was Italian and he wanted a certain girl, and he told her that he wanted her. This girl said she had a problem. She says, "Look, if you want me, you must come home and speak to my parents." So, this guy went there and they spoke and this and that. Then, finally, the father said, "Well, but why did you come here? What did you come for? What do you want?" And that guy was shy, but he had to say it. So he says, "Well, to tell you the truth, the reason I came here is that I want your daughter. I want to marry her, you see?" So, the father says, "Well, son, you must be pretty stupid if you want our daughter. Are you sure you want her? Because, look. She's pretty and all that, but she's sick! She's got a disease, a bad disease that she couldn't cure!" So, this guy figured, "Christ, this must be a good man. He said the truth to me!" But he wanted that girl, so he made up his mind. He says, "Well, Pap, do me a favor. What's this disease that she's got?" The father said, "Well, she's nervous. She has a disease of nerves. She's all nerves. And if she gets you when she's that way, she beats you up!" "Oh, is that all? Don't worry, Pap. Don't worry. I'll fix it. I'll fix her up!" So, finally, they made a fine wedding, and then they got married, and all that. Now the husband was a man, and he started to go out at night. He used to go to the Marconi Club up here, see? And he used to come home late, real late. And the wife used to yell at him, "Son of a bitch! Is this the time to come home?" She used to yell a lot, see? But the man started to come later the next day. He'd come later. He went to the club with his friends, other guys, you know, and he'd be late. When he was home, the girl had a stick and she hit him on the head. She yelled dirty words at him, and she hit him. She said, "You think you're kidding me! But you've got to come home early, or I'll fix you!" Well, that guy wouldn't say a word. Not a word! The night after, he was later than before, and she was behind the door. She was ready to beat him, see? But the husband grabbed her by the hair and then he beat her and beat her and beat her. Oh, boy! She was like dead. And then he went out to call her mother and father. He says, "Hurry! Peppinella's got that disease. She's in bed, and she wants help." So, they run there, and when they get there they found the wife. Oh, she was in bad shape! She was black all over! So, they say, "Peppinella, what's the matter?" And the girl said, "Oh, he ruined me, he beat me up, see?" So the parents got mad and the mother started to yell. She said, "You, idiot! Son-of-a-bitch! You stay there, and don't do nothing! Go get the doctor!" So, the doctor went there and he saw her, and he fixed her. "Don't worry," he says, "she's O.K. She'll be all right in three or four days." Now the husband, you know, he gave the doctor twenty dollars. That's a lot, twenty dollars. To pay him, he gave twenty dollars; but the doctor, "No, no. It's only five dollars. My job is five dollars, not twenty." But then the husband says, "I know it. I know doctor. But my wife gets this disease—this illness, you know, almost every day. She gets it, and every time she gets it, I have to beat her up, see? So, I pay you also for the next times, and I won't have to worry because you're already paid, see?" Now, his wife was listening to him, you know? She was in bed, but she could hear all right. So she started screaming from her bed, "Peppino! Peppino!" That was the name of the husband, see? "Peppino, get the rest! Take it, 'cause I haven't got no disease no more. It's all over now!" Well, that's how some women are.

8: *The Foolish Bride*

Tale Types: Th 1450 (Clever Elsie) and Th 1384 (The Husband Hunts Three Persons as Stupid as His Wife).

I found the combination of the above two types only among Italian-born Rosetans, while the second generation seems to know only the first part.

Informant: Filomena Pagano Gonfalone. Text obtained in the Rosetan dialect.

(B: Bianco;   F: Filomena)

F: My children used to like this one. They used to say, "Ma tell us the story of the wine all over! Tell us the story of the foolish wife!" I used to know it better once, though, now I'm getting old and no good!

B: But try, maybe you'll remember.

F: Shall I say it in here [the tape recorder]? Won't they laugh at me, the way I speak?

B: Of course, not. Try.

F: All right then. My mother used to tell me that some time ago, in those villages up there in Italy, they were stupid, see? They didn't know things like we do now. They were pretty foolish then, see? So, there was a family that had the *osteria* [tavern], and they were right on the square, in the village square, and the village was on top of a mountain, like Roseto Valfortore. They had an only daughter, and her name was Carmela. Carmela was pretty and very stupid, as stupid as a stupid chicken. But she was pretty and she had everything she should have, see? So the men in town had eyes and they saw Carmela was pretty, and they courted her a lot. To make it very short, one guy one morning takes his courage and goes to speak to the parents, to say that he wanted the girl, that is, you know? To do the *trasuta* [the traditional, formal request] had to be done on a Sunday night, and he did so. He went there on a Sunday night, and he ate with them and they said many nice things, and they laughed and they had a good time. Finally, he told them what he wanted. He said that he wanted to marry Carmela, see? He said, "I want to marry Carmela, and I came here to ask for your permission." And so the parents were happy because he was a wealthy boy, see? But they said they had to think about it a few days. They say, "Son, we want you to come back such and such day for the answer!" Because you don't want to look like you were waiting for that, see?

B: Yes.

F: People always do this. They never want to give satisfaction.

Well, he went again such and such a day and they said, "Yes. We like it." And to make it very short, they decided on the date of the wedding, to get married. And they had to decide upon so many other things, like the trousseau, see? You don't get married without a pair of pants, see? You need shirts, linens, towels, pants, night-gowns, see? All that was fixed up. Then they had a fine wedding, and they got married all right. After that, they had a banquet in the tavern, and the guests wanted to eat and drink, see? You don't eat all those fine things without drinking, right? And so they needed lots of wine. But the wine they had in the shop was finished, and somebody had to go fetch some more, or the guests would go away. Now, it's bad luck if your guests leave, see? They needed wine, and the father called the daughter and said, "Carmela, go down in the cellar for some wine! Here's a bucket." And Carmela went down-stairs in the cellar. The cellar is way down in the grotto, you know how it is up there in our villages, no? The cellar is a cave, cold, dark, right? So, Carmela had to go down a long, dark stair and then she started to fill the bucket with the wine. But, I told you they were nuts, no? The family was stupid. So was Carmela, and she started thinking, "God, I got married and now I may have a kid. And if I get a kid, I'll have to call him some name. Which name should I call him? Filippo? Gaetano? Peppino? Ciccuzzo? Yes, I believe I should call him Ciccuzzo, yeah!" She said, "Ciccuzzo! Cic-cuzzo, my sweet baby!" Then she thought, "What if Ciccuzzo gets sick? Oh, my God! How terrible! Because he may even die if he gets sick! And if he dies? Oh, if he dies, we would all cry. Cic-cuzzo! Ciccuzzo! Ciccuzzo, baby!" And this idiot girl, see, kept on crying and calling her baby. She cried, "Ciccuzzo, why did you die? Why did you leave your dear mother? Oh, my baby! Ciccuzzo!" And, to make it very short, we leave this idiot there. She even for-got about the wine, the wedding, and the banquet; and the wine was all over the grotto, all over. There was wine all over the floor, like a lake, like a big sea! We leave her there, and we go back up-stairs, right? The guests were starting to yell at the owner. They were thirsty, and they wanted wine. They said, "Get more wine!" And the man called his wife. Says, "Go down, will you? Go see our daughter, Carmela, why she isn't back?" And so the mother goes down the stairs, and she find Carmela crying. And, I told you they were nuts. This woman doesn't even mind the wine. All she does, she asks Carmela, "What's the matter? Why do you cry?" And Carmela tells her the story, says, "See? I got married now, and I may have a baby. Then I may call the baby Ciccuzzo. Then, Ciccuzzo may get sick and may die, see?" And what do you think the mother did? The mother cried, too! She did! She cried, "Ciccuzzo, why did you leave your grandmother alone? Ciccuzzo! Ciccuzzo!" All nuts! And the wine! The wine was all over! All over! But now we must leave these two idiots there, and we go back to the banquet, all right? Up there the guests were leaving already because they were thirsty, see? So, the father decided he had to go down himself to see what were those two damn women doing there, see? Well, he went there. But he was one of the family, see? So, he was nuts too! He found his women crying, and he forgot about the wine and the banquet and the guests. All he did was asking, "What's the matter? What's the matter?" And his wife, that other idiot, she says, "Oh, listen to this. Carmela got married, and she may get a child and the child may be called Ciccuzzo, and he may get sick and then he may die! See? He may die! Then, if he dies, we would all cry! We would cry: Ciccuzzo! Ciccuzzo! Ciccuzzo!" And that other fool, the father, he started weeping and mourning, too. "Ciccuzzo! Why did you leave your poor grandfather? Why did you die? Ciccuzzo! Ciccuzzo! Ciccuzzo!" And who thought of the wine? Nobody! Nobody! The wine was all over the cantina, all over the grotto. Now, that poor fellow up there was alone, the groom, I mean the husband, was alone because all the guests had left, see? He was mad; he didn't know what to do, and he went down, too. When he found those three fools there, crying, "Ciccuzzo! Ciccuzzo!" he was shocked. He thought, "These people must be out of their minds! These are nuts! Real, solid nuts!" The poor boy. He wasn't a professor or a genius, either, but he was sane, see? Those weren't! Well, he had to realize, he said, "These are nuts, and I've got to get out of here. I'm leaving before it's late!" And so, he left. But, before he left, he told those people there, "Look, I'm leaving. I won't come back to you unless I find three people in the world who are more stupid than you! If I find those three persons, I come back, but how can I find anybody so stupid? So, I'm leaving." He was right! He was mad at them, and he went away, see? See, how stupid some women are?

B: Sure.

F: Stupid, like stupid chickens! Well, let's leave them now. Let's go after the boy, the husband who left. Well, he was riding a mule, because he couldn't walk around the world, see? He had to go far, very far! He passed mountains and rivers, and towns and lakes. He ate and he slept and he went to the next village. And then he ate and slept and he left again. Every day the same thing. He

went always looking for stupid people; but he couldn't find anybody *that* stupid! One day, though, he was getting close to a village.
You know how it is in Italy, villages have walls and walls have
doors, arches, see? Like archways?

B: Yes.

F: Well. So, he was going to enter in this village one evening,
and he saw some people all well-dressed following a bride. Now the
bride was on a horse, see? She was on the horse and the groom
was on another horse, but they went slowly, and the others were
following and were crying, too. They stopped by the door, and they
wept even more. They looked desperate. The bride was in tears and
she screamed, "Poor me, poor me!" Now the fellow was curious.
He went there and asked a guy there. He says, "What's the matter?" That guy says, "Don't you see what's the matter? Don't you
see that the bride and the groom can't pass the arch?" "They can't
pass the arch?" "Sure! The arch isn't high enough, don't you see?
And the bride can't go out of town, she can't go to her new house
with her husband, see? Bad luck! Bad luck! She'll have to go back
to her father, now!" Of course, our fellow, he couldn't believe his
eyes, I mean his ears. He figured, "These people must be out of
their minds; this bride *is* more stupid than my wife, sure!" So, he
goes there, and he says that he knows how to fix the thing. And they
say, "Really? And how much do you want for it?" "I want a sack
of gold and one of silver." And that was a lot, see? But that was a
rich bride, and they paid for the gold and for the silver. And after
the guy had received the money, he said, "Now, get down." He said
to the bride that she had to step down from the horse, see? And the
husband, too, because they hadn't enough brains to know that, see?
They couldn't think of that! The nuts! So, they were surprised, but
they did as he wanted, and then he said, "Now, give me the horses."
And they gave him the horses. So he made the horses go through
the arch, see; without those idiots, the horses did fit, right? Then,
he says, "Now, you two pass here!" And they did it. And then he
says, "Now you. Take your horse and ride." And, to the husband,
"You, too, get on your horse and ride." And, you should see the
feast they made! They were all happy they could pass the arch,
see? The bride and the husband and all those other nuts there!
What a crowd of idiots! And they had paid, too; this is the best
part of all, see? To pay all that to pass that arch! And so, that fellow figured, "Those are the persons I was looking for; I think I
found them. That means my wife isn't that stupid after all. Let me
go back to her as I promised I would." And he went back. He went

back because he had found a bunch of people who were even more stupid than his wife, see? That's the story of the wine all over and the foolish wife.

9: *A Fool Had a Donkey*

Tale Type: Th 1682 (The Groom Teaches His Horse To Live without Food).

This tale is usually told among Italians as an example of enforced habits of frugality. Under Fascism, the fool was often Il Duce who was daily reducing the citizens' rations.

Informant: Rose Anicola De Bernardinis. Text obtained in the Rosetan dialect with frequent English words.

(B: Bianco;   R: Rose)

R: This was one of those fools, you know? Some people think they can get rich by not eating or something! Well, as Pap used to say—I don't remember the name of that guy, but let's call him— well, Pasquale? Is it all right?

B: Oh, sure!

R: Pasquale, yeah! Well, Pasquale was a cart driver who carried things from one village to another because in those days up in the mountains of Italy they didn't have any trains or buses. They were poor, see? So he used to drive his wagon with the mule—the donkey rather—from Roseto to Biccari and to Alberona. He was poor, too, see? Because they didn't pay much in those days, who gave them? And the donkey went very slowly, too, so he couldn't make too many trips a day! So, Pasquale thought that, to spare money and to make some pennies, he would reduce the food for the donkey! He would give him less straw, or whatever they give donkeys, who knows? Well, he thought, "Why should he eat better than me? No!" And the next morning Pasquale went to the donkey who slept just behind his room in those days, see? He went there, and he gave him less straw, say, he gave him two pounds—or two kilos, maybe—less, see? Two pounds less, I think. The donkey, well, he didn't know it was less because they didn't have a scale or anything to weigh it, right? And then donkeys are stupid, as my father used to say. My father had a donkey once, see? Well, the donkey didn't know it and, of course, he ate and kept quiet, didn't say anything, didn't protest, see? Now, Pasquale was expecting some protest, and he didn't get any! So he was happy. He went to his wife—let's call her Filomena—and says, "Filomena! Listen, we can give less food to that animal, so we can eat more!" See the idiots! Well, he was happy he had spared that little straw that morning. He was all happy. Next morning, he went to the donkey again, to bring him food, you know? And he figured, "What if I try to give him even less today? I'll try; then, if he says something, I'll give him more!" And he tried to give the animal another two pounds less, see? Another two or three pounds less. He gave him the straw and then he stayed there to see what would happen. Because that idiot thought the animal would say something, see? But, of course, not a word! The animal didn't notice it. Maybe his stomach noticed, see? but he didn't know it! And then, imagine Pasquale! He ran to his wife singing almost, you know? "I made it! I made it! He didn't say a word! I gave him only—only—well, let's say three pounds of straw—I gave him only three pounds of straw! And he didn't notice it! See? We can give him nothing even, and maybe he won't speak at all! I'll try tomorrow, oh, yeah, I'll try!" And they were so happy they had found this trick, see? So, when the next morning comes, Pasquale had been up all night for the joy, see? He couldn't go to sleep for the joy of what he had invented! He gets up, he shaves, he drinks his—not coffee; my father used to say they had no coffee then in Italy. He has his breakfast, anyhow, and he goes to see his donkey! But he didn't take any straw at all with him, see? He wasn't going to give anything to that poor animal! He just went to see the donkey, not to feed him, see? So, he went there and he says, "Good morning," and then he says, "Well, are you all right?" Now, the donkey made a move with the head that looked like "yes," but he didn't mean that! He didn't! But Pasquale thought he said, "Yes," and so he asked whether he was hungry, you know? He said, "Do you want to eat?" And at that moment, you know, the animal moved like this, and it looked like he says, "No," see? So Pasquale was happy and he went to his wife, Filomena. He says, "Filomena! Our donkey got used." She says, "Got used to what?" "To fast! See? He doesn't need any food, really, and we have been wasting all that good expensive straw! But now it's all over! Food is over! We're rich!" And the two went out and got drunk. They sang and they danced all night, see? Then they went to sleep. When he woke up, Pasquale went right to the donkey, and he found the donkey asleep, see? So, he smiled and he tiptoed back to the kitchen to his wife. Says, "Filomena, don't make all that noise, he is asleep! See how nice? He is asleep now, and we don't have to bother any more! He got so used now, he won't ask for more." And he went to do something in the cellar and then he had to go to the market, and so he was busy that day and he didn't think of the donkey any more. Then the night came and, of course, they went to sleep and they slept until next morning. Then Pasquale got up, and he got dressed. Then he thought he would go see his donkey because he had to go to Alberona and he would tell him to get ready to go, see? So he goes. When he gets there, he finds the animal asleep, again. This time he gets mad, see? He starts yelling, "What's the matter? Do you think you don't work anymore? Get up, wake up! Come on! Ah! Ah!—This is how they used to yell at donkeys up in Italy—Ah! Ah!" But there was no "Ah" and "Oh" that could do. So, he looks down. He tried to touch him, and he moves him. And can you imagine? The donkey was dead, dead like a stone of marble, like a piece of shit. Just like that! He was dead! And, of course, Pasquale started weeping and yelling, says, "Why did you do this to me? I had taught you not to eat. I had taught you to live without food, and you die like this? How stupid of you, and how ungrateful to your master!" And he cried, and he wept; and I think he is still mourning now, you know?

10: *The Father Sends His Daughter to a Convent School*

Tale Type: I could not find a specific type number for this tale on the Thompson's index. However, it should be included between Th 1628 (The Learned Son and the Forgotten Language) and Th 1628* (So They Speak Latin).

Informant: Mariantonia Casciano, "Puttanella."

Text obtained in the Rosetan dialect.

(B: Bianco;   P: Puttanella)

P: This one cannot be told in here [the tape recorder]. It's too dirty!

B: Really?

P: Of course! But I like jokes, see? This is the way I talk, and they call me "Puttanella" for this, see? Well, there was a man who had just lost his wife, and he was a widower, like me. I am a widow, too. His wife had passed away with a heart disease, see? And he was so sad all the time that he had no time to bring up his daughter. He had a little girl called Teresuccia and she was a nice girl, you know? His father thought, "I'm so desperate; I'm not able to bring her up, and I have to go to work so she will be in the street all the time. Poor Teresuccia. She won't learn nice things in the street! She won't become a nice young lady like her poor mother wanted. And I am a man. How can a man educate a girl?" And he was so worried, you know? Because he was a nice father, not like many who like to go to bed all the time with any whore they find! He didn't want to get married and give his daughter a stepmother, see? Stepmothers aren't very nice to stepdaughters, like Cinderella, you know that story?

B: Oh, I hope you tell me that.

P: If I can remember. But this poor man was decent, see? He wanted his daughter to become a fine lady, and so he thought about it and he thought. Finally, he says, "I know what I'll do! I'll take Teresuccia to a convent school. The nuns are fine ladies, and they will give my daughter a fine education. She'll learn how to talk nice, how to do things, how to cook, and all that. That's what I'll do!" And so, the poor man took his daughter one morning, and he gave her a bag of clean clothes and a few pennies, and he says, "Now we go to a place where you'll learn things fine." And they leave the village by mule and went very far, far away, until they went—to Napoli, I think. It was a city, with fine palaces and monuments, you know? Artistic! And they went to a palace where they found the convent, the house with the nuns. And so, they went in, and the father recommended that they teach Teresuccia fine manners, right? He had to pay, too, of course! Nuns want money, you know? They are ladies that need money. Anyway, he had to leave after that, and he went away. The nuns were glad they had Teresuccia because she was sweet, see? She was nice and good and she helped in the kitchen and all that. In other words, they liked the girl, and she was happy there. One day, though, the nuns had to call some workers in the convent because the palace was broken— not broken, but very old and in bad shape, see? They had to fix it, and they had to work there. So they called a few men from the city to work there. Now, of course, those were working men, like my poor husband was, see? Like all our men, right? Well, they don't talk Latin or Greek! No, sir! They talk like—well, simple! Plain, you know? Like me. I call things simple! Not vocabulary. Do you know what I mean?

B: Sure.

P: That's it! So, those men talked that way, and they went to work there. All day they were working and hollering like this, "Pete! Stop chatting and bring your ass here, will you?" Or they would say, "Hai, Phil! You damn prick! Is this the way to pull the rope?" And they said also, "That whore of your mother made you so stupid." They said, "Fuck" and "Shit," you know what I mean? I told you, it was dirty! [She laughs.] Well, the girl, you know, she heard all that, but she couldn't figure what it meant because she was growing as a fine lady, see? So she ran to the Mother Superior

to ask, see? She says, "Mother, what's a 'fuck'?" Just like that, she
asked for that, see? And that poor nun, what could she say?
She had no time to think about it, and so she said, "Well, 'fuck' is
——to—to take off one's hat, see?" And then the girl said, "And
what's a 'prick'?" My God! The poor nun jumped up, you know?
To hear that word from that innocent kid in a convent? The nun
didn't know what to say; but she had to make up an answer, so she
said, "Well, yes, of course, that's a—a hat, a man's hat, right." So,
the little girl saw that the nun knew all the words she didn't know,
and she went right on, see? She went on. She said, "And what's
a 'whore'?" "Oh, a—a whore? Well, yes, right! A whore is—is—it's
one of those, you know those wardrobes, it's a closet, that's what it
is!" "I see," said Teresuccia, "but what's an 'ass' now?" The poor nun
was almost fainting; she was passing away, see? She was shivering,
and yet she had to answer, or it wouldn't look good that a nun
didn't know words, right? What is she, an ignorant? So, she took
her courage, and she told her. "An 'ass' is the hanger, inside the
closet, see? A hanger, that's all." And that was all for that day
because the little girl was satisfied, see? She didn't suspect anything, see? She went to play and the nun went to lie down on a
couch, to rest. She had a headache by then, see? And so they went
on, and the workers left the palace because they had fixed it. Then,
of course, the girl was anxious to see her father again after months,
you know? And she wrote to her father to come to see her, that
she was grown up, and she was good at school, and all that. The
poor man had to borrow some money and he had to sell a few
things, too, to find the money for the trip, see? He wasn't wealthy,
he was a poor peasant, like my poor father, right? But he was
happy to sacrifice for the education of his daughter, so he goes to
see Teresuccia and he goes there to see her. When he rang the bell.
When he rang the bell, Teresuccia knew it already! She had been
at the window, you know, and she knew it! She was excited, oh,
boy! She went to open the door, and she jumped on her daddy,
and she kissed him, and this and that. Then, you know, she was
anxious to be nice to him and she went like this, "Daddy, please
fuck your prick now, fuck your prick, and put it in the whore's
ass, come!" See? She said so, and then she repeated, "Come on,
Daddy, fuck your prick, put it in the whore's ass, come on! Or give
it to me, and I'll put it in the ass!" And all that, see? Then—[she
laughs and can hardly speak]—well—what do you think? Her poor
old father there! He went pale, he turned red and yellow and
green! I think he dropped dead, honestly!

11: *It's Good They're Cherries!*

Tale Type: Th 1689 (Thank God, They Weren't Peaches).
Informant: Mariantonia Casciano, "Puttanella."
Text obtained in the Rosetan dialect.

(B: Bianco; P: Puttanella)

P: Anyway, this is even better [than the previous one]. Angelone used to tell me this one. Madonna! We used to laugh when he told the story of the cucumbers! Oh, boy! That's funny!

B: Well, tell it, tell it now, then.

P: I'll see if I can say it. The thing was in a village up in Italy, long, long ago! Long, long ago. Those days, you know, Italian villages used to have doors, you know? Huge, big doors that the enemies could not get in, or the robbers, because there were bandits, robbers. I remember that, I do! Not that they closed the doors, but I remember the bandits, yeah! Well, so they would lock those big doors. They had huge iron keys and gigantic locks, see? Well, this place I was telling you was a mountain village and all around there were mountains and more villages built on top of those other mountains, see? You could see those villages from your own window, see? Oh, I remember that! Anyway, this village was called—Angelone said—how did he say now? I believe he said San Bartolomeo—San— let's make it San Bartolomeo, yeah! Well, you see, at that time, they had just finished a war, a big war with a prince who came from Germany, a king, a German king. And they had won against the Germans, see? Like we won lately. But then, see? All the dead bodies were left in the fields, and they had no medical assistance and trucks and funeral homes at that time. So those corpses were going bad; they were stinking and they had worms! Oh, terrible! So, it happened that the rumor was that the plague was coming to the village, see? You know what's the plague? A dirty disease! Terrible! They all die!

B: Yes.

P: And some people were getting sick and the whole village was afraid the plague would come to town and would kill them all. So, like we have a mayor and the City Hall? They, too, they had some—some chief, like a duke, see? Like up in Roseto we have the Marquis Saggese, see? So, they had a chief and this chief wrote a letter—not a letter, a notice, that's a large notice that you put on the walls of the houses, see? So everybody that can read, reads it! Then, of course, poor peasants can't read and then they had men who went around the village with a trumpet, see? Oh, I remember that! Yeah! This man went around the streets and he called the people and he announced what he had to announce, see? Like: "Tomorrow there'll be a procession!" And things like that, see? Well, so, for those persons who couldn't read, there was this announcement in the streets. And so it happened in that village, see? Anyway, the order was that the doors had to be closed. The village doors had to be closed and nobody could go out because they could bring back infection, see? But nobody could come in either. Like the farmers from the mountains could not come to town and sell the fruit, for example, because they say that the fruit had the plague, too, see? The fruit had it. So, the population couldn't eat the fruit and could not go any place and all that. Now, one of those letters was put on the outside walls, too, near the big door, see? To tell the foreigners that they could not bring the fruit to town because the fruit had the plague, as I told you, see? And so, everything was fine. One day, though, two farmers came from the country and they wanted to sell their fruit. They had two huge baskets of fruit that they brought from the fields, see? They carried them on their shoulders, and that way, they entered the door that was open that minute. That minute, see? The guard—the sentinel, he was away for something, I can't remember what it was—but he wasn't there that minute and the two men went in! They went right in. And then, the letter was there, but they couldn't read it! Do you think they could read? Of course, not. So, they went in and they started to sell the fruit in town! See? Now, I forgot to tell you an important thing: the letter, the notice, said that whoever was caught selling fruit in town would be punished! He would be punished, do you know how he would be punished?

B: How?

P: [Laughs.] Well, listen. The guards would stick the fruit they wanted to sell into their ass! One by one, yes! One by one they would stick the fruit into their asses! [Laughs.] True! Well. Then we go back to those two. I forgot their names, too, but let's call them Ciccio and Martino, right? Martino and Ciccio. Now, Ciccio was selling cherries, see? Nice, red, hard cherries. And while he was selling them, the guard came back from—well, from where he was, and he yelled at Ciccio and Martino. He went like this, "You murderers! Criminals, dirty pigs! You want to kill us all, right? Didn't you see the notice out there? All of them, I'll stick all of them into your ass! And you, too [to Martino], you, too." So, anyway, a few more guards come and they grab the poor devils who didn't know what was going on and drag them to the police station! To the police station. At the police station, you know, the guard does it like this! He sits on a chair and makes Ciccio kneel down in front of him. Ciccio kneels down, see? And the guard has the basket with the cherries right here, at his side, and he picks them up, one by one! [Laughs.] He picks them up and sticks them right into Ciccio's ass! [Laughs.] See? And Ciccio started laughing, you know? He started laughing and, of course, the guard couldn't figure out why. He thought, "What the hell? Is he happy? Why is he laughing instead of screaming?" And so, he asks, he says, "You son-of-a-bitch, dirty idiot, what's the matter? How come you laugh?" And, well—can you imagine? Ciccio could hardly speak and kept on laughing. But then he said it. He said, "Well, of course, these are cherries. I'm thinking of Martino: He's got cucumbers in his basket!" [She laughs.]

12: *Ezzolle* (That's All)

Italian-American joke.
Told by Giovannina Martino in the Rosetan dialect. The words in italics are the original Italian-American words (e.g., *ezzolle*, that's all).

(B: Bianco; G: Giovannina)

G: This one is called "A Hundred Lire and *Ezzole*."

B: How do you say that?

G: Well, the husband wrote to his wife. He said, "Dear wife, I just send you a hundred lire and *ezzolle* [that's all]." Now, of course, his wife read the letter, and she saw that there was a hundred lire check, but she couldn't fine the *ezzolle*. It wasn't there! So she goes to her janitor, or the mailman, maybe. She says, "What do I do?" He says, "Go to the Post Office." She goes to the Post Office and she says, "My husband sent me a hundred lire check *ezzolle*. Give me a hundred lire *ezzolle*." And the clerk, you know, he took a hundred lire from the safe, and he gave her. This woman stayed on, waiting. She wouldn't leave, see? So the man says, "But I gave you the money." She says, "But my husband sent me *ezzolle*, too!" He says, "I gave you the hundred lire." "But I want *ezzolle!*" The clerk, "Well, I don't know what's *ezzolle*." The woman insisted, though, see? She was determined; she said, "What sort of clerk are you? Can't you give *ezzolles?*" Then the clerk got bored, and he got wise, too, see? He said, "All right, then, come over here, go around the counter and come here, I'll give you *ezzolle*. You want *ezzolle?* I give you *ezzolle!* I got *ezzolle!* [Laughs.] And he makes love to her, see? That's the *ezzolle* he had! Anyway, next day, this woman goes to *u cumbare* [godfather] and asks him to write a letter for her husband. Because, you see? She could read a little, but she couldn't write. I'm like that, too, you know? Well, anyway. So she wrote—*u cumbare* wrote—"Dear husband, I went to the postman and he gave me the hundred lire and *ezzolle*." Her husband in America read the letter, and he thought, "What did she get?" Well, anyway, after nine months, this woman has a baby and, you know, she was mad because she had nine already and she didn't need anymore. So she had *u cumbare* write another letter to her husband. She said, "Dear husband, send me the hundred lire, but don't send me the *ezzolle* anymore!"

13: *I Can't Hear You!*

Tale Type: Th 1777 A* (I Can't Hear You).
Informant: Costanza Falcone, "Connie."
Text obtained in the Rosetan dialect with frequent use of English.

(B: Bianco; C: Connie)

C: Oh, this one is funny! My father used to tell me many years ago, you know my father? The brother of my uncle! Uncle A. Z., you know him.

B: Sure.

C: My father says that up in Italy those priests are smart! They preach and they pray, they sing mass and all that, but they eat a lot, too! And they go to bed with the wives of the other men! Well, as I said, my father said that up in Roseto one day there was a priest, one of those priests. He had land and his house was full of any sort of good things. He had hams and salami, cheese, olives, everything! He had oil, too, olive oil, you know? They have good olive oil there. So he had lots of oil and he kept it behind the church because his house was too full with the rest of the things he had. So, he had noticed that his oil was diminishing that year and he hadn't touched it yet because he was still using the one from the previous season, see? Well, he saw that the oil was going and he was mad, because he suspected the sexton. But he wasn't sure, and he didn't know how to make the sexton confess it. To top all that, the priest had an affair with the sexton's wife, see? So, he didn't tell the sexton about the oil because he was afraid the sexton would tell him about his wife, see? So, the business went on and on. Until Christmas came and, of course, the sexton had to confess for communion, see? It was Christmas and he had to. So, the priest saw him coming, and he was happy because he figured, "Now, I'll serve him right! Now he has to confess it!" And so, the sexton kneels down in front of that window, you know? He stood there and waited, then he started confessing minor little things, see? Like: I dropped a dish in the kitchen, or I forgot to say goodnight to my wife, see? Minor things because he was a son-of-a-bitch, too, see? The sexton was like his master. So the priest waited and then he said, "Son, tell your brother confessor: Who took the oil from the jar?" But the sexton was a son-of-a-bitch, I told you! He says, "What? I can't hear you!" And the priest, of course, he repeated, he went: "Son, dear son, confess to God. Who took the oil?" And the sexton went right on, "I can't hear, I can't hear you. What?" Now the priest was getting mad, see? He got wise, see? But the sexton couldn't hear, he couldn't. Then the priest figured, "All right. He thinks he's smart, but he doesn't know how smart I am! I am a priest!" So, he sticks his head out of the other window and tell the sexton, "Listen, why don't you come in here and I come out there? This way. I'll show you how it's possible to hear from where you are now!" The priest thought to be smart, see? And the sexton, that's all he wanted! He said, "Yes." And they shifted, they changed. The priest went to kneel out there and the sexton went inside the box. All right. Then, the sexton spoke to the priest, he says, "You tell me now. Who fucks my wife?" Ah! The priest out there had no choice. He had to answer, "I can't hear! I can't hear you." So the sexton came out laughing and told the priest, "See? I told you I couldn't hear!"

VII

Folksongs

14: *Cecilia*

A love ballad popular throughout Italy and among Italian-Americans of all regional groups. I collected numerous versions of *Cecilia* in New York as well as in both Rosetos.

Bibliographical references: Constantino Nigra, *Canti popolari del Piemonte* (Torino, 1854–88), n. 3/a, p. 48; Gianbattista Bronzini, *La canzone epico-lirica nell'Italia Centro-meridionale* (Roma, 1961), I, 457–528.

The story has close analogues with Shakespeare's *Measure for Measure* and with the legend of Colonel Kirke as it is narrated in D. Hume, *History of England* (1685–88), LXII.

Informant: Giannina Castellucci.

Text obtained in the Rosetan dialect.

1. Oh, how greatly Cecilia weeps,
   Weeps for her husband
   Who is dying in jail
   And they want to take his life.

2. The story of Cecilia
   Is famous in the world.
   "Hurry, hurry, Cecilia,
   Hurry to the Captain.

3. Hurry to the Captain,
   The Captain of the King.
   Ask the Royal Captain
   If he can set me free!"

4. "I beg you, Royal Captain,
   I beg for your mercy.
   Peppino is in your prison,
   Won't you set him free?"

5. "Don't cry, sweet Cecilia,
   This grace I'll give to you:
   His freedom you will have
   If one night you sleep with me."

6. "Forgive me, noble Captain,
   It is not for me to say:
   I'll ask my dear Peppino
   His reply I'll bring back."

7. "Peppino, dear Peppino,
   These words he said to me,
   If I sleep with him one night,
   He says you will go free."

8. "Go there, go there, Cecilia,
   Go and spend one night with him,
   Don't mind, don't mind the honor,
   Only care about my life!"

9. "Listen, noble Captain,
   To what Peppino said,
   If only for one night,
   We go to bed and rest."

10. At the stroke of midnight,
    Cecilia gives a deep sigh,
    "What troubles you, Cecilia?
    Why do you sigh like this?"

11. "How can I feel, my Captain?
    My heart is full of pain.
    My husband is in prison
    And I am here with you!"

12. "Cecilia, oh, my Cecilia,
    Do not weep like this.
    There are princes, dukes, and barons
    Who want to mary you."

13. The morning comes at dawn,
    To the balcony she runs:
    And there below she sees
    Peppino's stake-pierced head.

14. "Oh, Captain, Oh, my Captain,
    You have betrayed me well!

You took away my honor
And you've cut Peppino's head!"

15. "Don't worry, sweet Cecilia,
Do not distrust me so:
As a prince and as a Captain
I shall be a husband to you!"

16. "Oh, I want no princes,
No captains and no dukes,
I want my dear Peppino
To whom I was wed."

17. She cuts all her hair,
She dresses like a man,
She pulls out a pistol
And kills the Captain.

18. The story of Cecilia
Is famous in the world,
The Captain of the King,
Was killed by her hand.

15: *St. Catherine the Sinner*

Italian religious ballad.

Bibliographic references: Giuseppe Pitrè, *Biblioteca delle tradizioni popolari siciliane* (Palermo, 1870–1913), II, no. 946; Raffaele Lombardi-Satriani, *Canti popolari calabresi* (Napoli, 1926–40), IV, 370–385.

This ballad is usually sung in a solo voice and to a simple and monotonous melody, similar to the recitation of litanies. I included it in this selection because it is one of the best-remembered songs among Italian-American women of all regional groups.

Informant: Maria Ronca (Protestant).

Original text in the Rosetan dialect.

(M: Maria)

1. One day it was the feast of Mary
And Caterina all in gold and silver,
All dressed up she walked into the church
Without even taking holy water.

2. She looked not at the Virgin's face,
She only looked at the handsome knights
And most of all at that noble knight
Who was kneeling down by the altar.

3. Caterina stared at that knight,
   But that knight saw none of this.
   He took the holy water and left the church,
   And Caterina stayed there and cried.

4. A confessor was in there, he was confessing,
   He said, "Caterina, why do you weep?"

   M: That confessor was Jesus Christ, see?

   "I cry because I am a great sinner
   And nobody wants to come to me!"

5. "Oh, Mother, Mother, there is a sinner,
   She is the worst of all the sinners,
   Why won't we forgive her,
   Why won't we forgive this sinner?"

6. "Son, oh, Son, if we want to save her,
   You must get dressed like a knight,
   You must get dressed like a knight
   And to her balcony you must go."

7. "Oh, Mother, Mother, what do you say to me?
   Caterina smells of mortal sin!"
   "Son, oh Son, if you want to save her,
   You must dress like a knight
   And hurry to the balcony of the sinner."

8. And Jesus Christ did this thing.
   Jesus Christ dressed like a knight
   To Caterina's window then he went,
   He went to the balcony of the sinner.

9. Caterina was at her window,
   She was watching people from up there,
   She saw the knight coming down the street
   And sent three maids to invite the knight in.

10. Caterina liked the handsome knight,
    She had him all in her heart.
    And each step that he had to climb,
    The knight got all covered with blood.

11. But Caterina saw none of this,
    "Oh, knight, dear knight, your sweet mouth,
    Your sweet mouth let me kiss."
    "Stay away! Stay away, stay away from me!"

12. "Sweet, sweet knight, listen to me,
    Is your person wounded or cut?"
    "I am not cut, and I am not wounded
    And I need no help from Caterina!"

13. "Sweet knight, sweet knight, listen to me,
    Let's leave all these words and talks,
    Let's leave all these words and talks
    And let's go to the table and eat."

14. He went to the table and he ate,
    And each dish that Caterina brought in
    Was all covered with blood,
    And Caterina understood none of this.

15. "Sweet knight, are you wounded or cut?"
    "Caterina, stay away from me,
    I am neither cut nor wounded,
    Stay away, your sin is too grave."

16. "Sweet knight, sweet knight, listen to me,
    Let's leave all this good eating,
    And let's go to bed and have a rest,
    Let's go to bed and let us rest."

17. The knight went to the bed of the sinner,
    Jesus Christ went to that bed,
    And as she was brushing the flies away,
    He nailed himself down as on a cross.

18. "Alas! Alas!" When Caterina saw him,
    "Who is this in my own house?
    Is he the true son of Mary?
    The true son of Mary came to me!"

19. All she had she gave to the poor
    And with a stone she hit her white breast.
    A golden chair was pulled down from Heaven
    And to Heaven like a saint she was borne.

16: *An American Family (Una famiglia di americani)*

Italian religious ballad of the emigration times. My informants remember the printed broadside that circulated in Roseto, Pa., until not long ago.

This text was sung by Filomena Pagano (age 80) in the Rosetan dialect and in the monotone, chant-like style typical of these ballads.

Oh, great Virgin of Mt. Carmel,
Oh, most glorious and fine queen,
You're your son's most worthy mother
And the Holy Ghost's bride.
Those who call you from their heart
Every day you'll grant them graces.
   Come and listen, you good people,
   What great miracle was to happen:
   Of Americans a whole family [returned migrants]
   They were saved by Maria.
   If you pray to her every moment,
   By Maria you'll be contented.
And that family though was pious,
Poor and hungry lived the life,
Then to America they did go
For to change their luck in life.
And with work and Mary's help
Rich indeed they were returning.
   And with great and mighty vessel,
   On the ship they went one day,
   And with the help of our Maria,
   They were sailing back to here [Italy].
   And with the air that was most windy
   Began to sail this noble ship.
Once it got on the deep blue sea,
Where you could not see no land,
For misfortune and bad luck,
A mighty storm began to blow,
And the wind that would not stop
A cruel tempest soon it brought.
And the ship went up and down
And two masts got blown away
And the water with the breakers
Right inside the ship was pouring.
Here they all began to cry
That they were all going to die.
   But the father of the family,
   Though he was all full of fear,
   He remembered the *abitino*
   Of Mt. Carmel that he wore,
   And he took it from his breast
   And he kissed it with devotion.
Then in tears he called so loud,

"Oh, dear Lady of Mt. Carmel,
I love you with strong affection,
Won't you save my poor life now,
And won't you spare this noble ship
That may bring us to salvation?"
   Oh, the miracle, oh, the miracle,
   At the top of a high, high mast,
   There appeared a burning fire,
   And a woman in there shined.
   And no one there could believe it
   But the Virgin was up there.
In the night the sea was black,
And the way was not secure,
But the shining lamp of Mary
Upon the sea she led the way
And for seventeen more days
The fine ship she made a-sail.
   Now the sea was good and quiet,
   For Maria the way she led.
   Every morning they did pray
   With full heart to the *abitino:*
   If you wear it all the time,
   Next to you will be Maria.
   Then to Sicily got that vessel,
   To the port for to land,
   And the lamp had gone away,
   And with joy they went back home.
Then the village they united
And Maria they celebrated,
All together they were singing
And a feast they gave the Virgin.
If this song on you you'll carry
You'll be safe from here to eternity.

VIII

Interviews in Roseto, Pennsylvania

(*excerpts*)

1. *The Yearly Cycle*

Informants: Anthony Zilio' Falcone, American-born, Protestant; Costanza Falcone, American-born, Catholic; Pasquale and Matilde Bozzelli, American-born, Catholic. The languages used were both Italian and English.

(B: Bianco; A. Z.: Anthony Zilio'; C: Connie)

B: So, what happened after supper, on Christmas night?

C: Oh, only until lately, but we used to bring *a fagghia* [a big branch of a tree], you know *a fagghia?*

B: Tell me.

C: Yeah! At midnight, yeah! When we went to mass? Pap would make it, you know? He would put oil and fat on it, 'cause, you see, Pap was working in the quarry over here, and he was an engineer, see? He used to clean the wheels and things, and with that grease, he used to make *a fagghia!* He used to take a big, big branch of a tree, see? Put all that grease and stuff on it. Then he would light it, you know? He would light it in the night, like a huge torch it looked! God! What a light, you know? At night! And he wasn't the only one; they would go around the streets the whole night with these things, all night! They would take them first to the church and leave them out of the church there, during the mass, see? Then, again, with *a fagghia* all around Roseto and Bangor. Remember that, uncle Tony? [She turns to A. Z., her uncle.] Then boy friends would take it to their girl friends, too, right?

A. Z.: Of course, I remember! I used to do it myself! Every

Christmas night! Yeah! Not any more, though. These idiots, these kids today. What do they do?

C: Pajama parties! That's what they do now! Graduation parties! The son-of-a-bitch party! And then, you know, the *fagghia*, they say it keeps the—the witches; it keeps them away! The *janare*, you know? The *janare*—the witches, yeah! They say so, yeah. I don't think it's true, but they say so, you know? Because these witches, they had to go to mass, see? They had to go to midnight mass, or they'd lose their power—their art! So, they say they'd be recognized by *a fagghia!* Well, who knows? That's what they say anyway.

A. Z.: Yeah! Look. I'm Protestant and these things are things— well, Catholic, see? Well, I did it too, but I didn't believe it because I didn't know, see? But *a fagghia* was good! Yeah!

B: I see. Are there any other fires that you used to make or that you still make during the year?

A.Z.: St. Anthony! Sure! That's my saint! I'm Anthony, too! But not the one from Padua, see? This is St. Anthony the Abbot, the seventeenth of January, yeah! He is an old man with a white beard, you know?

B: Yes, I know him. So, what happens then?

A. Z.: That they still do it! Do you know what they do over here? They——

C: [She interrupts him]—I'll tell you. They keep all the Christmas trees, see? Then the young people here, they gather them out, in the corners of the streets, see? In the corners, for safety, see? And then they pile 'em up, see? And then they make these big fires: Real huge fires! You should see, Carla! That's called *u foche de Sand'Andonie* [the fire of St. Anthony], and there's also a disease that's called the same, you know? Right, uncle Tony? *U foche?*

A. Z.: Yeah! That's different, that's when you get all red and your skin gets all red like fire, see? Like fire all over! It's bad!

B: Yes. Well, I think you already told me about the blessing of the throat for St. Blaise, on February third. Do you remember any rhymes for that?

C: There's something—there is, but I don't remember now.

B: And what about the *Candelora* (Candlemas Day: February 2)? Do you——

C: —that's the weather! How is it? *"Si c'e u sole a Cannelora* —[She starts a proverb.]

A. Z.: —*de l'inverno ascemo fora!* See? If there's sun for Candlemas Day, winter is over, see? But if it rains, then winter goes on, see? It's true, you know?

B: I see. Now, last night you told me about Carnival. What about Lent?

C: Wait! I forgot to tell you that for St. Blaise, we cook the *scocche* [a ritual bread for that day]. But before we didn't. There was a lady up here and she had this devotion, see? She was the mother of Luca Pasquale. You met him last night.

B: Bozzelli?

C: Right. She used to make them, all around, see? She used to make them, like a hamburger roll, but baked, you know? She used to stay in front of the church on St. Blaise Day, and as people came out of mass, she would give one *scocche* each, see? For nothing! Now she died, and we bake them for ourselves. But, uncle Tony. Do you know who makes them now? Mary Birth! Mary Luncheonette, yes! Mary Birth, her husband was Blaise; he died too. They're dry and tough. They almost choke your throat! They choke you! It's a devotion for St. Blaise who protects your throat, see.

B: I see. So, let's talk about Lent, now.

C: Oh, that we do!

B: What do you do? Do you observe it?

C: Yes, everybody.

B: And who is Lent? An old woman, maybe?

C: She used to be like that, yeah! Not now, see? When my mother was alive, she used to make the doll. Everybody used to at that time!

B: What doll?

C: The old lady! Lent. The old lady! Everybody did it. They'd hang 'em on a rope in the street, see? A rope across the street, from one roof to another, and the old lady in the middle with the potato and the feathers!

B: A potato?

C: Yeah! She had a skirt, see? Like this. And under the skirt, she had a potato, you know, a potato? Well, a potato and they used to pin seven feathers on it, seven feathers for seven weeks of Lent, see? And every week we would go there; we kids would go there and take one out, see? We would take one feather out! That was on Sundays.

A. Z.: Yeah! My wife, too, she did that. We used to have our doll out here. Not any more!

B: I see. And then, by Easter, she had no more feathers, right?

A. Z.: Sure! Then we'd burn it.

C: Yeah! My godmother used to do it, too. She loved me, you know, because I was born at Easter.

(B: Bianco;   P: Pasquale;   M: Matilde)

B: Did you use to put on fancy dresses and masks?

P: For Carnival? Yeah! We used to go door by door and knock, see? We used to put on a mask and then we used to wear trousers instead of skirts and skirts instead of trousers, see? Trousers were a Carnival costume for girls, see? Now it's for every day! Then we used to spread our faces with the black from the stove, yeah! Or we would wear an old straw hat or we would dress like a priest, or a devil, see? We'd knock at doors and those people would let us in, see? Then, we would dance there, and they would laugh, oh, they'd have a good time, I tell you! Because they couldn't tell who we were, see? We had masks! They had to guess and we would ask, you know, we'd go like this, "Hi, *cumpa* [godfather; nearly everybody was a godrelative to other people], give us a sausage, will you? Then, of course, they'd find out who we were, see? And, boy! That was great!

B: And what do you do for Easter?

M: We make bread with eggs. Bread with eggs. It's for Easter. We make bread and, instead of water, we put eggs, see? On Holy Wednesday, we make this bread with eggs that has to last for the whole week, see?

B: I see. And what do you do on Palm Sunday?

P: We go to church in the morning, at a quarter to seven, see? Then, priest comes out and blesses all the palms on the altar. Then, he blesses the wheat, you know? Then, before the mass begins, there are some fellows who distribute the wheat and the palms to all the people in the church. And we must keep those palms until the next Easter, see?

B: Does the priest go house to house?

M: Yes, to give his blessing. But now no more, lately yes, now no more. I don't know why! Before, he used to come on Holy Saturday. It was that way ever since I was a little girl, but it just changed now. Maybe last year or two years before that. They come around visitation and they bless your home and you pay your church dues. He blesses your home, and he asks if you went to church. Father Leone did that and the younger one, too. Up to two years ago, yeah! One priest goes one way and one the other, see?

B: Does he collect and bless cakes and Easter eggs?

M: Until last year, yeah! We used to put the bread with eggs, the wine, you know? The bottle with the wine, the hardboiled eggs, the salami, you know? We would take the best tablecloths we had for that, the best embroideries, handmade! The priest had to come, see? We fixed the house for the priest. But here the priests want money, see? Not so much the eggs, like in Italy! They want dollars. Cash! All like that!

P: He doesn't always ask for it!

M: Yeah! But you've got to give anyhow! You don't feel right if you don't pay, see? The priest comes and blesses your home, your food, and things, and you let him out with nothing? And then, you see, American priests haven't got the baskets no more. They have a little pocketbook now to put the money in!

P: Carla, things are changing and this priest here is trying to make everything American! Even when you die it's different. When you die, now, the undertaker takes care of everything. The people try to do things, but it's not easy 'cause he wants no mourning, no nothing! And you have to do things when they don't see you!

B: Like what?

P: Well, like—like—well, you put one dollar for *u male pas-sagge* [a dollar for the journey], but you've got to sneak it in a pocket, see? You put a dollar and a handkerchief in the pocket.

B: Why the handkerchief?

P: To clean his nose! And a book if the dead man reads, see?

2. *Traditional Games*

Morra or "Throwing Fingers." A traditional pastime very popular among Italian-American men. See Phyllis Williams, *South Italian Folkways in Europe and in America* (New Haven, Conn., 1938), p.108.

Informant: Donato Martino, American-born.

The interview was in English.

(B: Bianco;   D: Donato)

D: Oh, that's fun! *Morra* is fun! In other words, you play like this: you throw fingers, see? I'm gonna say—*cingue* [five]! Then, you throw and I throw, too. Together, see? But I throw, say, three and you throw two, and I'll say "*cingue!*" It's five, right?

B: Yes.

D: Then, maybe, you throw two and say "*sei*" [six] and I throw four, and I say "*cinque*" [five]. Then it's yours, see why? Because four and two is six! It's yours, then.

B: I see and then what happens?

D: Then, if I beat you with the *morra*, you stay on one side and I'll go to the next one, to the next man, see? But we have sides, see? If I win, I'm boss and you're second boss. Let's try: *Quatto* [four]!

B: Two!

D: See? I beat you 'cause I threw one and you threw three!

Makes four, so I'm boss! I'm boss! Then, we may throw and both win. Then, we'd say, *"Uno pe d'uno"* [one each]. Don't you say the wrong number though! Watch!

B: All right. But tell me, do people play this game in English?

D: No! Only in Italian. And then, if you throw all five fingers, you'll say *"Tutt'a morra"* [the whole morra]. Then, you play boss and second boss. And, you know, they have all the drinks. If there's ten guys, they get ten glasses of wine, or beer, see? Better wine, though. You put 'em on the table, ten glasses. And say that I'm boss, all right? Well, say I invite her [his wife Rose] for a drink, and there's ten people: five on one side and five on the other. Then, I play with her and I beat her. See? Then, I go to the next person and maybe he beats me, this time! So, he goes to the guy next to me, till the one side is down! Then, if I win, I'm boss and then we've got to go for second boss! Everybody throw fingers and we count: one, two, three, four, six, see? Say it makes twenty-five! The one who is twenty-five is second boss. Now the glasses. You're the second boss and you invite, say, him [his son] for a beer; and I say, "No! He doesn't drink! This other guy drinks." That is one of my guys 'cause I'm boss and I decide! See? The whole thing is to try to get that side that lost to fly. They call "fly" that they don't drink, see? You'll try to get your side to drink and let 'em go dry! Sometimes, you know, they go dry for hours, you know? All afternoon even! Yeah! Oh, in hot days, oh, boy! That's fun, I enjoy that! Sometimes the boss has to drink all the glasses! He gotta drink and it's pretty hard, see? But it's fun.

B: I see. Can you play this game with other kinds of drinks? Soft drinks or whiskey?

D: No! Wine! Or at least beer.

B: Do the German or the Welsh men around here play this game with you?

D: No. This is only ours. It's Italian, see? Italian people always group together; the others don't. See? We gather in a home and play games, we play cards, we play. Or we gather at the Marconi Club, you know? And on Sundays and the Fourth of July, on Columbus Day, on Our Lady of Mt. Carmel Day.

3. *Storytelling*

The informant touches important aspects of storytelling habits in the community—his father's role as an important narrator, the informant's own similar role, usual audiences, place and time for storytelling, languages used, and transmission.

Informant: Carmine Malpiedo.

Text obtained in English.

(B: Bianco; C: Carmine; R: Rose)

C: Ev'ry generation is changing, changin', changin'! Before, the men were giants! The men and women *evene gevande* [were giants]! Tall, beautiful! My father used to say it: "*Alti, belli,*" he said; and now they're cuccuricù!

B: Cuccuricù?

C: They're . . . weaker! In other words, Pap said, it's gonna come the time the world will get wiser and weaker, yeah! And, it's comin'! Ever heard before they're gonna go to the moon? Lot of people is smart, wise, you know? They try to invent something else, and weaker. My father said so, and I knew my father! I could spot my father miles away! Other boys couldn't spot their father.

B: Did your parents speak good English?

C: Pap did, pretty good, yeah. Not Mam. Mam, she spoke better than my mother-in-law, though, yes. Her mother [his wife's] didn't speak, my mother could speak, not good, you know, but you could understand.

R: Because she worked in the mill!

C: She worked in the mill [his own mother] and then she was in New York City for a number of years, you know?

B: I see.

C: Because, if one is always with Italians, you can't learn, see? Now, my mother-in-law, she always raised the family, she never moved. She used to go to Italian stores and buy stuff and all that story, and then, you know, we always had to spend the evenings with our folks. Like we say, New Year's Day. We would go out and would go visit. Her uncles—I had no uncles—they all lived around here, and we'd play cards, we'd drink, we'd tell jokes till two, three o'clock in the morning. Also, we used to go house to house.

B: Oh, tell me this.

C: See? We used to go to Bangor Junction! We used to go to see zi' Fulippe [Uncle Philip], zi' Ntonie [Uncle Anthony] and so on. Then, by the time you had to have dinner, you either were drunk, or you couldn't eat! You couldn't, 'cause you go to places there and they all give you something. They all give you something. Then, we would sit and tell stories, like I told you yesterday.

B: Yes, you were telling me. Wouldn't you tell about that now?

C: Well. My father, in wintertime, we used to sit around the stove. That's when we had all our work done, and he would tell us the story. When it was about eight o'clock, he'd say, "Now, tomorrow." He'd do certain jobs, my sisters had to do their jobs and

tomorrow night we would continue the story. So, we would wait
for that night to come and we used to sit wait . . . and wait . . . what
would be the end of the story.

B: And did he know a lot of them?

C: Oh, yeah! He knewed a lot. A lot of stories!

B: All of them from Italy?

C: Oh, naturally. He all learned them in Italy!

B: Would he say the stories in English sometimes?

C: No. No. In Italian.

B: And did you tell them to your children?

C: I told my children in English. I told them in English.
I used to tell also when I was a boy, you know?

B: Oh, really? Tell me.

C: We didn't go to school. We would sit in the woods
somewhere, and I would say the stories. I would tell the boys the
story to pass time, see? That's why I kept on rememberin'.

B: Now, I wonder whether some of those boys have learned
the stories.

C: No! No! Those, they are almost all dead.

B: But do you think they told the stories to their children?

C: No! No. You see? They weren't those people! They used
to go out, playin' cards—they'd drink—or they turned out to be
runnarounds. They never stayed with the family, you see? But I
repeated the stories that Pap told me many, many times after!
Many, many.

B: In English?

C: In English. Oh sometimes, I put in an Ittalian word.
I wasn't that smart in English! Then, I would say, so, so.

B: Well, let's start with the one which you like best.

C: Well, once my father told us a story abbout a maggic
landern [magic lantern].

B: Oh, that must be good!

C: And, believe it or not, I saw the story in the movie
picture!

B: Really?

C: Yeah. The exactly story that Pap told me, told us
kids, we saw it in the movies: *La Lenderna maggica* [The Magic
Lantern].

B: Tell me this one.

C: Yeah, but, see? I have to think abbout—that's way
back! Way back, way back. And, oh! You are running that thing
now?

B: Yes.

C: Oh, shut that off now!

B: No, no. That's good for me.

C: Yeah? Well. I had run down to the movin' picture and by eight thirty I had to be home, otherwise the door would be locked, and I'd go for a whippin'!

B: Yes.

C: And, I used to beat my sisters, see? My sisters used to go out and I used to beat them up!

B: Really?

C: Yeah! And one Saturday night the story that Pap had told us, there it was, on the screen! Exactly the same thing! And it was played by an actor—he was a very good actor—Jack Hock, I think it was the name. He was the man that was supposed to be, the big, the big deal!

B: Yes. And where did you see this picture. In Roseto?

C: In Bangor. In Bangor there was a place, they used to call him the "music hall."

B: Well, couldn't you tell the *Lanterna Magica* now?

C: No. I can't think about it just now. But, I can think about *Aspre Agrimante, U rre tre portualle* [The King and the Three Oranges]. . . .

B: How many times did your father tell you this story?

C: Well, a year in and a year out! Because, one story he made it last, maybe, a week!

B: Really?

R & C: Yeah!

C: Sure! Otherwise, he would run short. Like Saturday: no stories. Sunday: no stories. Just durin' the week, to keep us in the house, because it was cold out.

R: You know, *zi' Filumeja Macaluso* [Aunt Filomeme Macaluso]? They'd come, and . . .

C: Oh, yeah! The neighbors, they'd come.

R: And, what ye call 'em? *Donna Ciccia.*

C: Yeah, the neighbors, they always used to come down to hear the stories. There was a lady there, they called her *Donna Ciccia, "Mo, zi' Luigi, stasera dici u rumanze?"* [Now, tonight, Uncle Louis, will you tell us a tale?]

B: I see. And did your mother also tell stories?

C: No, my father.

B: Isn't that something? And he learned them when he was a boy, right?

C: When he was a boy, *a la massarija* [at the farm], 'cause he used to work out.

B: But he didn't read them, he heard them.

C: Well, my father didn't know how to read or write! So, when he'd sit out in the country, at night, while they cooked, or they took care of the animals, they'd sit and they would say the stories. And he remembered them and he told those to us.

B: And you remember.

C: And I remember, yeah. Yeah, I remember. I remember.

B: Does your sister also remember?

C: Well, if you would mention them, they would remember loads. Like *Aspre Agrimande, U re tre portualle, The Magic Lantern,* and *The Two Cavalere, The Fisherman;* they would remember them, I mean, not the whole story.

B: Would they tell them?

C: No, no! Not the whole story, no.

B: You are the storyteller, eh? So, you took after your father, then?

C: Yeah! I remember, I remember 'em well!

B: How old was your father, when he died?

C: Seventy-three.

B: And your mother?

C: Seventy.

B: I'd like to know something about their lives, you know?

C: They worked very hard. My father came to this Roseto, here. He was a stranger. And they used to call my mother *"Margarita a Forestera"* [the stranger].

B: Yes.

C: Because they were all from Roseto, Italy, except my mother, and they used to call her "Margaret the Stranger." "Margaret the Stranger."

B: Right.

C: My father used to work and—not that he became a millionaire—but they used to pay all those bills and they figured that the Malpiedo family had a lot of money! [He laughs.] We were the only strangers. Well, there was some Sicilian families, afterwards. A few.

B: Yes, but from that place, what's the name you said?

C: The name of this family?

B: No, I said, what's the name of the village near Salerno.

C: Postiglione.

B: And, from that place.

C: Nobody!

B: You were the only family.

C: The only one. My uncle. Where I live today, this used to be my uncle's home. And when he died, he left everything to his brother, that's my father. Naturally, my father died, then we all shared what he had and what my uncle had.

B: Yes, and you were saying that your father worked very hard, here in the slate?

C: He only worked in the slate mines.

B: He never worked in a mill?

C: Never.

B: And did you always work in a mill?

C: I have. I have five trades. The union trades. I can do anything. I work in the mill, fix sewing machines, put blouses together, managing the shop, work on smith work, *terazo* floors.

B: What?

C: *Terazo*, concrete floors. I made all the concrete floors in the school. I picked that all myself. I picked up myself. I figured: this here was done by a man and, if it breaks, gotta be fixed by a man! So I am always trying to save a nickel and see if I can fix it. If I break it, I save money, I don't pay to fix it, so I always fix it.

B: I see. Did your father also do this?

C: My father, my father took care of the house, he used to build the chicken houses, you know? And he always had a hammer and a saw, and I learned that from him. And I plaster and I paint.

B: And do you make your own wine?

C: I did, before. I don't do it anymore. But you see? When I had wine. I had a lot of friends! Yeah! But now we travel and the wine would spoil.

B: I see. Well, let's tell more stories now.

C: Oh, no! Not now! I am tired, and it's always a long story, like I told you. Go ahead with her now [he indicates his wife]. And then, it wouldn't even fit in the thing there, I can see.

B: Oh, don't bother with that. I can turn it. Actually, I must.

C: Yeah, but I'll rest now.

A Note on the Methods

I STARTED with the Italian Roseto, making several trips there in 1965, 1967, and 1968, for a total of about six months in the town. My stay in the American Roseto also lasted nearly six months, divided into four trips during the year 1965–66. Formal and informal interviews, as well as participant observation methods, were all used according to the particular situation I met in approaching my informants. In both places I lived in private homes and in the local boarding house, and I participated in most of the important events of the two communities—attending weddings, funerals, city council meetings, parties at the Marconi Club and the Knights of Columbus Hall, even harvesting crops in the sunny fields of Apulia, and from sitting by the kitchen fire or in the *osterias* in wintertime to the long summer sessions spent on the front porches in the humid, hot nights of the American Roseto.

In setting up my network of informants, I tried to follow some consistent lines according to place of birth, family ties, neighborhood, occupation, and age group. I also tried to secure at least a few outstanding talents in each folklore genre. I avoided concentrating too much on this effort for fear of getting an unrealistic and episodical, though appealing picture of the situation. Interviews took place at almost anytime and anyplace in the two Rosetos, while during my previous field work in New York and in Chicago, the sessions were mostly held in the evenings after work and dinner.

Informants in both towns generally responded with pleasure and even with enthusiasm, rarely showing any embarrassment at being taped and only becoming hesitant when the interview focused on material that they considered obscene or, in America, "un-American." In the latter cases, I never insisted on keeping the tape recorder running and either took notes on a pad, or else tried to memorize the information and write it down soon after the session. In many cases, however, I found that the tape recorder was less conspicuous than a notebook. This was partly due to the magic power traditionally attributed to written material and partly to the fact that the machine's functioning did not interfere as much as my writing did with the continuity of my rapport with the informants, who could thus receive my uninterrupted attention. As a rule, the informants' attitude was one of diligent cooperation, mixed with visible pride at helping "the American education" and pleased vanity at being able to hear their own voices played back on the tape recorder in some cases. As a result, I could secure practically any kind of information I wanted.

Obtaining situations suitable to the various topics of the interviews was a constant problem and for this purpose it was necessary to visit most people several times. An engagement party, a picnic, or a Sunday family reunion were ideal settings for choral singing, or sessions of joke-telling and anecdotes, while the more somber description of cures and the narration of long fairytales required a different atmosphere. Lullabies, for instance, were told more willingly and naturally if the woman had a baby on her lap. The evil eye, too, was a touchy subject that could only be broached in the proper atmosphere, with some motivation and usually in the presence of not more than one or two informants.

Some informants were eager to show me, as an Italian coming from Rome, that their isolation from the Old Country had not made them forget their Italian identity, as if I were the personification of the Italian nation. These, however, were mostly people with strong middle-class ambitions, such as quarry and factory owners, building contractors, and other kinds of notables; and I questioned the sincerity of their feeling. The Venetian informants from the town of Pen Argyl, only two miles from Roseto, mostly fell into this category and they proved also to be the most difficult persons to interview because they were difficult to guide and seemed instinctively eager to give me what they thought was a proper portrait of themselves. Out of six interviews with informants from Veneto I only drew scanty information outside of folksongs, and these sounded for the most part as though they had been filtered through the mass media. In addition, there was an evident effort on their part to distinguish themselves from the southern Italians, whom they significantly referred to as "Moroccans."

Several letters addressed to relatives and friends, as well as photographs and spoken messages on tape collected during my field work in Roseto Valfortore, greatly helped me in establishing connections in Roseto. Being from Rome also gave me considerable advantages in both places, for while I was not a stranger from the

North I was sufficiently removed from Roseto to justify my interest in learning about their culture. This was also a positive factor in America, where anyone coming from any Italian village is always regarded as a potential immigrant into the settlement. The fact that I could speak their dialect besides English was of fundamental importance in Roseto where no other level of Italian language would have been useful. In addition, being a woman gave informants of both sexes more confidence in and a feeling of ease with me.

I rarely used the questionnaires and finding lists, which I had previously drawn up, in the presence of informants, but their usefulness before and after each interview was always substantial. It helped me to keep track of what I was obtaining from the various groups and to cover as completely as possible a comprehensive and comparable body of information.

The extension of this investigation, based on two related and yet distant groups, required vast documentation which I secured through recorded tapes and other devices. The recorded collection of Italian-American folklore totals one hundred and forty-eight tapes. I used a portable UHER 4,000–Report, both electrically and battery operated, and a portable CGE, four-track, electrical. The tapes contain narratives and songs of all kinds, games, riddles, proverbs, rhymes, life histories, interviews on the *rites de passage*, and accounts of historical events. The other data consist of a variety of materials: field journals, longhand notes taken during the interviews, and sources such as the Easton and Bangor libraries, local newspapers, the City Council, and the Recorder of Wills Office of Northampton County. There are objects such as amulets, broadsides, manuscripts, books of prayer, newspapers, embroideries, scrapbooks, calendars, letters, and photographs, collected both during the interviews and through a notice published in the local newspaper, *The Bangor Daily News*. Presently, the collection is deposited at the Archivio Ethnolinguistico of the Discoteca di Stato in Rome.

In this book I have tried to identify and discuss traditional values and orientations of American Rosetans and I gave, when possible, the folklore evidence of the observations I was making. My frequent references to the past were intended to offer analogy or contrast with the subject matter under discussion, as I am convinced that the present can be understood only when it is considered together with the past. My original intention was to do my study of Rosetan culture and of its process of adaptation to American society totally on the basis of folklore data. As my work progressed, however, I realized that just using folklore texts would reveal only a very partial picture. Without an attempt to complete that picture with as many other aspects of present life as possible, those folklore texts would be a series of lifeless relics and the result would be one of cultural immobility, a sort of disorganized mosaic of survivals from the Old Country. I became convinced that in order to attain validity folklore studies today must include all ways of thinking, feeling, and acting of a given individual or group, and thus I made the widest use of informal interviews with Rosetans in Italy and in America. I felt that learning the various ways of testing the evil eye or just checking on all the folktale types circulating in the community, without seeking the relationships between such findings and the society that holds them, would lack relevance, and for this reason I let the Rosetans speak about their own culture, their problems, and their hopes.

As a complete treatment of the culture of both Rosetos was not possible here, I used Roseto Valfortore as a constant frame of reference, as a starting point, to follow the development of the Rosetan group in America. The other Italian groups I had previously met in urban areas of the United States and Canada also supplied useful background data to compare with the Rosetan findings. While the perspective of this study permitted me to include only a tiny part of my extensive folklore collection, I hope I have succeeded in offering an honest and valid portrait of the people of Roseto, Pennsylvania. These people are now my friends. They correspond with me, they talk about me, and they visit me when they come to Italy in the summer months. A few years have passed since I did my field work in Roseto but its human, warm reality is still as close as ever.

Selected Bibliography:
The Italian Immigration to America

1. *Works with Specific Reference to Italian-American Folklore*

Agonito, Rosemary. "Il Paisano: Immigrant Italian Folktales in Central New York," *New York Folklore Quarterly*, XXIII, No.1 (1967), 52–64.

Benigni, V. "Patron Saints," *Catholic Encyclopedia*, XI (1911), 563.

Bianco, Carla. "Il folklore degli emigrati italiani in America," Lares, XXX, No.3–4 (1964), 148–152.

_____. *Roseto, Pennsylvania, 19 giugno 1966.* Milano: Edizioni del Gallo, 1967.
Preface by Prof. Alberto M. Cirese. One day of field work in the Italian-American community: journal, recordings, photographs of the day.

Barrese, Pauline. "Southern Italian Folklore in New York City," *New York Folklore Quarterly*, XXI, No.3 (1965), 184–193.

Bernardy, Amy A. "La 'Donna Lombarda' nel Canadà," *Atti del III Congresso di Arti e Tradizioni Popolari* (Rome, 1963), pp. 524–534.

"Calling on the Devil to Cure Disease," *Journal of American Folklore*, V (1892), 238.
A judicial case arising from a superstition episode in New York City. In English.

Dorson, Richard M. "Dialect Stories of the Upper Peninsula: A New Form of American Folkore," *Journal of American Folklore* LXI (1948), 113–150.
Includes 84 items from various ethnic groups; nos. 17, 60, 61, 62, and 63 are in Italian.

"Festa: Festival of San Gennaro, New York City," *New Yorker*, XXXIII (October 5, 1957), 34–36.

Francello, Elvira, "An Italian Version of the 'Maid Freed from the Gallows,'" *New York Folklore Quarterly*, II, No.1 (1946), 139.
A good version of the song both in Sicilian and in English.

Garofalo, Alexander, "The Oven of the Seven Montelli," *New York Folklore Quarterly*, II, No.4 (1946), 272–275.

An Italian tale of the supernatural told in English by an Italian resident of New York City.

Grieco, Rose. "They Who Mourn: Italian-American Wakes," *Commonweal*, LVII (March 27, 1953), 628–630.

Recollections from the author's childhood.

———. "Wine and Fig Trees," *Commonweal*, LX (June 4, 1954), 221–223.

On wine-making.

Hoffman, Dan G. "Stregas, Ghosts, and Werewolves," *New York Folklore Quarterly*, III, No.4 (1944), 325–328.

An Italian from Cansano, Napoli, and now resident in Brooklyn, tells a few anecdotes in English.

Irving, Elizabeth A. "Where the Players Are Marionettes and the Age of Chivalry Is Born Again in a Little Italy Theatre on Mulberry Street," *Craftsman*, XII (1907), 667–669.

About the Sicilian puppets in New York City at the beginning of the century.

———. "The Story of a Transplanted Industry: Lace Workers of the Italian Quarter in New York," *Craftsman*, XII (1907), 404–409. Italian girls making laces in New York follow traditional patterns.

"Italian Festivals in New York," *Chautauqua*, XXXIV (1901), 228–229.

Italian-American Folklore. Collected by Indiana University students. Arranged by subject matter at the Archive of the Folklore Institute, Bloomington, Indiana. It is mostly in English.

Jagendorf, M. "Italian Tales in New York City," *New York Folklore Quarterly*, XI, No.3 (1955), 177–182.

Jones, Louis C. "Italian Werewolves," *New York Folklore Quarterly*, VI, No.3 (1950), 133–138.

Kafka, John. *Sicilian Street.* n.p., n.d.

The story of a puppeteer immigrant from Enna, Sicily, who continues the tradition of ancient puppetry in his theatre in Brooklyn.

Kimball, Charlotte. "An Outline of Amusements Among Italians in New York," *Charities*, V, No.12 (August 18, 1900), 1–8.

Lubell, Samuel. "Rhode Island's Little Firecrackers," *Saturday Evening Post*, CCXII (November 12, 1949), 31, 174–178.

Musick, Ruth Ann. " 'The Ring' in 'European Folktales in West Virginia,' " *Midwest Folklore*, VI, No.1 (Spring, 1956), 29.

North America. U. S., Wisconsin, Italian, and Finnish Immigrants. Four tape rolls, dual track, collected by Tom Bartom from relatives. Folksongs, beliefs, customs, and related experiences. In Archive of Traditional Music, 66–4–14 (75).

Ondis, A. Lewis. "Peter's Sandals," *New York Folklore Quarterly*, XVII (1961), 226–228.

Ramirez, Manuel D. "Italian Folklore from Tampa, Florida," *Southern Folklore Quarterly*, V (1941), 101–106.
Brief information on the Italian settlement in Tampa. There are three Italian songs in Sicilian dialect. Rather poorly transcribed.

———. "Italian Folklore from Tampa, Florida," *Southern Folklore Quarterly*, XIII (1949), 121–131.
A very good description of Sicilian life in Tampa.
List of 116 Sicilian proverbs in Sicilian and in English translation.

"Religion of Lucky Pieces, Witches and the Evil Eye," *World Outlook*, III (October, 1917), 24–25.

Simmons, Donald C. "Anti-Italian-American Riddles in New England," *Journal of American Folklore*, LXXIX, No.313 (July–September, 1966), 475–479.

Speroni, Charles. "The Observance of St. Joseph Day Among the Sicilians of Southern California," *Southern Folklore Quarterly*, IV (1940), 135–139.
In English, with bibliographical reference. Some quotations in Sicilian dialect.

———. "Five Italian Wellerisms," *Western Folklore*, VII (1948), 54–55.

———. "The Development of the Columbus Day Pageant of San Francisco," *Western Folklore*, VII (1948), 325–335.

Spicer, Dorothy Gladys. "Health Superstitions of the Italian Immigrant," *Hygeia*, IV (May, 1926), 266–269.

Trop, Sylvia. "An Italian Rip Van Winkle," *New York Folklore Quarterly*, I, No.1 (1945), 100–105.

Urick, Mildred. "The San Rocco Festival at Aliquippa, Pa.: A Transplanted Tradition," *Pennsylvania Folklife* (Autumn, 1969), 212–216.

Voiles, Jane. "Genovese Folkways in a California Mining Camp," *California Folklore Quarterly*, III (1944), 212–216.

Williams, Phyllis. *Southern Italian Folkways in Europe and in America*. New Haven: Yale University Press, 1938.
Originally published by the Institute of Human Relations. Reissued by Russell and Russell, New York, 1969, with an introduction by Francesco Cordasco.
A handbook for social workers, visiting nurses, school teachers, physicians.

2. *The Italian-Americans: Social, Economic, and Political Aspects*

Auerback, M. S. "Monograph on Roseto," New York *Times* (December 15, 1919).

Baily, Samuel L. "The Italians and Organized Labor in the United States and Argentina, 1880–1910," *The International Migration Review*, I, No.3 (Summer, 1967), 56–65.

Barzini, Luigi. *The Italians*. New York, 1964.
A best seller on Italian culture and history.

Bennet, Alice. "Italian-American Farmers," *Survey*, XXII (May, 1909), 172–175.
Why Italian-Americans are rarely employed in farming in the U. S. Successful Italian farmers in America.

Bercovici, Konrad. "Italians in the United States," in *On New Shores* (New York, 1925), pp. 84–100.
An interesting cultural analysis of the Italian group in the U. S. Old-fashioned but useful for critical insights into the culture.

Bernardy, Amy A. *Italia randagia attraverso gli Stati Uniti*. Torino: F.lli Bocca Ed., 1913.

Boheme, Frederick G. "The Italians in New Mexico," *New Mexico Historical Review*, XXXIV, No.2 (April, 1959) 98–116.

Breed, R. L. "Italians Fight Tuberculosis," *Survey*, XXIII (February, 1910), 702–704.

Browne, Henry J. "The Italian Problem in the Catholic Church of the United States," *The Catholic Historical Society, Historical Studies and Records*, XXXV (November, 1927), 46–72.

Buscemi, Philip A. "The Sicilian Immigrant and His Language Problems," *Sociology and Social Research*, XII (November, 1927), 137–143.

Campisi, Paul J. "The Italian Family in the United States" in *Selected Studies in Marriage and Family* by Winch, Robert F., and Robert McGinnis (New York, 1953), pp. 126–138.

———. "Ethnic Family Patterns: The Italian Family in the United States," *American Journal of Sociology*, LIII (May, 1948), 443–449. Reprinted in Milton L. Barron, *American Minorities*. New York, 1957.

Candido, Salvatore. *Los italianos en America del Sur*. Montivideo: Instituto Italiano di Cultura, 1963.

Carlevale, Joseph William. *Americans of Italian Descent in New Jersey*. Clifton, New Jersey, 1950.

Carter, Hugh and Berenice Doster. "Residence and Occupation of Naturalized Americans from Italy" in *Immigration and Naturalization Service Monthly Review*, IX, No.1 (July, 1951).

———. "Social Characteristics of Naturalized Americans from Italy," *Monthly Review, Department of Justice, Immigration, and Naturalization Service*, VIII, No.11 (May, 1951), 145–152.

Cerase, Francesco P., "L'Emigrazione di ritorno nel processo di integrazione dell'emigrato: una prima formulazione," *Genus*, XXIII (1967), 7–28.

———. "A Study of Italian Migrants Returning from the United

States," *The International Migration Review*, I, No.3 (Summer, 1967), 67–74.

Child, Irving Long. *Italian or American? The Second Generation in Conflict in New Haven*. New Haven: Yale University Press, 1943. Reissued in 1970 by Russell and Russell, New York.

Ciampis, Mario do. "Note sul movimento socialista fra gli emigranti italiani negli U. S. A. (1890–1921)," *Cronache meridionali*, VI, No.4 (April, 1959), 255–273.

Cordasco, Francesco and Salvatore LaGumina. *The Italian Experience in America: A Preliminary Bibliography*. Leiden, The Netherlands: E. J. Brill, 1969.

Covello, Leonard. *The Social Background of the Italo-American School Child*. Leiden, The Netherlands: 1967.

With an introduction by Francesco Cordasco.

A study of the southern Italian family mores and their effect on the school situation in Italy and in America. Originally a Ph.D. dissertation, New York University, 1944.

Cunningham, George E. "The Italian: A Hindrance to White Solidarity in Louisiana, 1890–1898," *Journal of Negro History*, L (January, 1965), 22–37.

On the lynching of several Italians during strike disorders.

D'Amato, Gaetano. "The Black Hand Myth," *North American Review*, CLXXXVII (April, 1908), 543–550.

Dickinson, Jean Y. "Aspects of Italian Immigration to Philadelphia," *The Pennsylvania Magazine of History and Biography*, XC (October, 1966), 445–466.

Dies, Martin. *The Trojan Horse in America*. New York, 1940. On the Fascist activity of the Italian Consulates in the United States.

Dore, Grazia. *La Democrazia Italiana e l'Emigrazione in America*. Brescia: Morcelliana, 1964.

The various Italian governments and emigration.

Duffield, Marcus. "Mussolini's American Empire: The Fascist Invasion of the U. S.," *Harper's Magazine*, LCIX (November, 1929), 661–672.

Fenton, Edwin. "Italians in the Labor Movement," *Pennsylvania History*, XXVI, No.2 (April, 1959), 133–148.

Fucilla, Joseph G. "Anglicization of Italian Surnames in the United States," *American Speech*, XVIII (1943), 26–32.

Gans, Herbert J. "Some Comments on the History of Italian Migration and on the Nature of Historical Research," *The International Migration Review*, L, No.3 (Summer, 1967), 5–10.

_____. *The Urban Villagers: Group and Class in the Life of Italian-Americans*. New York: Free Press of Glencoe, 1962.

Ginger, Mina C. "In Berry Field and Bog: The Seasonal Migration of Italian Pickers to New Jersey, Its Profit, Its Cost, Illiteracy, and Disease," *Charities*, XV (November, 1905), 162–170.

Gisolfi, Anthony M. "Italo-American: What It Has Borrowed from

American English and What It Is Contributing to the American Language," *Commonweal*, XXX (July, 1939), 311–314.

Howe, Maude. "From Italy to Pittsburgh: Where the Pennsylvania Italians Come From," *Lippincott's Monthly Magazine*, LXXIII, No.434 (February, 1904), 200–209.

Ianni, Francis A. J. "Italo-American Teen-agers," *Annals*, CCCXXXVIII (November, 1961), 70–80.

————. "Residential and Occupational Mobility and Indices of the Acculturation of an Ethnic Group: The Italo-American Colony of Norristown, Pa.," *Social Forces* (October, 1957), 65–72.

The Italian Experience in Emigration. A special issue of the *International Migration Review*, I, n.s., No.3 (Summer, 1967).

Jones, H. D. *The Evangelical Movement Among Italians in New York City.* New York, 1933–1934.
Committee of the Federation of Churches of Greater New York and the Brooklyn Church and Mission Federation. A rich source of information on the phases and entity of the movement at the time.

Kingsley, H. L., and Carbone, M. "Attitudes of Italian-Americans Toward Race Prejudice," *Journal of Abnormal Social Psychology*, No.33 (1938), 532–538.

Koren, John. "The Padrone System and the Padrone Banks," *Bulletin of the Department of Labor*, No. 9 (1897), p.123.

LaGumina, John Salvatore, ed. "Ethnicity in American Political Life: The Italian-American Experience," *Proceedings of the First Annual Conference of the American-Italian Historical Association.* New York, 1966.

Livi-Bacci, Massimo. *L'Immigrazione e L'Assimilazione degli Italiani negli Stati Uniti e le Statistiche Americane.* Milano: Giuffre, 1961.

Maiale, Hugo V. *The Italian Vote in Philadelphia Between 1928 and 1946.* Philadelphia: University of Pennsylvania Press, 1950.

Mariano, John Horace. *The Second Generation of Italians in New York City.* Boston: Christopher Publishing House, 1971.

Morgan, A. "What Shall We Do with the Dago? Prisons Should Not Be Comfortable," *Popular Science Monthly*, XXXVIII (December, 1890), 172–179.

"Mulberry Bend from 1897 to 1958," *Saturday Evening Post*, CCXXXI (August 2, 1958), 34–53.
A description of life in Mulberry Bend, an Italian enclave in New York.

Nelli, Humbert S. "Italians in Urban America: A Study in Ethnic Adjustment," *The International Migration Review*, I, No.3 (Summer, 1967), 38–55.

————. "Italians and Crime in Chicago: The Formative Years, 1890–1920," *American Journal of Sociology*, LXXIV (January, 1969).

Norman, John. "Repudiation of Fascism by the Italian-American Press," *Journalism Quarterly*, XXI (March, 1944), 1–6.

———. "Pro-Fascist Activities in Western Pennsylvania During the Ethiopian War," *Western Pennsylvania Historical Magazine*, XXV (1942), 143–149.

Palmieri, F. Aurelio. "Italian Protestantism in the U. S." *Catholic World*, CVII, No.638 (May, 1918), 177–189.

Pantaleone, Michele. *Mafia e Droga*. Torino: Einaudi, 1966.

Pisani, Laurence Frank. *The Italian in America*. New York: Exposition Press, 1957.

Psathas, George. "Ethnicity, Social Class and Adolescent Independence from Parental Control: A Study of the Southern Italian and Eastern European Jewish Ethnic Groups in New Haven," *American Sociological Review*, XXII (August, 1957), 415–424.

Radin, Paul. *The Italians of San Francisco: Their Adjustment and Acculturation*, California Relief Administration, Cultural Anthropology Project, Monograph No. 1. San Francisco, 1935.

Reed, Dorothy. *Leisure Time of Girls in a "Little Italy."* New York: Columbia University Press, 1932.
Research was done in East Harlem, a really homogeneous group at the time. Quite a good source of information.

Rolle, Andrew F. *The Immigrant Upraised: Italian Adventurers and Colonists in an Expanding America*. Norman: University of Oklahoma Press, 1968.

———. "Italy in California: *The Pacific Spectator*, IX, No.4 (Fall, 1955), 409–420.
A great deal of information on the North-Italian farming colonies in the west such as the "Italian Swiss Colony."

Sartorio, Enrico. *Social and Religious Life of Italians in America*. Boston: The Christopher Publishing House, 1918.
Very interesting source of information for the new religious tendencies developing at the time among the Italian-Americans.

Schiavo, Giovanni. *The Truth About the Mafia and Organized Crime in America*. New York: The Vigo Press, 1962. Interesting but not sufficiently focused on socioeconomic factors in Italian life as a related, important aspect of the question.

Sondern, Frederic, Jr. *Brotherhood of Evil: The Mafia*. New York: Farrar, Strauss, and Cudahy, 1959.

Sweet, Mat McDaniel. *The Italian Immigrant and His Reading*. Chicago: The American Library Association, 1925.

Tait, Joseph Wilfrid. *Some Aspects of the Effects of the Dominant American Culture upon Children of Italian-Born Parents*. New York: Teachers College, Columbia University, 1942.
Scientifically organized. Difficulties of assimilation on the part of the young Italian-Americans.

Tomasi, S. M., and M. H. Engel. *The Italian Experience in the United States*. New York: Center for Migration Studies, 1970.

Valletta, Clement. "Italian Immigrant Life in Northampton County, Pa., 1890–1915," *Pennsylvania Folklife,* First Part (Autumn, 1965), 36–45; Second Part (1966), 39–48.

Vecoli, Rudolph J. "Contadini in Chicago: A Critique of the Uprooted," *Journal of American History,* LI (December, 1964), 404–417.

Velikonja, Joseph. *Italians in the United States: A Bibliography.* Carbondale, Illinois: Southern Illinois University, 1963.

Weld, Ralph Foster. *Brooklyn in America.* New York: Columbia University Press, 1950.

Whyte, William F. *Italians in the U. S.: Street Corner Society.* Chicago: The University of Chicago Press, 1943. Revised edition, 1955.

    The social structure of an Italian slum.

Wright, Frederick H. "How to Reach Italians in America? Shall They Be Segregated, Missioned, Neglected or Welcomed?" *Missionary Review of the World,* XL (August, 1917), 588–595.

3. *Autobiography and Fiction*

Carnevali, Emanuele. *A Hurried Man.* Paris: Three Mountains Press, 1925.

    A book of poems and prose reflecting the author's life in America.

Corsi, Edward. *In the Shadow of Liberty.* New York: The Macmillan Company, 1935.

    A description of the immigrant's experience: habits, beliefs, episodes, etc.

DiDonato, Pietro. *Immigrant Saint: The Life of Mother Cabrini.* New York: McGraw-Hill Book Company, 1960.

Mangione, Jerre. *Mount Allegro.* Boston: Houghton Mifflin Company, 1942.

    The life of a large Italian-American family originally from Sicily. There is much information about habits, customs, and beliefs.

Pagano, Jo. *Golden Wedding.* New York: Random House, 1943.

    Case history of an Italian-American family.

Panunzio, Constantine. *The Soul of an Immigrant.* New York: The Macmillan Company, 1921.

    A famous autobiography, rich in cultural insights.

Pellegrini, Angelo. *Americans By Choice.* New York: The Macmillan Co., 1956.

    Profiles of Italian immigrants in different parts of the United States.

————. *Immigrant's Return.* New York: The Macmillan Company, 1953.

    Immigration at the age of nine. Fictionalized, but rich in information and insight.

Index

Agriculture, 15, 143*n*3
American dream, 45, 46. *See also* Myth of America
American Family, An: text, 204–6
American Protective Association, 9
American society: antagonism toward, 123; Rosetans and, 125–26
Anecdotes. *See* Jokes and anecdotes
Animal tales, 75, 77
Aristocracy, Italian, 4
Army, Italian, 32
Artisans, 25

Babies, 94, 108–9
Ballads. *See* Emigration songs; Songs
Bandit stories, 83
Bangor, Maine, 20
Bangor, Pennsylvania, 22, 31
Bangor Daily News, 64
Bangor High School, 30
Bird and the Magic Liver, The: text, 161–68
Birth, 107–11
Black Americans, 59–60
Boston, Massachusetts, 8, 20
Bozzelli family, 15, 26
Bozzelli, Matilde, 207
Bozzelli, Pasquale, 207
Brazil, 6
Bread, 99
Brides: as immigrants, 48–50, 112, 116; and wedding customs, 113
Bruno Comes Back from America, 41–42
Buffalo, New York, 8

Campanilismo. See Regionalism
Capitol Slate Quarry, 26
Capobianco family, 26
Capozzolo, Joseph, 26
Carnevali, Emanuel: poem by, 46–47
Carnivals. *See* Festivals
Casciano, Mariantonia "Puttanella," 195
Castellucci, Giannina, 183, 200

Catholic church, the: in Roseto, Pa., 25, 105
Catholic cult, the: and magic, 84
Catholics: number of, in Roseto, Pa., 30
Cecilia: text, 200–2
Change, cultural, x, xii, xv; in traditional beliefs and customs, 119–20
Chicago, Illinois: immigrants in, 8; as setting in tales, 82
Children: as storytellers, 77; parental authority over, 124–25; role learning of, 126
Christian Democratic Party, 16
Christmas, 120
Christmas Eve: powers of witches on, 90, 91
Christ Stopped at Eboli, 44
Church attendance, 29, 104–5
Churches: in Roseto Valfortore, 25, 145*n*3
Cirino, Mrs. Sabatino, 62
Cirino, Onorio, 62
Citizenship, American, 32
Class antagonism, 4. *See also* Social distinctions
Clergy, 16
Cleveland, Ohio, 8
College attendance, 62, 138
College students: among Rosetans, 30–31; leaving Roseto, 142
Columbia Fire Company, 25
Columbus School, 25
Communal aspects of life, 121
Communication: channels of, in Roseto, Pa., 30
Communist Party, 16
Contact with Italy, 51–52, 141. *See also* Letters; Travel to Italy
Cultural isolation, 123
Cures, 103
Customs: origins of, 106–7

D'Avanzo family, 28
De Bernardinis, Rose Anicola, 190

De Cesari, Luigi, 65
Death: rituals of, 116–19
De Franco Meat Market, 30
Devils, 90
Dialect, Rosetan: and recent immigrants, 28–29; survival of, 74
Dialects, Italian: and standard Italian, 70, 150n2; as "secret" language, 73; differences in, and effect on storytelling, 80. *See also* Language
Di Capua, Prince Bartolomeo, 13, 19
Diet. *See* Food habits
Di Salerno, Prince Sanseverino, 19
Donatelli, maestro, 31
Dowry, 39, 40

Easton, Pennsylvania, 20
Education: in Roseto Valfortore, 19; in Roseto, Pa., 30; interethnic contact through, 62; role of mother in, 124; traditional view of, 136–38; impact of, 141
Education Act of 1962, 19
Elite groups, 28
Emigrants, 8, 44–45. *See also* Returned migrants
Emigration, x, 5–6; practical problems created by, 37; scarcity of males as result of, 42; cost of, 147n8
Emigration agents, 8
Emigration songs, 37–40
Emigration stories, 41
Engagement, 112–13
English, the, as immigrants, xi
Entertainment, 138–40
Ethnic differentiation, 132. *See also* Interethnic contact; Regionalism
Ethnic in-group: function of, 8; importance of, 53
Evil eye, 85; practice of, 94; protection against, 95; test for, 95, 96, 98; and pregnancy, 107; attracted by wealth, 131
Exorcism, 84
Ezzolle (That's All) : text, 197–98

Falcone, Anthony Zilio', 53, 110, 129, 179, 182, 184, 207
Falcone, Costanza, 198, 207
Falcone, Guiseppe, 65
Falcone, Leonardo, 31, 146n11
Falcone, Lorenzo, 28, 31
Family, the: traditional role of, xiv, 30, 122–25; change in, 125–26, 141
Family reunions, 29
Fascism, xiv
Father: as family authority, 125

Father Sends His Daughter to a Convent School, The: text, 192–94
Fertility potions, 107
Festivals, 120–21; in Roseto, Pa., 29; Festa del Carmine, 120, 152n55
Finelli family, 30
Fisherman, The, 81; text, 168–76
Food habits, 134–36; among Rosetans, xi, 16, 19; traditional, 108, 151n33
Fool Had a Donkey, A: text, 190–92
Foolish Bride, The: text, 186–90
Formula tales, 78
Founders of Roseto, Pa., 31
Fox and the Ricotta, The: text, 176–79
Funerals, 118–19

Games, traditional, 211–12
Garibaldi, 59; as "liberator of slaves," 60–62
Garibaldi and the Freedom of Slaves, 83
Germans, the, as immigrants, xi
Ghosts, 90
Giacquinto, George, 32
Godfather: as source of loan, 8; role of, at weddings, 114
Godmother: role of, at births, 110; role of, at weddings, 110
Gompers, Samuel, 9
Grandparents, 76

Historical traditions, 83–84
Holy Week, 120
Honeymoons, 107
Houses: described, in Roseto Valfortore, 13–14; described, in Roseto, Pa., 24–25
Hungarians, the, as immigrants, 7

I Can't Hear You!: text, 198–99
Illiteracy: among Rosetans, 19; among immigrants, 50; semi-, defined, 146n5
Il Progresso, xiv
Imgaro, maestro, 31
Immigrants: adjustment to American life, xi; disillusionment of, xiii, 46; urbanization of, 7; temporary, 7; geographical distribution in U.S., 8–9; hostility toward, 8–9; recent, 28; arrival of, 50; adherence to tradition among, 50; in the South (U. S.), 60
Immigration: distribution by decades, 6–7; time of, as social factor, 28; patterns of, 48; recent, and traditions, 80
Immigration laws, xii, 32, 144n6

Immigration policy: attacks on, 9–10
Individual behavior, 121
Industries: lack of, in Roseto Valfortore; in Roseto, Pa., 26
Interethnic contact: conflict as result of, 31, 53–54, 56–57; at present, 58–59, 62
Intermarriage: among immigrant groups, xi, 7–8; among Rosetans, 74. *See also* Intermarriage
Italian empire: 1936 proclamation of, 4
Italianism: as American concept, xiv
Italians and the Invention of Music, The, 83
It's Good They're Cherries: text, 195–97

Jehovah's Witnesses, 30, 106
Jokes and anecdotes, xii, 82–83

Kennedy, John F., 43, 44
Killing the Returned Soldier, 41
Knights of Columbus Hall, 32, 218
Know Nothing movement, 9

Landowners, 15, 16
Land redistribution, 15
Land Reform Act, 16
Language: Italianization of foreign words, 71–73. *See also* Dialects
Language difficulties: reflected in songs and jokes, 73; in church, 105–6
Law and state authority, 127–28
Legends: as social defense, 59; as part of repertoire, 75, 78; saints', 83; about devils and witches, 89–90
Letters: from immigrants to Italy, 50–51
Levi, Carlo, 3, 4
Little Italy: inaccuracy of term, xiii, xiv; as village and kinship clusters, 7
Lodge, Henry Cabot, 9
Love potions, 115–16
Lullabies, 123

Magical morbidity, 94
Magical-religious lore: in new land, 86–87; spells and cures, 100–1
Magical-religious world view: and the Catholic cult, 84; in new land, 85; as kept by Rosetans, 90; and animal talk, 99–100; among third generation, 101; and religious affiliation, 103–4
Magic tales, 75; and recent immigration, 80; comparative length of, 82

Male population: scarcity of, as reflected in folklore, 42–43
Malpiedo, Carmine, 80, 82, 161, 169
Man Who Went to Church, The: text, 179–82
Marconi Club, 25, 29, 114, 218
Marriage: attitudes and practices surrounding, 107, 111-12; arranged, 116. *See also* Intermarriage
Martellotti, Carmela, 8
Martino, Donato, 211
Martino, Giovannina, 197
Martocci-Capobianco American Legion Post, 32
Mass, the: ritualism of, 84
Mass media: impact of, on traditional culture, 76, 141; effect on oral traditions, 77. *See also* Television
Medicine: distrust for, 108; traditional lore on, 132–34. *See also* Cures
Michigan State University Concert Band, 31, 146n11
Middle Ages: Roseto Valfortore during, 19; customs dating from, 106
Middle class, 16
Midwives, 110
Migration. See Emigration; Immigration
Money, 131
Mother, Give Me a Hundred Lire: as recorded in Roseto, Pa., 37–38
Mother's Curse, 38
Munaceddi, 85–86
Musicians, 31
Mussolini, Benito, x; on peasant fecundity, 4–5
Mythical new land: as subject of songs, 35–36
Myth of America: dual nature of, 43–47

Names, family: social distinction of, 28
Naples, Italy, 48
Narration: among Rosetans, 74. *See also* Oral tradition; Storytelling
Narratives: concerning migratory process, 35; type distribution, 81; characters in, 83
Native air, 44, 45
Nervous Wife, The: text, 184–185
New Crucifix, The: text, 183–184
New Immigration, the, 6
New Year's celebrations, 120
New York, New York, 82
Nicknames, 28

Northampton County, Pennsylvania, 20, 21
Northerners (Italian), 65
Nuptial procession, 114

Old people: as storytellers, 75; regard for, 76
Oral tradition: forms of, and migration, 34; effect of mass media on, 77; shift in action to new milieu, 82; distribution among sex and age groups, 150n8. *See also* Narratives; Storytelling
Others: concept of, 123, 128; distrust of, 129

Paese: term, as used in Roseto, Pa., 30
Pagano, Filomena, 135, 204
Passing of the Great Race, The, 10
Peasants, Italian: poor condition of, 3–5; view of U.S. of, 40, 43; and dominant classes, 122; as term, defined, 144n1
Pennsylvania Dutch settlements, 21
Philadelphia, Pennsylvania, 8, 20
Physicians, in Roseto, Pa., area, 26
Pius X High School, 25
Policelli, Giovanni, 28, 31
Politics, 127, 128
Pope John XXIII, 43, 44
Population: of Roseto Valfortore, 20; of Roseto, Pa., 21
Pregnancy: attitudes and practices surrounding, 107–11
Presbyterian Church, 25
Presbyterians, 30
Privacy, 121
Protestant churches, 9
Protestants, 30, 103–4
Proverbs: on "promised land," 36; on peasant lot, 36–37; on law and state, 127–28; as medical advice, 133–34

Racial discrimination: Italian-Americans as victims of, 60; and the Garibaldi legend, 61–62
Reading habits, 138–39
Regional groups: among immigrants, x, 143n4
Regionalism: in Italian society, xiv; reflected in stories, 41; and interethnic conflict, 53; in Roseto, Pa., 73–74
Relatives: contact among, 51, 52; differentiated behaviors toward, 126–27

Religion: attitude toward, 106. *See also* Magical-religious world view
Religious songs, 106
Returned migrants: as folklore subjects, xii–xiii, 40–42; numbers of, 144n4
Rinaldo, Prince Dottor Domenico, 19
Romantic tales, 78
Rome, Italy, 20
Ronca, Maria, 202
Rosato, Nicola, 28, 31
Roseto Cornet Band, 25, 31
Roseto Golden Jubilee, 32
Roseto Hotel, 25, 114
Roseto, Pennsylvania: founding of, xi, 28, 31; Italian atmosphere of, xiii–xiv; village affinity of, 7; ethnic homogeneity in, 7, 21; geographic situation, 20–21; public buildings in, 25; history of, 32; future of, 141–42
Roseto Valfortore, Italy: geographic situation, 11; aspects of life in, 11–19; town layout, described, 13; history of, 19–20; effect of emigration on, 20

Sacred objects, 86, 87, 89
Saggese family, 13, 16
Saggese, Marquis Filippo, 20
St. Catherine the Sinner: text, 202–4
Saints: and magic practices, 100, 116; in Rosetan folklore, 105
Salesian Sisters Convent and Kindergarten, 25
Sbrocchi, Lucia, 78
Schools: in Roseto Valfortore, 14; in Roseto, Pa., 25
Second generation: change in norms among, xii; and interethnic contact, 62; image of Roseto Valfortore among, 65; and Italian language, 72–73; and traditional narratives, 79; and magic tales, 82; attitude toward wealth, 131; critical of younger generation, 141; term, defined, 143n8
Serpent, The, 80
Sex groups: effect of emigration on, 75
Sharecroppers, 15
Sicilians, 60
Social distinctions: in Roseto Valfortore, 16; in Roseto, Pa., 26–27, 28; need for status reflected in legends, 59–60
Socialist Party, 16

Social life: in Roseto Valfortore, 14; in Roseto, Pa., 22; street, decline of, 29
Songs: comparative length of, 38. *See also* Emigration songs
South, the (Italy), 3
South America, 35, 36
Spaghetti dinners, 29
Sterility, 107
Stoddard Slate Company, 26
Storytellers, 75
Storytelling, 74–80; aspects of, described, 212–17
Supernatural tales, 78
Superstition, 83

Tedesco family, 30
Tedesco, Ferdinando, 26
Television, 76–77
Theatre, 120
Three Oranges, The, 80
Toronto, Ontario, 20, 32
Transmission of folklore, 73, 74
Travel to Italy, 141; frequency of, by early immigrants, 32; current, 65–68
Trousseau, 113, 114–15
True stories, 83

Unions, 9

Values, 53
Vario, Fred, 31, 64

Washington, D. C., 20
Wealth, 130, 131
Wedding customs, 111, 113–115
Welsh, the, as immigrants, xi
Werewolves, 90, 92–94
What Is the World Doing?: text, 182–83
Widows, 113
Witches, 90–92
Women: as immigrants, 7; social life of, 14–15; and travel, 32; as narrators, 77–78; employment of, 26, 123–24; traditional role of, 123–24
Work: attitudes toward, 130–31
Work songs, 129
World War I: effect on emigration, 5–6; uncertainty during, in Roseto, Pa., 32
World War II: revival of emigration after, 6; travel to Italy after, 32; Rosetan soldiers in Roseto Valfortore, 62–64; effect on the two Rosetos, 64–65

Yearly cycle: celebrations during, 120, 207–11